Julien Audebert

À Verdun poussent des obsidionales, fleurs aux graines transportées depuis leur milieu d'origine sous les semelles des soldats, les sabots des animaux de guerre. Sous ce titre générique, Julien Audebert a peint pas moins de quarante pièces sur plaque de cuivre, le métal des obus de 14-18[1]. Tiges irradiant de nuances de brun et de vert où s'accrochent en guise de pétales des tons jaune vif, violets, roses ou blanc rosé, bleutés. Feuilles et épines sur fonds sombres lourds ou agités d'ocre, de vert mousse ou d'eau. Cet herbier, l'artiste en a observé la vie sur le champ de bataille vallonné par les bombardements de la Grande Guerre quelques années plus tôt, lors de séances photographiques de nuit avec un éclairage pauvre, des torches dans le creux de cratères adoucis par le temps. *Nocturne*[2] fixe l'image de troncs d'arbres qui semblent chercher racines dans une coulée d'obscurité. Si la beauté des fleurs veloutée par l'huile répond à la profondeur noire de la photographie, aussi intense que celle de la *Crucifixion* (1475-1480) du retable d'Issenheim, leurs écarts ont un fond commun et invisible, l'homme.

J'irai fleurir vos tombes

Corinne Rondeau

Pas question ici de stigmatiser l'oubli d'une terre de morts sous la nature, ni la métamorphose niaise du désastre en écologie bienheureuse et condescendante. Ce n'est pas non plus une série de fleurs commémorant – une fois de plus – la souffrance humaine. La disparition qui semble être l'affaire de Julien Audebert est sans romantisme, sans lyrisme, sans mélancolie, et possiblement sans mémoire. Elle a quelque chose de non-immédiat, mais dès qu'on porte les yeux dessus on ne s'en remet pas. Il faut dire que le rendu particulièrement parachevé des pièces, souvent à des échelles inhabituelles, soumet le regard à une intrigue, non tant comme un détail dans l'image, plutôt comme une absence, un film à suspens sans suspens mais pas sans inquiétude.

Le mot « disparition », qui ne s'arrange pas avec celui d'histoire, s'arrange davantage avec le rire effroyable du personnage éponyme de *Toby Dammit* de Federico Fellini, cher au cœur de l'artiste. Ce moyen-métrage de la fin des années 1960, qui appartient à un film à sketches adapté de quelques *Histoires extraordinaires* de Edgar Allan Poe, est sous-titré : *Ne pariez pas votre tête avec le diable*. Terence Stamp est Toby Dammit, icône du cinéma britannique invitée à Rome pour des interviews, Ferrari à la clé. Acteur damné d'un monde de pacotille et de morts-vivants, Toby est hanté par la vision d'une petite fille à l'apparence surexposée de lumière dont la robe blanche accentue un monde de carton-pâte, et entourée d'un aéropage de trognes immodérément maquillées qui passent la singularité à la broyeuse, clichés vivants à l'heure de la société du spectacle. Dimension hallucinante, apparence outrancière n'y sont pas de simples illusions, mais un moyen de supporter, voire survivre, dans un monde asphyxié de questions indiscrètes et de m'as-tu-vu. Lors d'une émission TV, on demande à la vedette si elle croit au diable : passant alors d'une torpeur d'addictif à la concentration, Toby, avec une douceur inattendue, répond affirmativement quand bien même il ne croit pas en Dieu. La petite fille est une image de Méphistophélès, et *Toby Dammit* une version contemporaine de Faust. Si tous les chemins mènent à Rome, certains prennent la tangente, suivant une lumière avec l'espoir de crever la paroi des illusions avec l'illusion elle-même. Toby en paie le prix fort. Lancé, pied au plancher, cheveux au vent, pour rejoindre la vision « heureuse et sympathique » du diable via une berge sans pont, un fil métallique invisible lui tranche net la tête qui, après un rire de fou et la fuite à tombeau ouvert, roule au pied de l'ange maléfique telle une sentence dans le silence retrouvé de la nuit. On ne sort pas d'un monde dont la réalité est dévoyée par la représentation car le monde de camelote derrière soi existe toujours. Le saut de Toby Dammit est une tentative désespérée pour atteindre la vérité de l'image : le comble de la surface et des effets de lumière au pays de valeurs culturelles irréelles, ou quand l'appétit d'illusion fait perdre la tête.

Ce détour n'est pas aussi indirect qu'on pourrait le croire. D'un abord visuel qui capture le regard, l'intrigue d'une absence peuple les images de Julien Audebert, qui utilise de nombreux procédés photographiques quand il ne peint pas, et majoritairement deux médiums, film et livre. Toute la singularité des pièces relève d'une sorte de court-circuit : la dimension temporelle du film ou du livre est réduite à une unité figurative : une photographie unique. Mais cette photographie a une particularité : elle est rendue possible par des techniques de la photographie argentique à une époque où elles sont en train de se raréfier, voire de disparaître. Ce choix de techniques, qui demande du temps pour changer la nature du rendu de l'image, implique de se dégager d'un monde d'images pixellisées et d'affirmer un retour à une corporéité de l'image. Il y a, dans la production de Julien Audebert, une procédure à rebours qui transforme la nature de l'image d'origine du travail – numérique – en une nature qui fut celle de l'origine du monde moderne reproductible – argentique. Ce n'est pas un goût pour les vieilles choses, mais une façon d'interroger la production des images actuelles dont le problème n'est pas la prolifération, mais la disparition. Dès lors il n'y a pas à s'étonner qu'une de ses premières œuvres porte sur un essai abondamment commenté de Walter Benjamin, *L'œuvre d'art à l'époque de sa reproduction mécanisée (Pour W. Benjamin)*[3]. Texte intégralement reproduit sur une page A4 par un procédé photographique. Inutile d'écarquiller les yeux, le texte n'est pas lisible sans loupe. Les retours à la ligne donnent une apparence d'effacement dans le blanc restant, comme des pas se perdraient sous les reflux de la mer au bord d'une plage.

Le texte est surface avant d'être contenu, ce qui oblige le spectateur à s'attarder d'abord sur sa dimension perceptuelle et renverser le commentaire comme ce qui la fait exister. Le lecteur est emprisonné par la surface. Le choix d'un texte devenu surface n'est pas un déni de sa valeur signifiante, mais une façon d'imposer une histoire contemporaine à son contenu : la valeur de l'œuvre d'art est proportionnelle au nombre d'idées qui lui sont raccrochées et surtout reproduites, un peu comme les images ne cessent de se multiplier sur le web ou comment retrouver l'ici et maintenant d'une image, autrement dit sa matérialité photographique, ce qui a pour conséquence de déplacer la critique de la perte de l'aura de Benjamin. Cela ne pose pas à nouveaux frais le problème de la perte de l'originalité, ni la question de la domination du discours sur le regard, comme s'il fallait toujours opposer l'image à la réalité ou la raison à la sensibilité. Bien plus impertinente, lorsqu'on crée des images à une époque qui ne cesse d'en produire, est la répétition de l'histoire de la photographie qui n'a pas arraché la mort au présent. Bien au contraire, le présent photographié lui est voué. Chez Julien Audebert, la mort est celle de l'image, pas du monde, et si les rares corps qu'on discerne dans ses pièces sont effacés ou d'une présence de figurants, c'est pour signifier que la simultanéité des images assèche l'expérience. La question la plus banale qui en surgit est celle de Walter Benjamin dans *Expérience et pauvreté* : sommes-nous encore capables de comprendre une histoire ? Je préciserais pour que la question prenne toute sa gravité dans notre présent et au regard de cette œuvre : sommes-nous encore capables de fabriquer des images dans un monde de pixels ? Le tour de force d'une telle fabrique étant de tirer l'image de sa disparition.

La photographie de *Studio*[4] est une des plus surprenantes. Le « démontage-remontage » de *La Corde* d'Alfred Hitchcock est une composition de plans en version numérique qui organisent en perspective l'appartement où un meurtre a été commis à l'insu des invités d'une soirée bourgeoise. En sélectionnant des détails de qualité optimale, le plus petit détail pixellisé étant d'une qualité égale au plus grand, l'image repose sur une tête d'épingle, et croît en proportion de la qualité visuelle qui l'uniformise. Le résultat est un « faux-plan » d'un format à taille humaine, 90 × 190 cm. Mais ce qui fait l'intrigue, c'est la surprise inquiète du spectateur se découvrant au bout de l'exploration à la place du coffre hors-champ où est dissimulé le mort. Son regard est du côté du cadavre, encore en situation verticale, l'image étant horizontale, un peu comme si, pour expliciter ce « tableau de figures humaines », portrait trivial car hors peinture de genre, l'artiste avait retiré à *Un enterrement à Ornans* (1849-1950) la tombe au ras de la composition de Gustave Courbet. Pas de doute, chaque image ainsi traitée est le lieu d'un

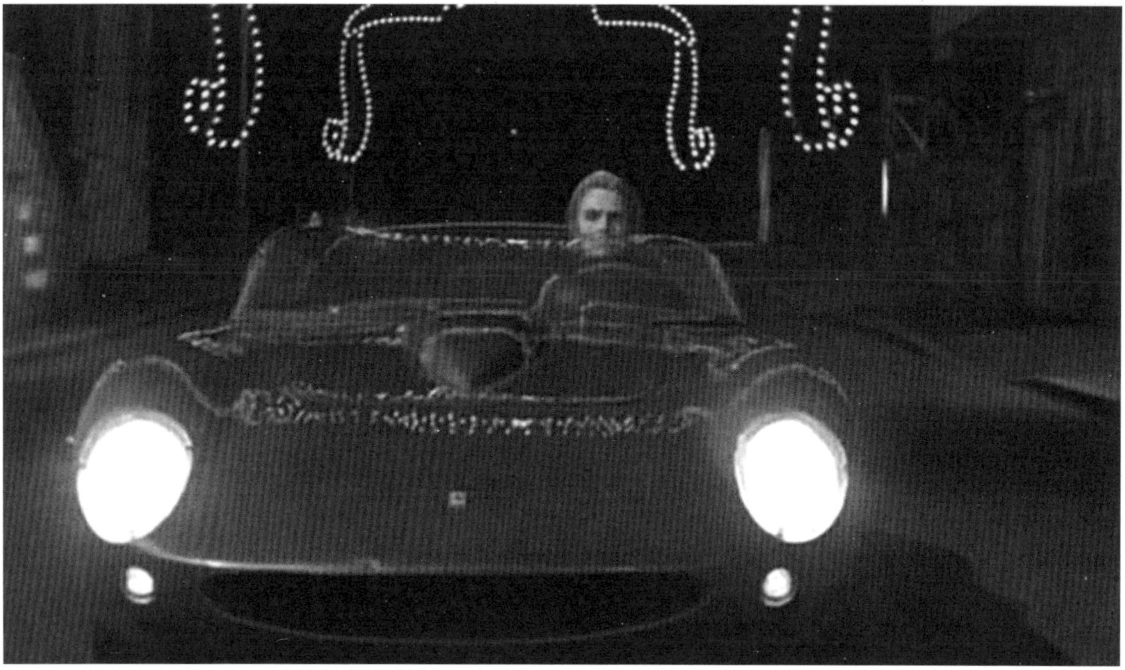

Images statiques par *Toby Dammit*, épisode de Federico Fellini dans le film à sketches *Histoires extraordinaires* (1968) / Stills from *Toby Dammit*, Federico Fellini's episode in the portmanteau film *Spirits of the Dead* (1968)

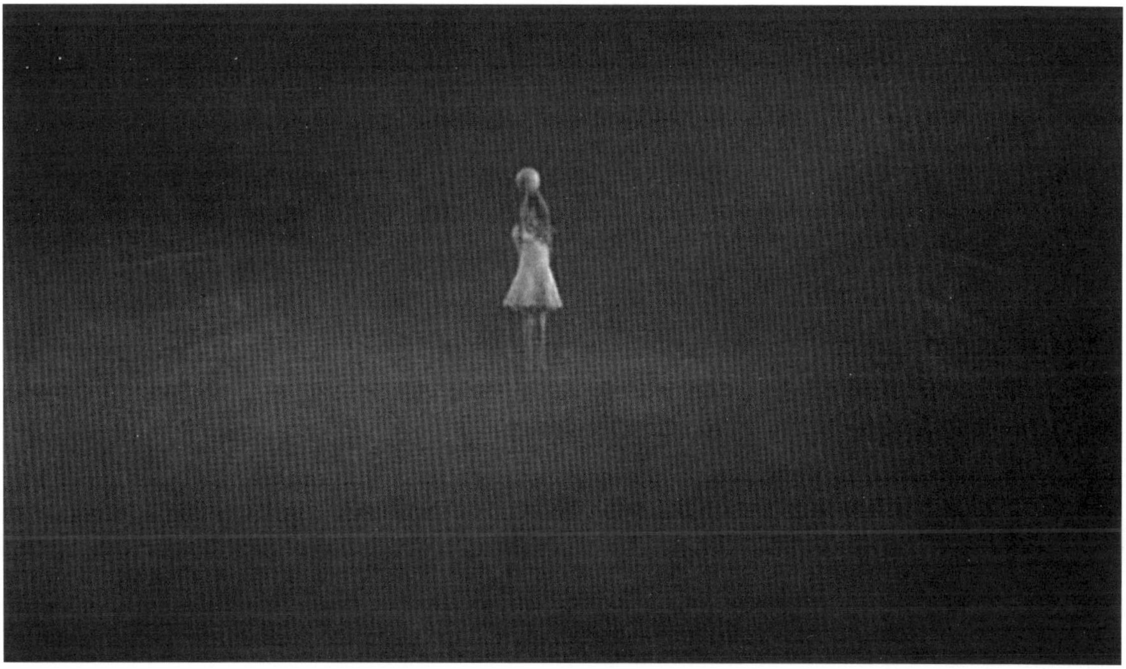

crime parfait, un crime que personne ne voit car la logique des causes et des effets est complètement renversée, voire éludée, alors même qu'elle ne cesse d'appeler le spectateur.

Côté spectateur une sorte d'inquiétude dans tous les cas fondée. La disparition lancinante d'éléments et scènes auxquels il accroche son regard lui suggère des corps engloutis par l'histoire, pas celle avec un grand H, une encore à écrire de la représentation.

Julien Audebert appartient à la famille du photographe documentaire qui fixa sur du bromure d'argent le monument d'un monde qui n'existe plus, un Paris vidé de vie, Eugène Atget. À une différence près, désormais il s'agit d'un monde éclaté par la pixellisation, un monde qui a détruit le temps de sa propre lecture. Ce n'est pas la fin du monde, c'est le monde rétréci pour le meilleur (ou pour le pire). Un monde qui a déjà eu lieu comme dans *Le Chariot de Mars*[5] qui a pour substrat le documentaire sur la Bibliothèque Nationale d'Alain Resnais, *Toute la mémoire du monde* (1956), qui commence par une phrase off, « parce que leur mémoire est courte les hommes accumulent d'immenses pense-bêtes », et que suivent des images de livres entassés comme un trésor de guerre dans les caves arc-boutées de la Nationale, amas classés au fil d'un travail infini de catalogage qui fait tenir le savoir aussi droit qu'un livre sur un rayon de bibliothèque. Mots emprisonnés laissés à la liberté interprétative des lecteurs, chaque consultation créant un nouvel ordre de lecture. Avec l'image numérique, Julien Audebert ne manifeste pas autre chose que ce qui vient à manquer, la lecture. Et il le fait selon une temporalité qui prend en charge une totalité, avec de surcroît le médium déferlant d'une économie de la visibilité.

Dans *Le Chariot de Mars*, la lecture est en trois temps, trois localisations différentes du magasinier dans son activité de transition : retirer du rayon le livre demandé par le lecteur, dont le titre évoque l'image de Mars, lourde d'une symbolique guerrière ; mettre le livre dans le chariot avec sa couverture blanche, détail intrigant dans un monde gris ; et sa fuite, de dos, au fond d'un couloir en perspective qui l'emporte vers un lecteur. Mais y a t-il un lecteur au bout du couloir ? Julien Audebert transmue la question en : comment sortir d'un monde d'images qui n'est qu'image quand le spectateur est hors-champ ? Comment trier des images qui renferment peut-être un moment révélateur, tel le « premier écrit de Rimbaud dans un obscur journal des Ardennes [...] » Ce que *Toute la mémoire du monde* traduit à son tour : « qui sait ce qui demain témoignera le plus sûrement de notre civilisation. »

Julien Audebert consacre un long et minutieux travail de repérage parmi quantités de photogrammes, la plupart du temps de culture cinéphilique : *La Corde* d'Alfred Hitchcock, comme on vient de le voir. Les deux versions de *L'homme qui en savait trop*. *M le Maudit* de Fritz Lang. *La Règle du jeu* de Jean Renoir. *À bout de souffle* de Jean-Luc Godard. *Soy Cuba* de Mikhaïl Kalatozov et *Le Cuirassé Potemkine* de Sergueï Eisenstein. *Le Jour le plus long* et *Libération*, chacun d'un collectif de réalisateurs, américains et soviétiques. Que ce soit l'image reconstituée de l'appartement de *La Corde*[6], la scène de la tentative d'assassinat dans le Royal Albert Hall, combinée entre la version de 1934 et celle de 1956[7], l'ensemble des plans autour de l'école d'Elsie Beckmann, où se mêle incognito à la foule son meurtrier[8], une scène de chasse où sont rassemblés lapins et canards dans une agitation de sauve qui peut la vie[9], la rue de Paris où Jean-Paul Belmondo se fait tirer dans le dos, vidée de toute trace de corps[10], les escaliers d'Odessa lors de l'insurrection de la ville roulant jusqu'à la révolution cubaine dans un chaos absolu[11], le rétrécissement géographique des champs de bataille d'est en ouest[12], la réduction passe par un choix de plans qui s'organisent selon la logique du « démontage-remontage » proche du collage autour du maître mot, la mort. Si chacune de ces images est une invention qui joue à plein du rapport cher à Benjamin entre proximité (je reconnais) et éloignement (que voir ?), c'est moins pour créer une origine perdue que pour s'en détacher. Il ne s'agit pas simplement de jouer avec une image du passé, dont on voit bien qu'elle a un point de ralliement, le crime parfait, mais de la choisir précisément en la faisant passer à un autre statut par l'entremise technique de production. Se rappeler comment sont faites les images est de la plus haute importance à une époque qui cherche surtout des contenus d'actualité, comme pour se rassurer que le monde soit toujours là.

Le travail de Julien Audebert est un procédé qui fonctionne comme un générateur d'images, à la manière de Raymond Roussel avec un autre médium tout aussi inflationniste et funèbre que l'image, le langage. Michel Foucault en décrit ainsi le principe : « pas doubler le réel d'un autre monde, mais dans les redoublements spontanés du langage, *découvrir* un espace insoupçonné et le *recouvrir* des choses encore jamais dites[13]. » Le trouble de la production du jeune artiste s'objective alors par la porosité d'une double temporalité : le temps de ce qui a lieu (l'effacement à la source de la question : que voir ?) et le temps qui a eu lieu (la trace à la source de ladite reconnaissance).

Le procédé implique une aporie dont le dispositif imagier confine la critique au malaise : comment dépasser un monde d'images avec une image de plus ? En ne conservant rien du montage, sinon le montage. Ce paradoxe consiste à travailler au cœur de l'impossibilité, et par exemple par le rappel que la page d'un livre peut aussi être une image, surface blanche ou couverte de hiéroglyphes qui efface toute possibilité de déchiffrement. Un peu comme si le héros de *La Jetée* (1962) de Chris Marker, cet homme marqué par une image d'enfance, ne la retrouvait jamais, et que sa conclusion ne pouvait jamais s'énoncer : « il comprit qu'on ne s'évadait pas du temps, et que cet instant qui lui avait été donné de voir enfant et qui n'avait cessé de l'obséder, c'était celui de sa propre mort. » Le travail de Julien Audebert consiste à sortir de la boucle des images, sortir du piège de notre temps, reprendre

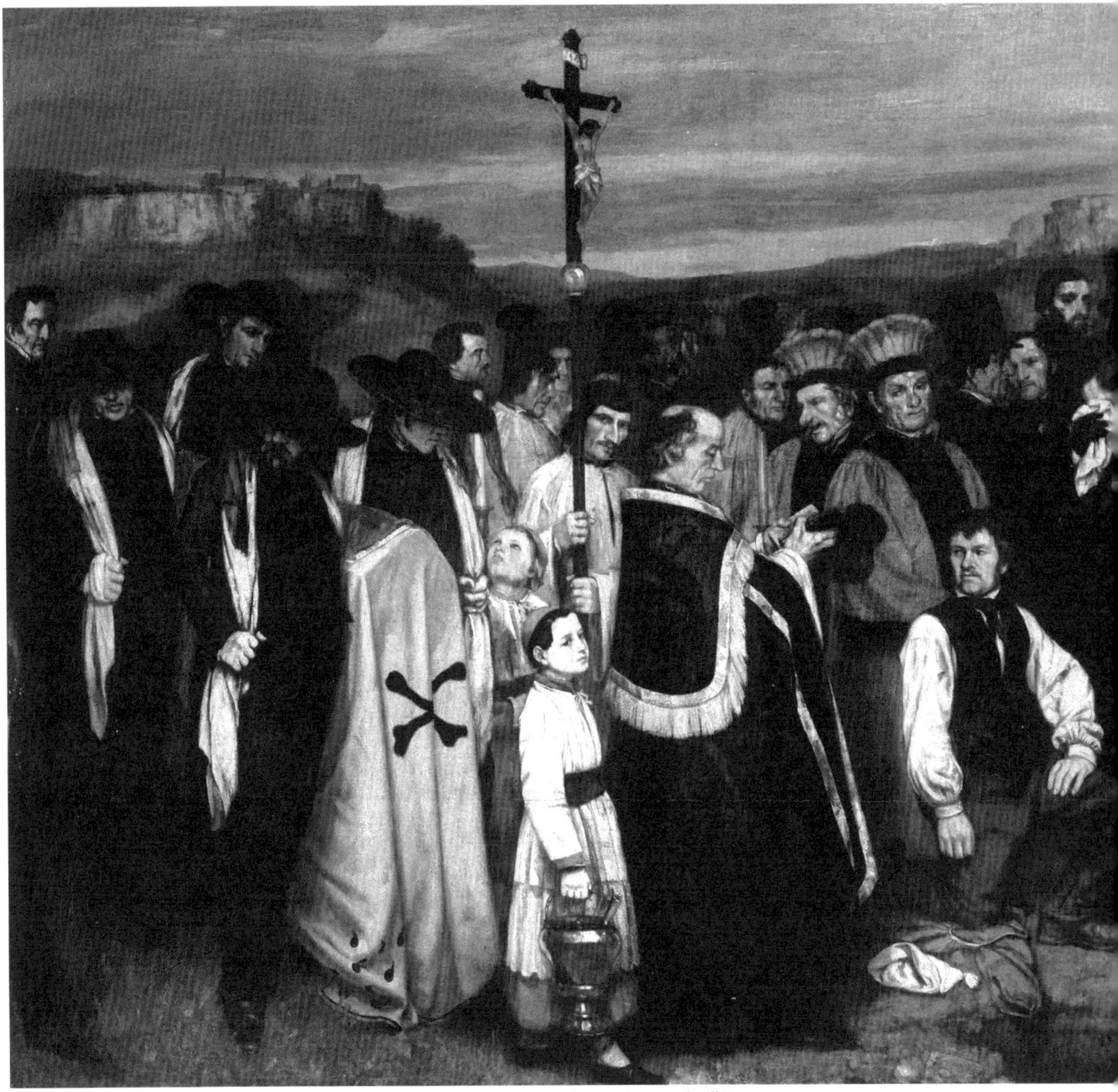

Gustave Courbet, *Un enterrement à Ornans* / *A Burial at Ornans*, 1849–50. Paris, Musée d'Orsay

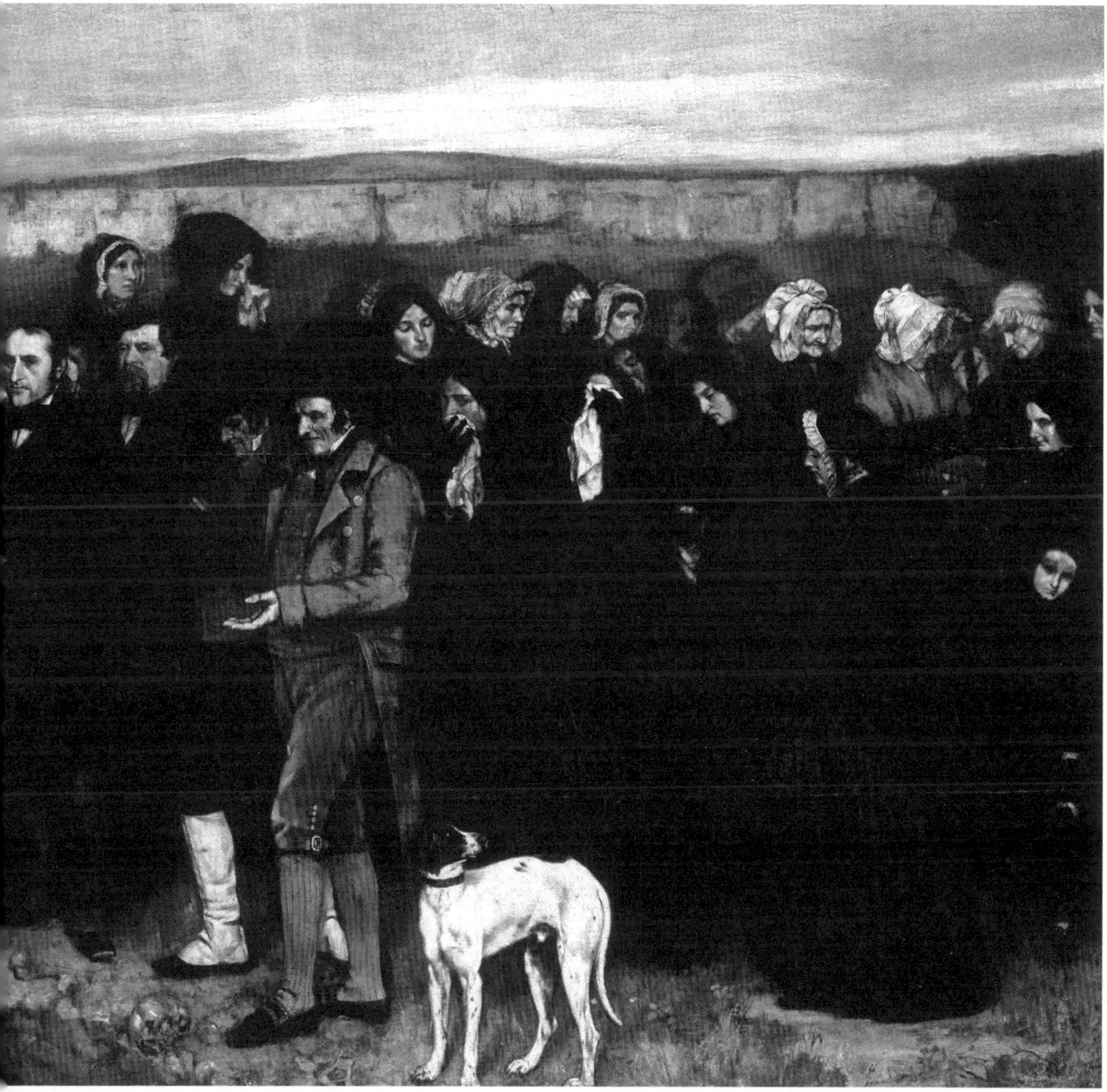

le contrôle d'une expérience perceptive, mais à même le monde des images. Si Atget réalise la disparition de l'homme au cœur de l'architecture hybride de l'ancien et du moderne, Audebert cèle la disparition de la réalité aux prises avec la représentation, poussant au bout la critique de Paul Valéry dans *La Conquête de l'ubiquité* qui, en 1928, ramenait les émotions brèves et brutales de la modernité à une « absurde superstition du nouveau[14]. » Walter Benjamin, commentant l'écrivain sétois, fait de ces chocs une rechute dans la barbarie. Dans le silence des images, l'intrigue ouvre à son tour une scène. Il ne fait aucun doute que le jeune artiste est revenu sur les lieux du crime en observateur des symptômes de notre civilisation et en critique acerbe de la disparition d'un sujet privé de la capacité du sens. « Le sentiment est tout quand tout le reste manque[15]. »

D'où la perfection de ses images qui joue au premier abord avec le règne du visuel, enjeu de la popularisation dans une société du spectacle, qui bute aveuglément sur la paroi des illusions au ras de laquelle roulent les têtes. Or cette qualité de perfection, qui ne fait pas l'économie d'un certain état de fait, est moins la doublure d'un monde désenchanté que d'une âme vouée au diable : ne faire qu'un avec ce qu'on voit est mortel. La totalité agite le rêve désespérant d'un Faust. Sa démonstration mobilise moins des images de crime qu'un crime d'image. Ce que Julien Audebert cherche avec une acuité folle, c'est le cadavre de toute interprétation de l'histoire. L'intrigue jamais visible, évitant soigneusement au spectateur le plaisir d'un détail métonymique, flotte délocalisée, détemporalisée, dans la composition d'une totalité apparemment insignifiante. Avec la possibilité de nouvelles existences, l'abolition de toute appartenance à un espace et un temps déterminés accomplit une totalité qui offre à un monde d'images l'issue qui coûta sa tête à Toby Dammit. Car la lecture est le dernier refuge de l'Inaccessible, au point de nous faire oublier dans le bain des nouvelles technologies les contours de notre propre histoire, et ainsi de réduire toute possibilité d'écart entre le visible et le sujet du regard. Une phrase de Siegfried Kracauer signe cette continuité subjective postmoderne de Valéry à Benjamin et de Fellini à Audebert, « jamais encore une époque n'a été aussi peu renseignée sur elle-même. »

La lecture que je propose est renforcée par un ensemble de pièces qui ont majoritairement trait à des livres qui sont des faits de civilisation, comme la Bible[16]. Selon la mise en page apparaissent des trous en place du mot « Dieu » dans des formats carré parfait ou A4, des blocs de signes plus que de signifiants.

Les faits de civilisation qu'utilise Julien Audebert, films et livres, sont des totalités qui se déplient dans ses images et proposent au spectateur de faire d'une disparition une origine. Mettre les mains sur un cadavre c'est interroger les causes de la mort. Sa dernière production en date, composée, tel un collage, d'images documentaires sur l'origine du feu dans les cavernes, en est une nouvelle démonstration. *Premier feu* (2021) cherche dans l'absence des hommes du passé la condition de l'apparition de la représentation. Les archéologues dont on voit les silhouettes sont moins les acteurs potentiels d'une découverte que des objets dans une image, figurants davantage que déchiffreurs. Conformément à la conclusion de Michel Foucault dans *Les Mots et les choses*, *Premier feu* pourrait bien être le dernier feu de notre civilisation. « L'homme est une invention dont l'archéologie de notre pensée montre aisément la date récente. Et peut-être la fin prochaine. » Ces silhouettes ne sont pas les seules. On en retrouve la cour médiatique sur un green de golf face à la crème d'un sommet international dans *Summit* (2016). Silhouettes de pouvoir guère différentes du pouvoir médiatique : faire de la figuration pour faire voir des images. Disparition du pouvoir comparable à celle de Gene Kelly dans la reconstitution de la rue en Technicolor d'*Un Américain à Paris* (1951) de Vicente Minnelli[17], qui vaut la peine qu'on précise le contexte invisible à l'image : « le *soft power* américain, ce processus de domination culturelle enclenché à partir du plan Marshall et qui trouvera un parfait allié dans le cinéma[18]. »

Le mot clé du travail de Julien Audebert, celui de *totalité*, s'apparente à la destruction de la pluralité des hommes, et de toute politique. Une totalité qui joue à effleurer le processus d'une téléologie pour mieux le mettre en échec. Ainsi des images de révolutions, d'insurrections, comme la série de onze feuilles barytées reconstituant en feuilles d'or les barrières de la Commune vues de dos[19]. Si aucun homme n'est voué à la destruction d'un système, il suffit qu'il s'en fasse témoin pour relancer son récit. Le pouvoir du témoin est sa faiblesse même, son extrême fragilité, sans peur d'y interposer un corps, afin de mettre en échec la représentation. Voici ce qu'est la production de Julien Audebert : une façon de faire effraction dans le système à partir de la totalité. Au lieu de jouer à en combler les trous, il le vide sans se – nous – ménager. De la même façon qu'avec *Red sunset over a lake* (2011), 211 cartes postales trouées par un tir de carabine dont la trajectoire traverse le paquet d'images, de la première – un coucher de soleil –, à la dernière – un crépuscule. Trajectoire qui fait le lien vide de 211 cartes postales et par la déchirure du papier glacé un autre canal temporel. Tuer le cliché pour reconstituer du temps est une façon de se libérer d'une vieille inquiétude : toutes les mutations qui affectent le savoir de l'homme jusqu'à son expérience propre et qui manifestent sa différence au cœur du semblable, ne sont jamais qu'une possibilité de changement, de simples re-dispositions d'un point de vue. Trouver la force d'être responsable des images que l'on regarde, cesser d'en chercher et d'en faire des réparations. C'est à quoi nous conduit la production de Julien Audebert au cœur de l'inquiétude : un déplacement de point de vue, si léger soit-il, au moyen de procédures techniques d'images qui nous entraînent vers la disparition. « Si ces dispositions venaient à disparaître comme elles sont apparues, si par quelque événement dont nous pouvons tout au plus pressentir la possibilité, mais dont nous connaissons pour l'instant encore ni la forme ni la promesse, elles basculaient, comme le fit au XVIIIe siècle le sol de la pensée classique, – alors on peut bien parier que l'homme s'effacerait, comme à la limite de la mer un visage de sable[20]. »

1 *Obsidionales*, 2019-2020.
2 *Nocturne*, 2015-2016.
3 *L'œuvre d'art à l'époque de sa reproduction mécanisée (Pour W. Benjamin)*, 2003.
4 *Studio*, 2006.
5 *Le Chariot de Mars*, 2018.
6 *Studio*, 2006.
7 *Royal Albert Hall*, 2005.
8 *Reconstitution du meurtre d'Elsie Beckmann*, 2004.
9 *La Règle du jeu*, 2007.
10 *Campagne Première*, 2006.
11 *1925-1964*, 2008.
12 *Est/Ouest*, 2012.
13 Michel Foucault, *Raymond Roussel*, Paris, Gallimard, 1992.
14 In *Préambule du Catalogue de l'exposition d'art italien*, Paris, Gallimard, 1935.
15 Siegfried Kracauer, *L'ornement de la masse. Essais sur la modernité weimarienne*, Paris, La Découverte, 2008.
16 *Livres*, 2003-2012.
17 *Danse américaine*, 2015.
18 Julien Audebert, http://julienaudebert.com/works/danse-americaine/
19 *L'histoire retournée*, 2011-2017. La série comprend : *Charonne, Saint-Sébastien, Castiglione, Royale, Voltaire-Lenoir, Chapelle, Madeleine, Allemagne-Sébastopol, Puebla, Concorde, Vendôme*.
20 Michel Foucault, *Les Mots et les choses*, Paris, Gallimard, 1966.

Verdun, where obsidional flowers grow seeds once scattered by soldiers' boots or hooves of war animals. *Obsidionales* is the generic title under which Julien Audebert has painted no less than fourteen pieces on copper plates, the same metal World War I shells were manufactured with.[1] Stems radiating shades of brown and green where bright yellow, purple, pinkish, or pink white and blue tones cling as petals. Leaves and thorns on dark backgrounds heavy with or disquieted by ochre, moss, or water green. The artist observed this herbarium's life on the hills of the Great War bombings battlefield a few years earlier, during night photography sessions with poor lighting, torches in the hollow of craters softened by time. *Nocturne*[2] sets the image of tree trunks whose roots seem to grow in a flow of darkness. If the beauty of the flowers' velvet rendered by the oil echoes the black depth of the photograph, as intense as that of the *Crucifixion* of the Issenheim altarpiece (1475–80), their differences have a common and invisible ground: Man.

I'll Go Place Flowers on Your Graves

Corinne Rondeau

Forgetting a land of the dead underneath nature should not be stigmatized nor should the disaster be naively turned into a blessed and condescending eco-friendly feeling. We are not facing yet another series of flowers commemorating—once again—human suffering. The disappearance that seems to be Audebert's concern is deprived of romanticism, lyricism, melancholy, and possibly even memory. There is something non-immediate about it, but as soon as you lay your eyes on it, you won't recover. It must be said that the particularly complete rendering of the pieces, often on unusual scales, subjects the gaze to an investigation, not so much into a detail in the image, but rather into an absence, a suspense film whose plot isn't suspended but nonetheless worrisome.

The word *disappearance* that is out of tune with that of *history* echoes the terrible laughter of the eponymous character of Toby Dammit by Federico Fellini, cherished by the artist. This mid-length film from the late 1960s, which belongs to a portmanteau film adapted from some of Edgar Allan Poe's *Extraordinary Stories*, is sub-headed: *Never Bet the Devil Your Head.* Terence Stamp is Toby Dammit, icon of British cinema invited to Rome for interviews, Ferrari into the bargain. A damned actor in a world of junk and the undead, Toby is haunted by the vision of a little girl overexposed to flashing light whose white dress highlights a world of cardboard-paste, and is surrounded by an aerompy of immoderately made-up trognes that grind singularity, clichés coming alive at the time of the society of the spectacle. In such an hallucinating dimension, outrageous appearances are not simple illusions but a way to endure, even survive, in a world asphyxiated by indiscreet questions and show-offs. During a TV show, the star is asked if he believes in the devil: then going from an addictive torpor to concentration, Toby, with an unexpected sweetness, answers affirmatively even though he does not believe in God. The little girl is an image of Mephistopheles, and Toby Dammit a contemporary version of Faust. If all roads lead to Rome, some take the tangent, following a light in the hope of breaking the wall of illusions with the illusion itself. Toby is paying a high price for it. Launched hair in the wind, putting the pedal to the metal, to join the "happy and sympathetic" vision of the devil driving on a bank without a bridge, an invisible metal wire cuts his head clean which, after a mad laugh and a flight at breakneck speed, rolls at the feet of the evil-angel judgement in the newfound silence of the night. We do not leave a world whose reality is distorted by representation as the world of junk behind us still exists. Toby Dammit's leap is a desperate attempt to reach the truth of the image: the climax of the surface and the effects of light in the realm of unreal cultural values, or when the appetite for illusion makes one lose one's head.

Such a detour isn't as implicit as one may think. From a visual approach that captures the eye, investigating what's missing is dynamics that reside in the images of Audebert who uses many photographic processes when he does not paint, and mostly two mediums: film and book. The whole singularity of the pieces relies on a sort of short circuit: the temporal dimension of the film or book is reduced to a figurative unit: a unique photograph. Yet this photograph is created thanks to film photography techniques at a time when they are becoming rarefied, disappearing even. Choosing techniques that need time to change the nature of the image rendering, the artist has to free himself from a world of pixelated images and assert a return to their corporeality. In Audebert's work, a reverse procedure turns the nature of the original image of the work—digital—into one that was that of the origin of the modern, reproducible world—analog. It is not due to a taste for old faded things, but his way of questioning how current images are produced, when the problem is not that they proliferate but that they disappear. It is therefore not surprising that one of his first works relates to a widely commented essay by Walter Benjamin, *L'œuvre d'art à l'époque de sa reproduction mécanisée (Pour W. Benjamin)*.[3] Text reproduced in full on an A4 page by a photographic process. There is no need to widen our eyes; the text is not readable without a magnifying glass. The remaining white seems to erode as the line breaks, much like footsteps wear away under the ebb of the sea.

The text is surface before content, which forces the viewer to first dwell on its perceptual dimension and then reverse the commentary as much as what makes it exist. The reader is trapped by the surface. The choice of a text that has become a surface is not a denial of its significant value, but a way of imposing a contemporary history on its content: the value of the work of art is measured up to the number of ideas that it triggers and especially reproduces, a bit like images do not stop multiplying on the web or a way to find the here and now of an image. In other words, its photographic materiality, which results in shifting the criticism of the loss of aura, according to Benjamin. This does not raise the issue of the loss of originality at extra costs, nor asks how the gaze is dominated by discourse, as if one still had to oppose the image to reality or reason to sensitivity. Much more impertinent, when it comes to creating images at a time that never ceases to produce them, is the repetition of the history of photography that has not torn death away from the present. Quite the contrary in fact the present photographed is a tribute to death. With Audebert, death is that of the image, not of the world, and if the rare bodies that we discern in his pieces are erased or whose presence is but of film extras, it is to signify that the simultaneity of images dries up experiences. The most banal question that comes to mind then is that of Walter Benjamin in *Experience and Poverty*: are we still able to understand a story? In order for the question to assume greater significance in our present and in view of this work, it needs to be more specific: are we still able to make images in a world of pixels? The amazing feat of such a factory is to pull the image out from its disappearance.

Studio photograph[4] is one of the most surprising. The "editing–unediting" of Alfred Hitchcock's *Rope* is a composition of film shots in digital version that arrange in perspective the apartment where a murder was committed without the guests of a bourgeois party knowing about it. By selecting details of the highest quality, the smallest pixelated detail's quality matching that of the largest, the image could rest on a pinhead, and grows in proportion to the visual quality that standardizes it. The result is a human-sized "false plan," 90 × 190 cm. But what really sets the investigation into motion is the worried surprise of the viewer who discovers himself right at the end of the exploration instead of the off-screen chest where the dead body is hidden. His gaze is on the side of the corpse, still in a vertical position, the image being horizontal. It feels a little as if, to explain this "painting of human figures," trivial portrait because outside of the Genre painting, the artist had removed the tomb at frame level of Gustave Courbet's composition of *A Burial at Ornans* (1849–50). Undoubtedly, each image thus treated is a perfect crime scene, a crime that no one sees because the logic of cause and effect is completely reversed, even if it does not cease to drag the viewer in.

On the viewer's side, a kind of well-founded anxiety lies. The aching disappearance of elements and scenes on which our gaze is hooked evokes bodies engulfed by history, not the one with a capital H but the history of representation which has yet to be written. Audebert belongs to the family of documentary photographers who fixed on silver bromide the monument of a world that no longer exists, Paris emptied of life, Eugène Atget. With one difference, now it is a world shattered by pixelation, that has destroyed the time of its own reading. It's not the end of the world, it's the world shrinking for better (or for worse). A world that has taken place already as in *Le Chariot de Mars*,[5] which has as substrate the documentary on the National Library of Alain Resnais, *All the Memory in the World* (1956), which opens on a voice-over sentence, "because their memory is short, men accumulate immense sticky notes," followed by images of books piled up like a war treasure in the arched cellars of the National Library, archived clusters thanks to an infinite work of cataloguing that urges knowledge to hold itself as straight as a book would on a tidy library shelf. Words entrapped thus left to the readers' interpretative freedom, each book consultation creating a new order of reading. With the digital image, Audebert does not exhibit anything other than what comes to be lacking, reading. And he does so according to a temporality that supports a totality, thanks over and above to a medium washing over sparse visibility.

In *Le Chariot de Mars*, the reading follows three steps, three different locations of the storekeeper in his transition work: remove from the shelf the book requested by the reader, whose title evokes the image of Mars, heavy with war symbolism; put the book in the cart with its white cover, intriguing detail in an otherwise gray world; and his flight, from behind, at the end of a hall in perspective that carries him towards a reader. But does a reader stand at the end of the hallway? Audebert reshapes the question thus: How to get out of a world of images that is only image when the viewer is off-screen? How to sort images that perhaps contain a revealing moment, such as the "first writing of Rimbaud in an obscure notebook of the Ardennes." What *All the Memory in the World* translates in its turn: "who knows what tomorrow will most surely bear witness to our civilization."

Audebert devotes his long and meticulous localization work to quantities of photograms, most of the time of cinephilic culture: *Rope* by Alfred Hitchcock, as we have just seen. Both versions of *The Man Who Knew Too Much*. *M* by Fritz Lang. Jean Renoir's *The Rules of the Game*. *Breathless* by Jean-Luc Godard. *I Am Cuba* by Mikhail Kalatozov and *Battleship Potemkin* by Sergei Eisenstein. *The Longest Day* and *Liberation*, each of a collective of directors, American and Soviet. Whether it is the reconstructed image of

Rope's apartment,[6] the assassination attempt scene in the Royal Albert Hall, combined between the 1934 version and the 1956 version,[7] the set of shots around Elsie Beckmann's school,[8] where her murderer mingles incognito with the crowd, a hunting scene where rabbits and ducks are gathered in a life-saving agitation,[9] the street of Paris where Jean-Paul Belmondo is shot in the back, emptied of anybody traces,[10] the stairs of Odessa during the insurrection of the city rolling until the Cuban revolution in absolute chaos,[11] the geographical narrowing of the battlefields from east to west,[12] the reduction goes through a choice of angle shots that are organized according to the "unset/reset" logic close to collage around one key word: death. If each of these images is an invention that makes the most of the relationship dear to Benjamin between proximity (I recognize) and remoteness (what to see?), it is less to create a lost origin than to tear oneself apart from it. It is not messing around with an image of the past, which we can clearly see has a rallying point, the perfect crime, but rather choosing it precisely while giving it another status through technical production. Remembering how images are made is of the utmost importance at a time mainly looking for fresh content, as if to comfort oneself with the idea that the world is still here.

Audebert's work is a process that works as an image generator, similar to Raymond Roussel but with another medium just as inflationary and macabre as an image: language. Michel Foucault describes the principle as follows: "not to double the reality of another world, but in the spontaneous repetitions of language, to discover an unsuspected space and to cover it with things never uttered before."[13] The blur of the young artist's work can thus be objectified given the porosity of its double temporality: the time of what is taking place (the erasure at the source of the question: what to see?) and the time that has taken place (the trace at the source of said recognition).

The process involves an aporia whose imagery device confines criticism to malaise: how to overcome a world of images with one more image? By retaining nothing of the editing, except the editing. This paradox lies in working at the heart of the impossible, and for example as a reminder that the page of a book can also be an image, white surface or covered with hieroglyphs impossible to decipher. A little as if the hero of Chris Marker's *La Jetée* (1962), marked by a childhood image, would never find it, and that his conclusion could never be stated: "he realized that we do not escape from time, and that this momentary vision given to him as a child and that had never ceased to obsess him, was that of his own death." Audebert's work consists in getting out of the loop of images, freeing oneself from the trap of our time, regaining control of a perceptual experience, but keeping in touch with the world of images. If Atget realizes the disappearance of man at the heart of the hybrid architecture of the old and the modern, Audebert seals the disappearance of reality struggling with representation, pushing to its limits Paul Valéry's criticism in *The Conquest of Ubiquity* which, in 1928, reduced the brief and brutal emotions of modernity to an "absurd superstition of the new."[14] Benjamin, commenting on the writer from Sète, sees these shocks as relapses into barbarism. In the silence of the images, the plot in turn unlocks a scene. The young artist undoubtedly returned to the crime scene by observing the symptoms of our civilization and as a sharp criticism of the disappearance of a subject unable to understand. "The feeling is everything when everything else is missing."[15]

Hence the perfection of his images which plays at first glance with the reign of the visual, which is at stake when a society of the spectacle popularizes everything, and which stumbles blindly on the wall of illusions at the edge of which the heads roll. But this perfection quality, which does not ignore a certain state of affairs, is less the lining of a disenchanted world than of a soul devoted to the devil: to be one with what we see is lethal. Totality disrupts the despairing dream of Faust. Its demonstration summons less images of crime than an image crime. What Audebert seeks with insane acuity is the corpse of any interpretation of history. The plot is never visible, rather it carefully denies the viewer the pleasure of a metonymic detail, it floats relocated, detemporalized, in the composition of a seemingly insignificant totality. Thanks to the possibility of new existences, the abolition of all belonging to a given space and time fulfills a totality that offers a world of images the outcome that cost Toby Dammit his head. Because reading is the last shelter of the Inaccessible, to the point of making us drown in new technologies the memorable contours of our own history, thus reducing any possible distance between the visible and the subject of the gaze. A sentence by Siegfried Kracauer points out this postmodern subjective continuity from Valéry to Benjamin and from Fellini to Audebert: "never before has an era been so little informed about itself."

The reading that I propose is reinforced by a set of pieces that mainly relate to books that are facts of civilization, such as the Bible.[16] Depending on the layout, holes are created to replace the word "God" in perfect square frames or A4 formats, blocks of signs more than signifiers. The facts of civilization used by Audebert, films and books, are totalities that unfold in his images and urge the viewer to see disappearance as an origin. To put one's hands on a corpse is to question the causes of death. His latest production, composed, like a collage, of documentary images on the origin of fire in the caves, is a new demonstration of this. *Premier feu* (2021) searches in the absence of men of the past how representation appeared. The archaeologists whose silhouettes we see have less the potential of actors of a discovery than that of objects in an image, extras rather than decipherers. In accordance with Foucault's conclusion in *Les Mots et les choses*, *Premier feu* may well be the last sparkle of our civilization. "Man is an invention whose recent date is easily shown in the archaeology of our thought. And may be ending soon." These silhouettes are not the only ones. We find their media courtiers on a golf green facing the elite of an international summit in *Summit* (2016). Silhouettes of power are hardly different from the power of the media: playing walk-on parts to make one see images. Disappearance of power comparable to that of Gene Kelly in the reconstruction of the street in Technicolor of *An American in Paris* (1951) by Vincente Minnelli,[17] which makes it worth clarifying the invisible context in the image: "American soft power, this process of cultural domination initiated from the Marshall Plan and which will find a perfect ally in cinema."[18]

The key word of Audebert's work, that of *totality*, is akin to the destruction of men's plurality, and of all politics. A totality that fondles the process of a teleology to better put a spoke in its wheel. Thus images of revolutions, insurrections, such as the series of eleven barium sheets reconstructing in gold leaf the barriers of the Commune seen from the back.[19] If no man is doomed to the destruction of a system, it is enough for him to witness it in order to revive its account. The power of the witness is his very weakness, his extreme fragility, without fear of interposing a body, in order to defeat the representation. Here's what Audebert's production is: a way of breaking into the system seeing it as a whole. Instead of playing to fill in the holes, he empties it without sparing himself—us.

In the same way as with *Red Sunset over a lake* (2011), 211 postcards are pierced by a rifle shot whose trajectory crosses the pack of images, from the first—a sunset—to the last—a twilight. A shot that binds 211 postcards around an empty spot and creates another temporal channel thanks to the tear in the glossy paper. Killing the cliché to reconstruct time is a way of freeing oneself from an old anxiety: all the mutations that affect man's knowledge up to his own experience and that manifest his difference when surrounded by "seem-ilarity" are but a possibility of change, simple re-locating of one's view point. To be strong enough to take on responsibility for the images we look at, cease looking for them and fix them. This is what Audebert's production leads us to at the heart of our anxiety: a shift in vantage point, however slight it may be, thanks to image technical processes bringing about disappearance. "If these tendencies were to disappear as they appeared, if by some event the possibility of which we could at best foresee, but of which we still know neither the form nor the promise, they would change, as did in the eighteenth century the roots of classical thought,—then one can well bet that man would fade away, as would a face of sand at the edge of the sea."[20]

1 *Obsidionales*, 2019–20.
2 *Nocturne*, 2015–16.
3 *L'œuvre d'art à l'époque de sa reproduction mécanisée (Pour W. Benjamin)*, 2003.
4 *Studio*, 2006.
5 *Le Chariot de Mars*, 2018.
6 *Studio*, 2006.
7 *Royal Albert Hall*, 2005.
8 *Reconstitution du meurtre d'Elsie Beckmann*, 2004.
9 *La Règle du jeu*, 2007.
10 *Campagne Première*, 2006.
11 *1925-1964*, 2008.
12 *Est/Ouest*, 2012.
13 Unless otherwise noted, original texts in this essay are rendered in English by the translator. Original quote in Michel Foucault, *Raymond Roussel* (Paris: Gallimard, 1992).
14 Original quote in *Préambule du Catalogue de l'exposition d'art italien* (Paris: Gallimard, 1935).
15 Original quote in Siegfried Kracauer, *L'ornement de la masse. Essais sur la modernité weimarienne* (Paris: La Découverte, 2008).
16 *Livres*, 2003–12.
17 *Danse américaine*, 2015.
18 Julien Audebert, http://julien audebert.com/works/danse-americaine/
19 *L'histoire retournée*, 2011–17. The series includes: *Charonne, Saint-Sébastien, Castiglione, Royale, Voltaire-Lenoir, Chapelle, Madeleine, Allemagne-Sébastopol, Puebla, Concorde, Vendôme.*
20 Original quote in Michel Foucault, *Les Mots et les choses* (Paris: Gallimard, 1966).

35-37
Campagne Première

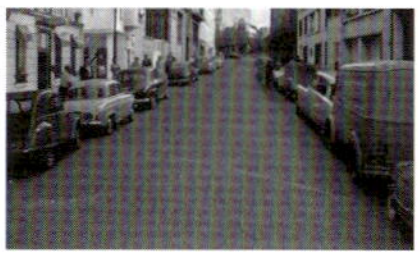
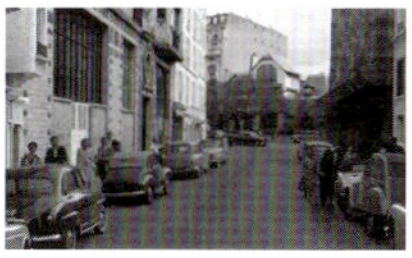

39-41
Written ornaments – Shelf

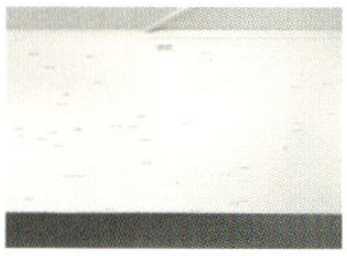
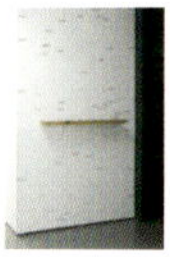
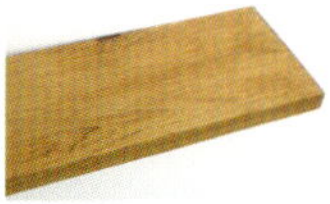

43-47
Reconstitution du meurtre d'Elsie Beckmann

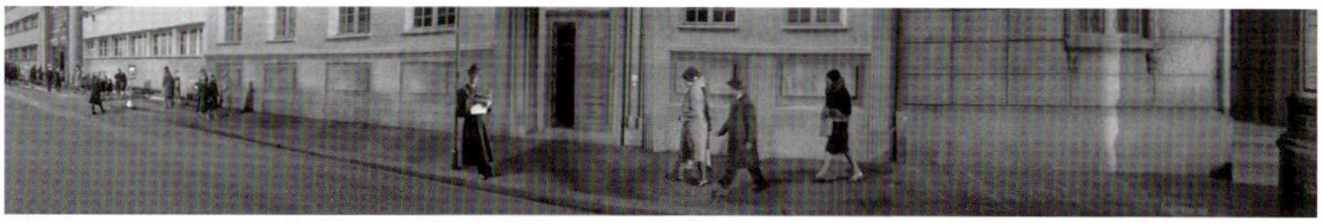

48-53
Inside the letter (The clue)

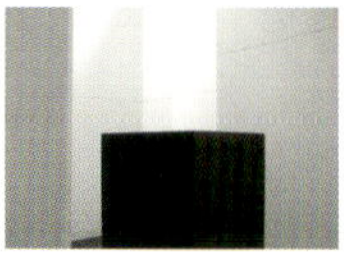
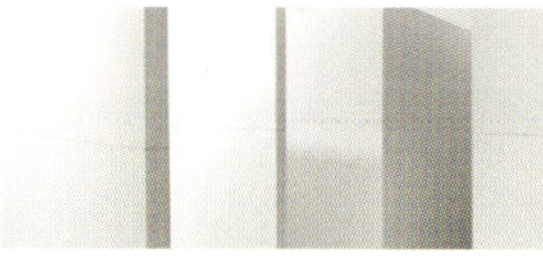
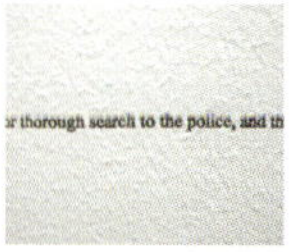

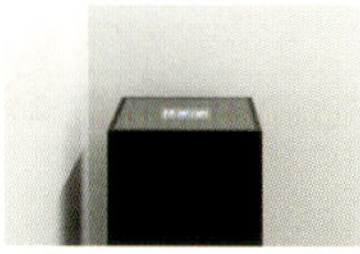

48-53
The clue (bladerunnerblowup)

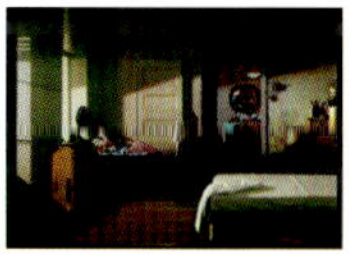
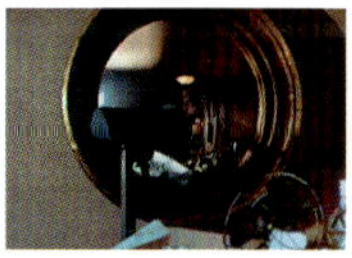
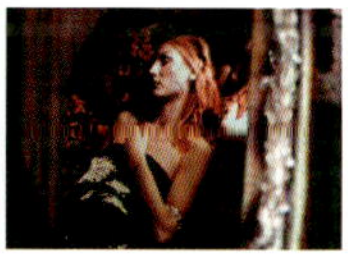

55-59
Royal Albert Hall

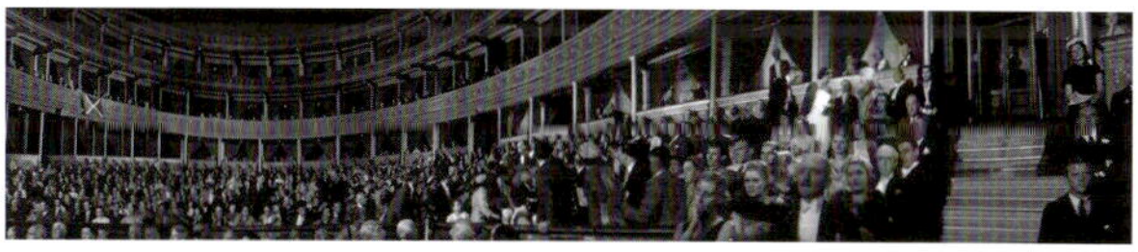

61
Narcisse/Echo

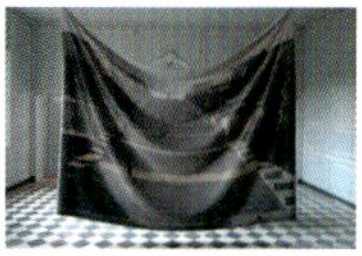
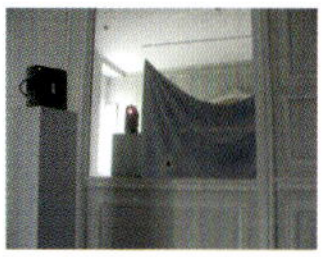

63-65
Studio

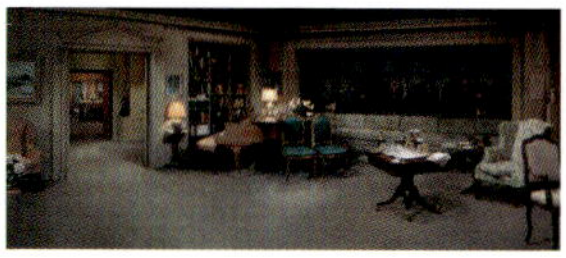
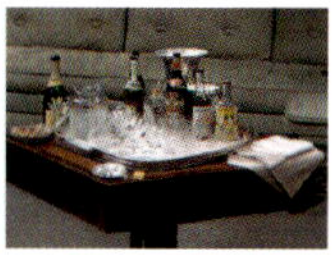

Dream never end

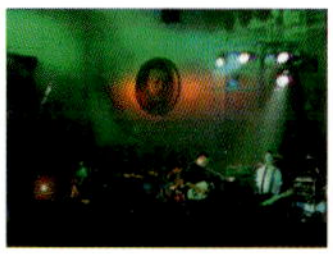

Campagne Première, 2006
Tirage Lambda / Lambda print, 77 × 121 cm

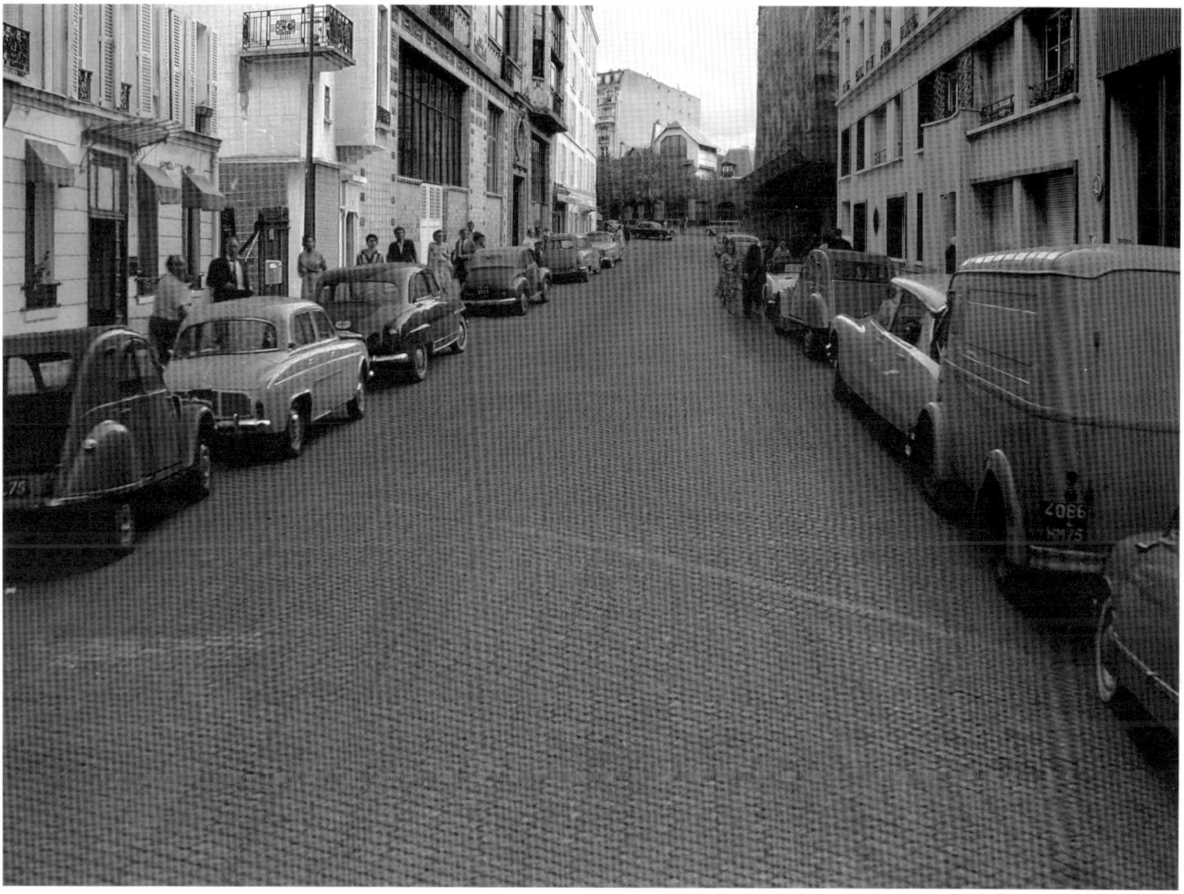
4086
MM75

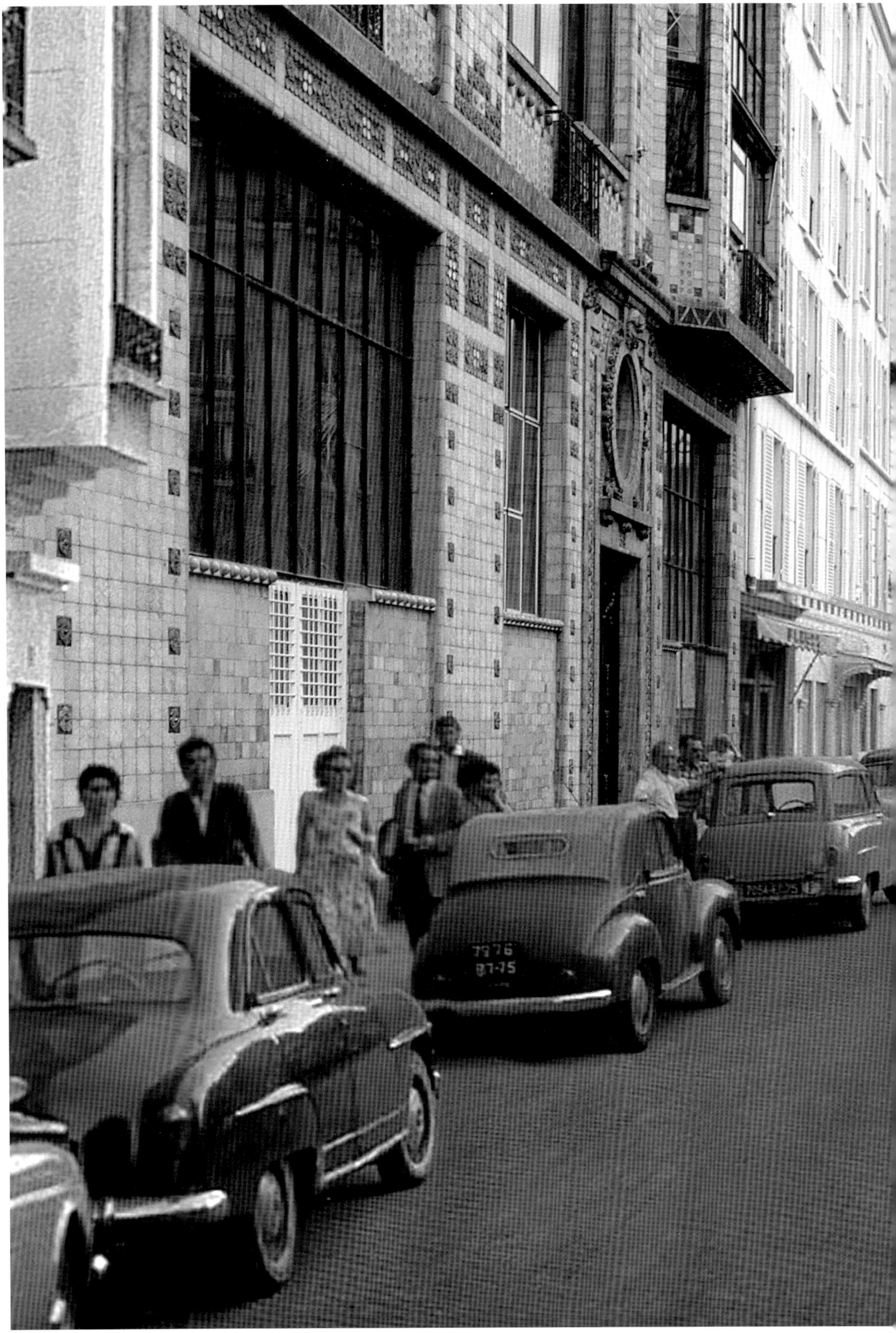

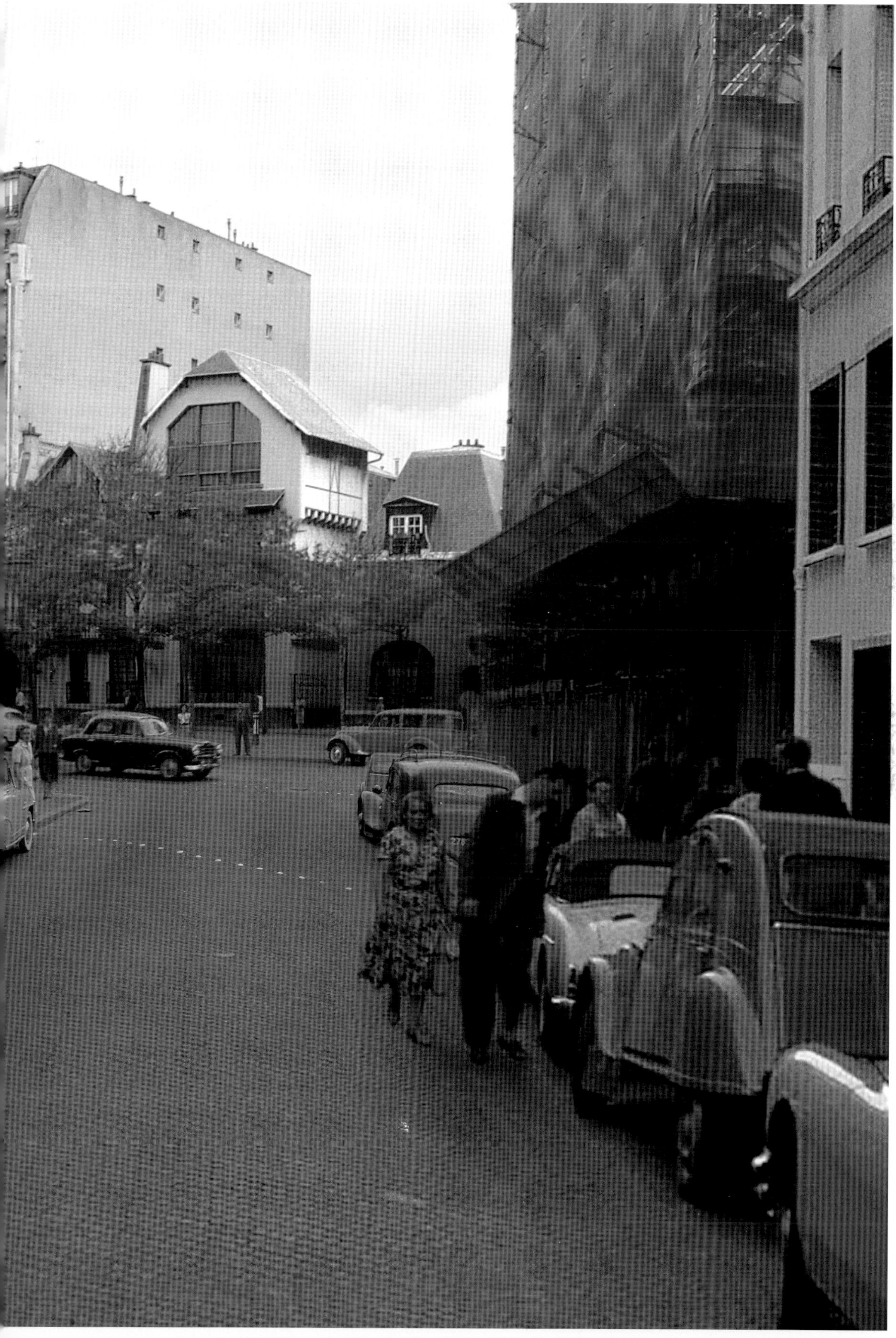

Written ornaments – Shelf, 2008
Encre sur mur, étagère en chêne peinte / Ink on wall, painted oak shelf, dimensions variables / dimensions variable

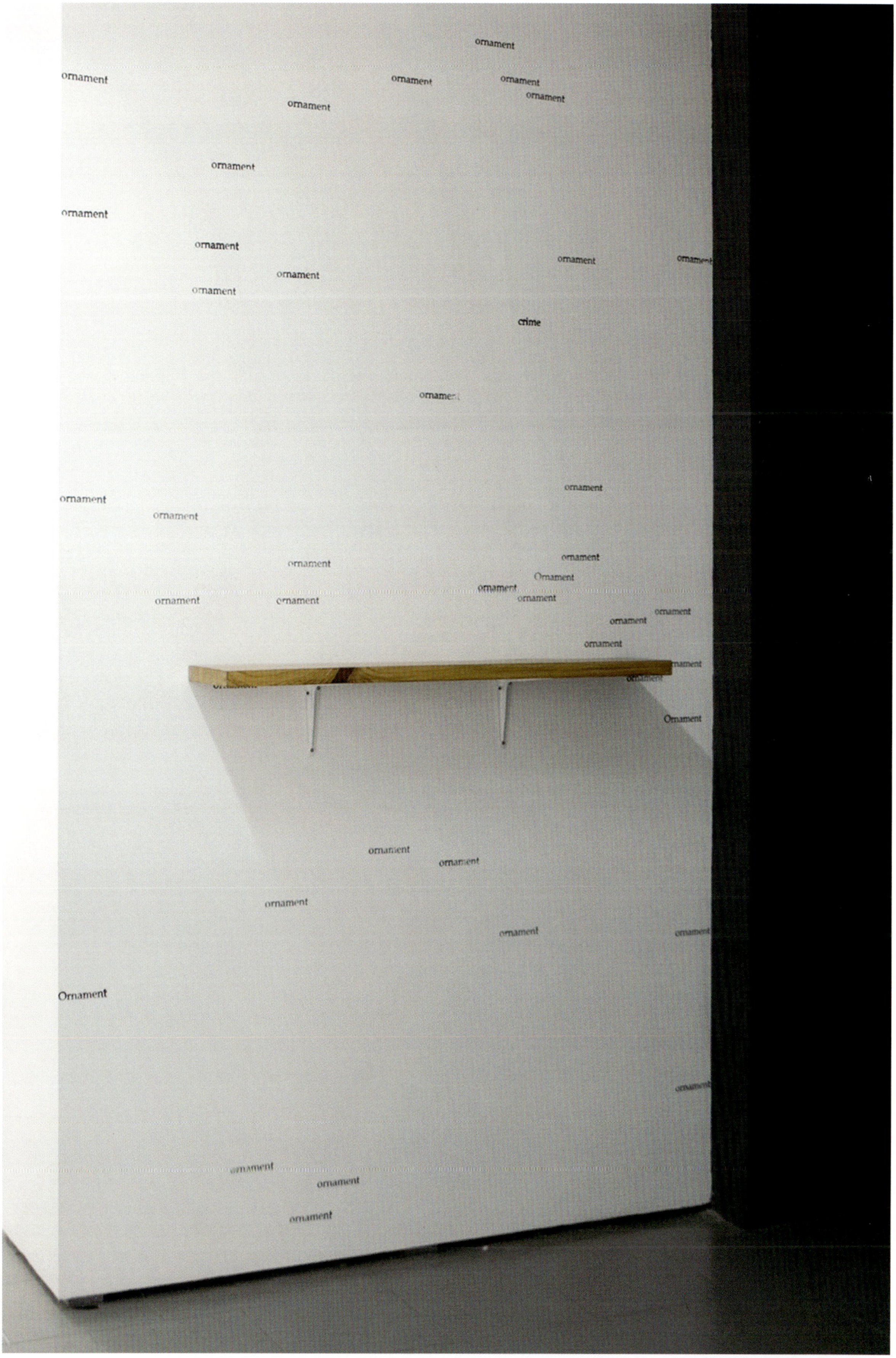
ornament
ornament
ornament
ornament
ornament
ornament
ornament
ornament
ornament
ornament
ornament
crime
ornament
ornament
ornament
ornament
ornament
ornament
Ornament
ornament
ornament
ornament
ornament
ornament
ornament
Ornament
ornament
ornament
ornament
ornament
Ornament
ornament
ornament
ornament

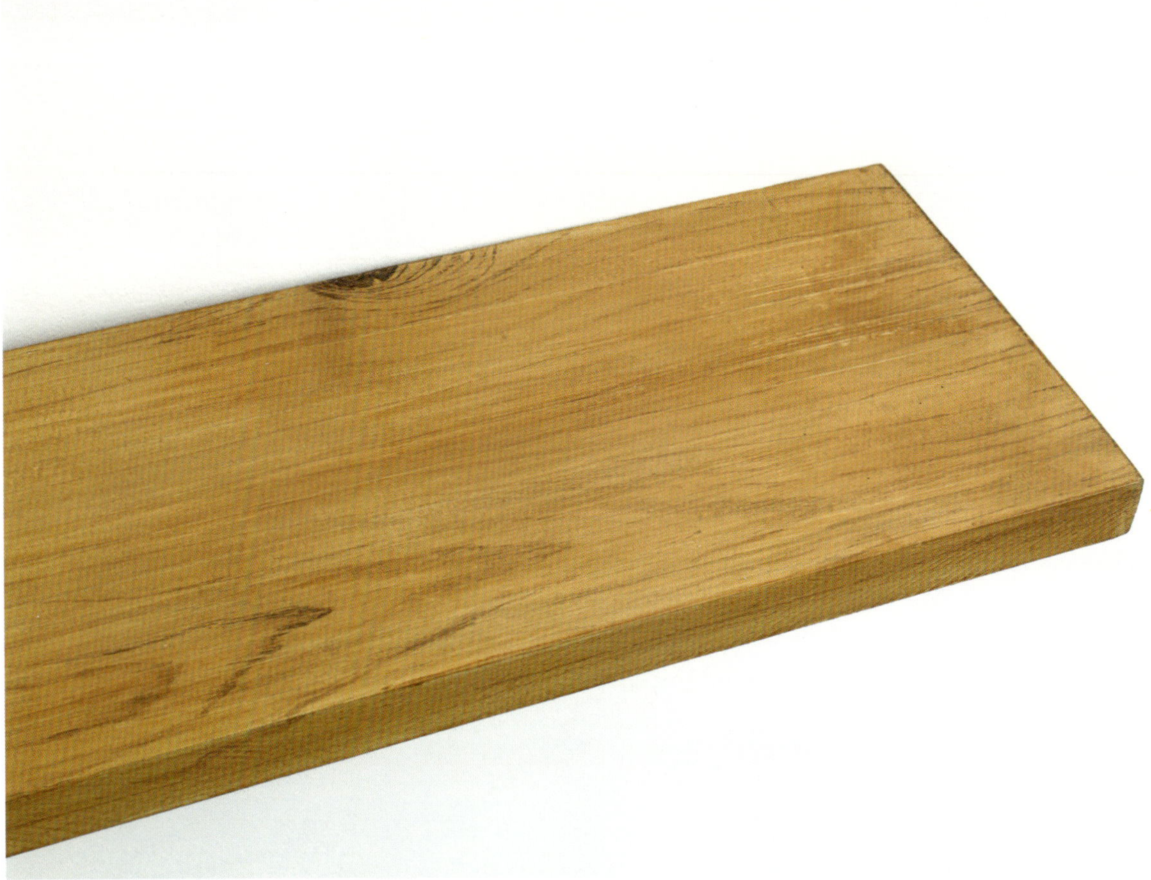

crime

ornament

rnament

ornament

ornament

Ornament

Reconstitution du meurtre d'Elsie Beckmann, 2004
Tirage Lambda / Lambda print, 60 × 240 cm

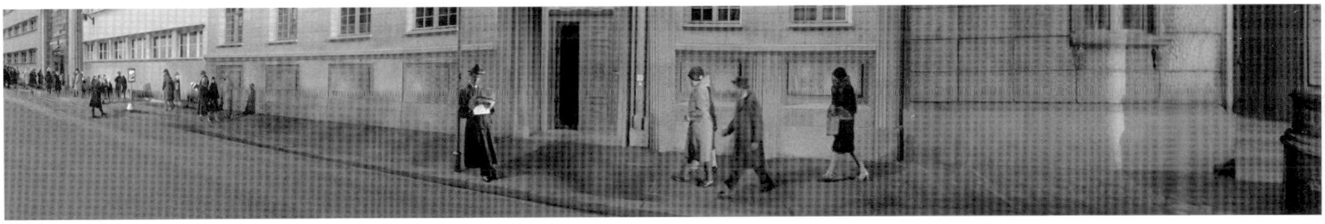

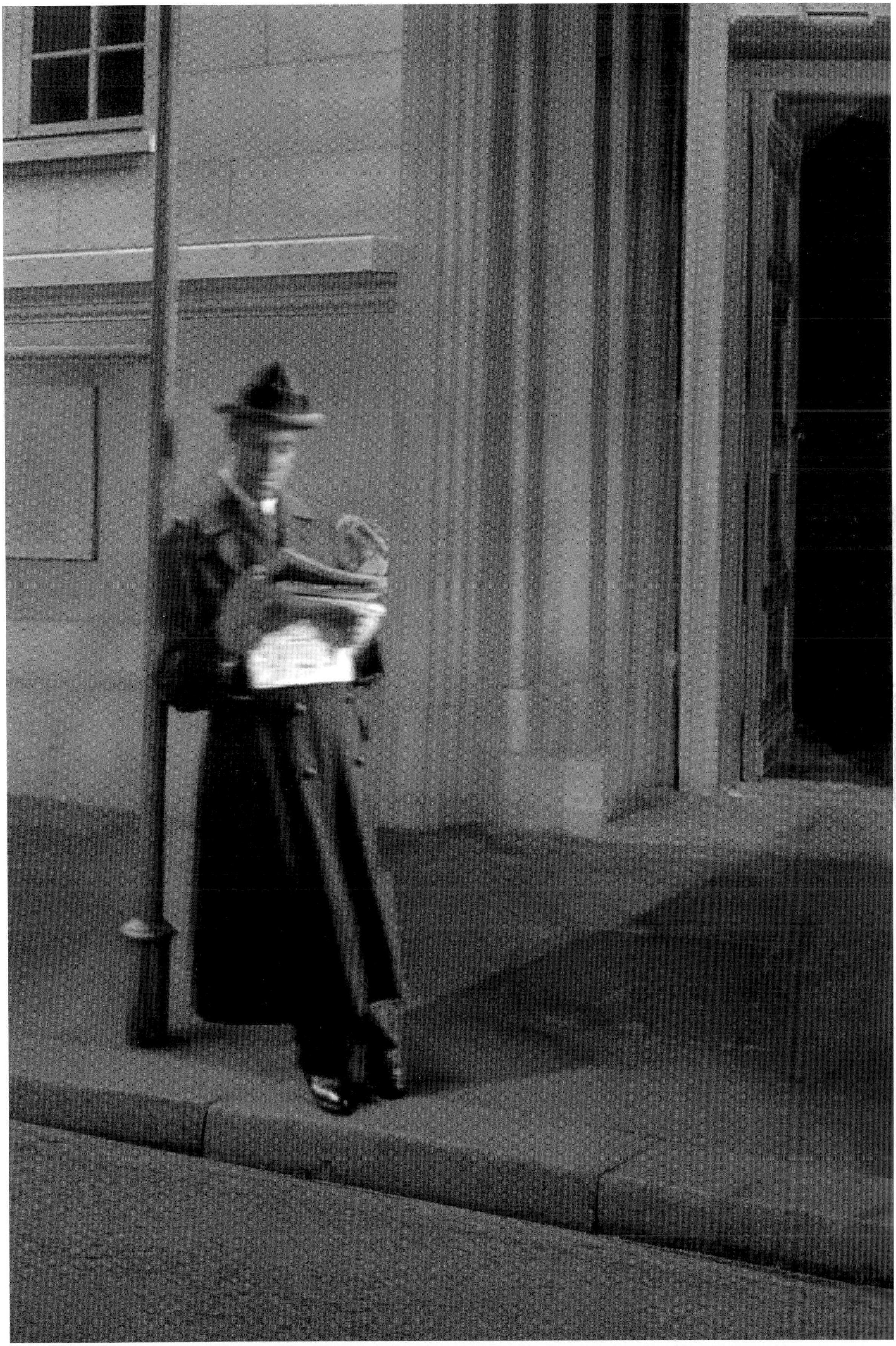

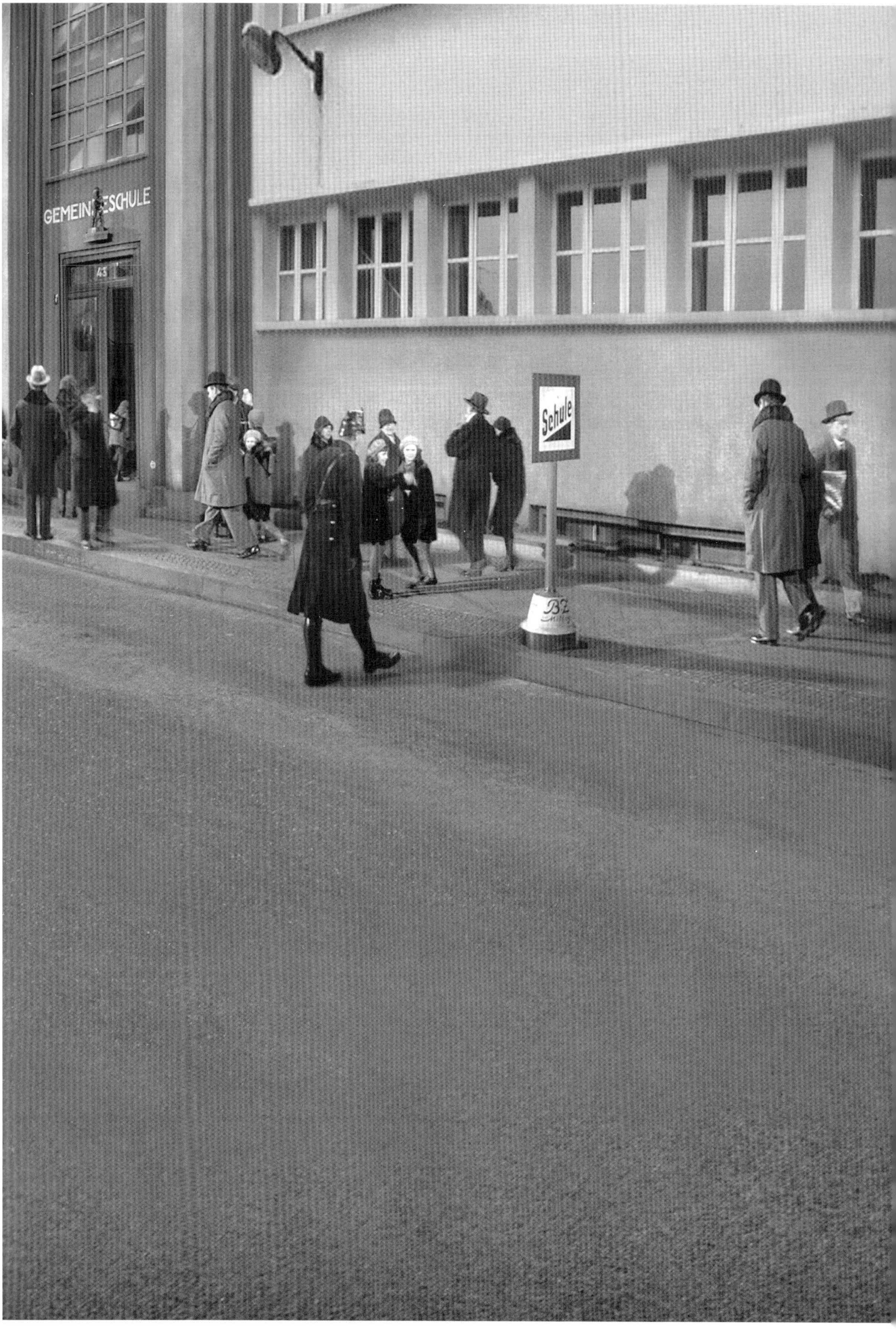
GEMEINDESCHULE
43
Schule

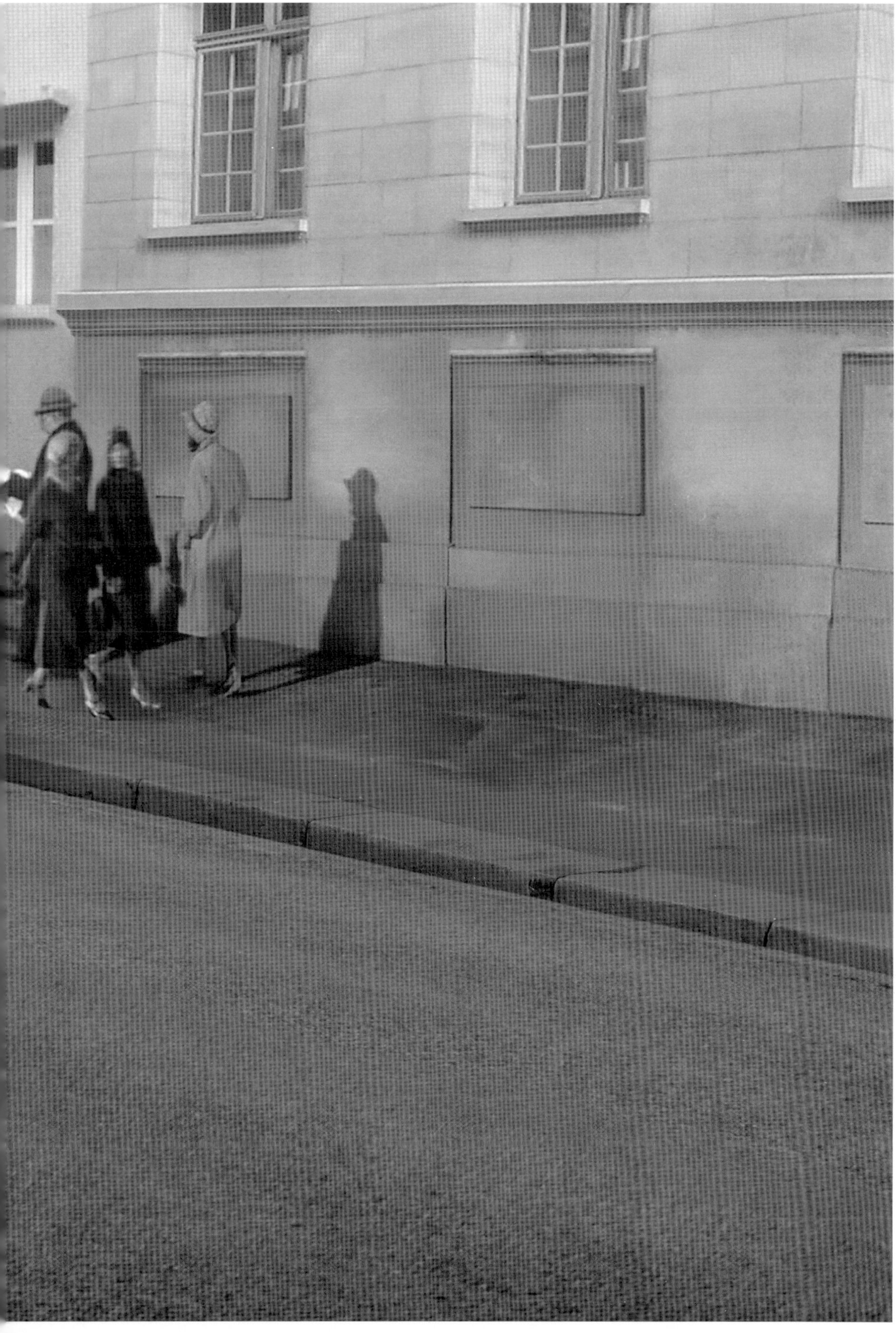

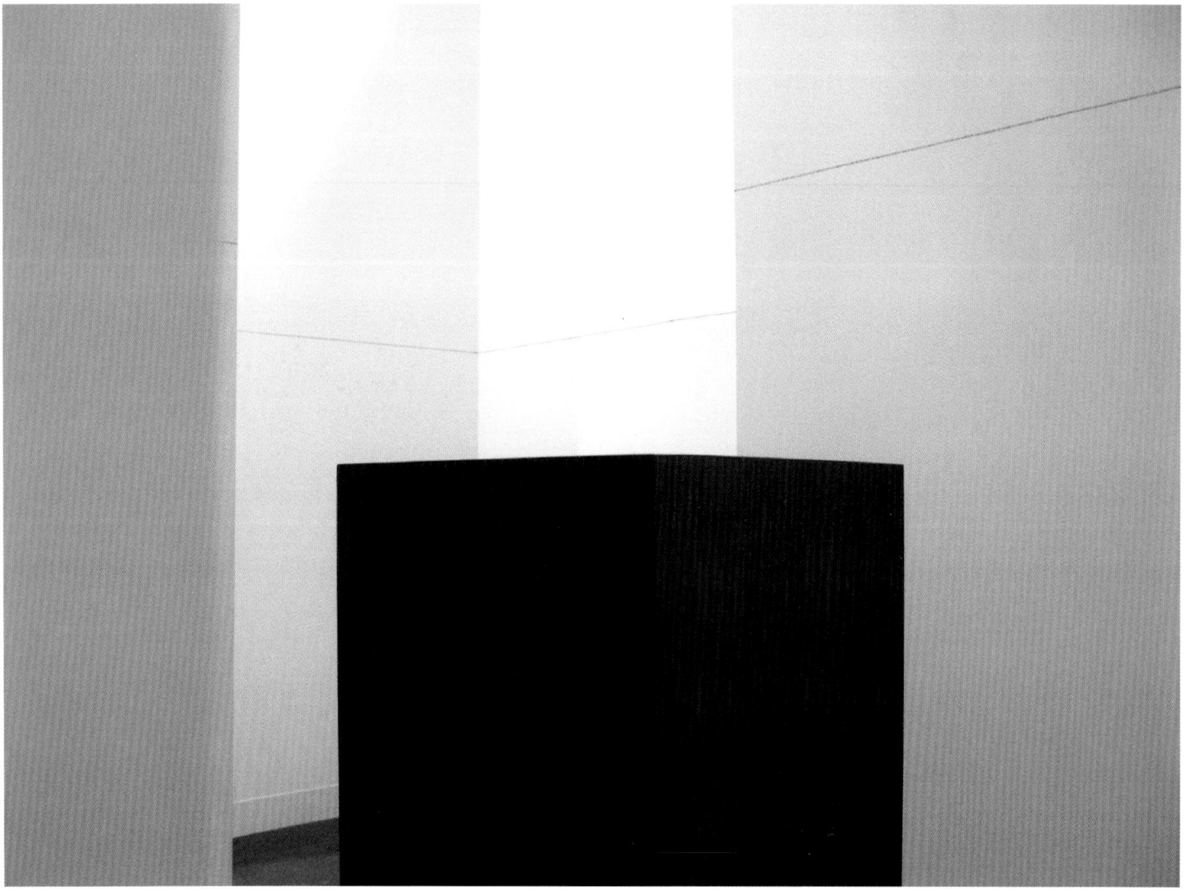

Inside the letter (The clue), 2008
La Lettre volée d'Edgar Allan Poe tamponnée sur mur, ektachrome (*bladerunnerblowup*) sur socle avec table lumineuse / Edgar Allan Poe's *The Purloined Letter* stamped on wall, illuminated Ektachrome on plinth, murs / walls: 540 × 540 × 270 cm, Socle / Plinth: 101 × 51 × 39 cm

The clue (bladerunnerblowup), 2008
Plan-film ektachrome / Ektachrome sheet film, 13 × 18 cm

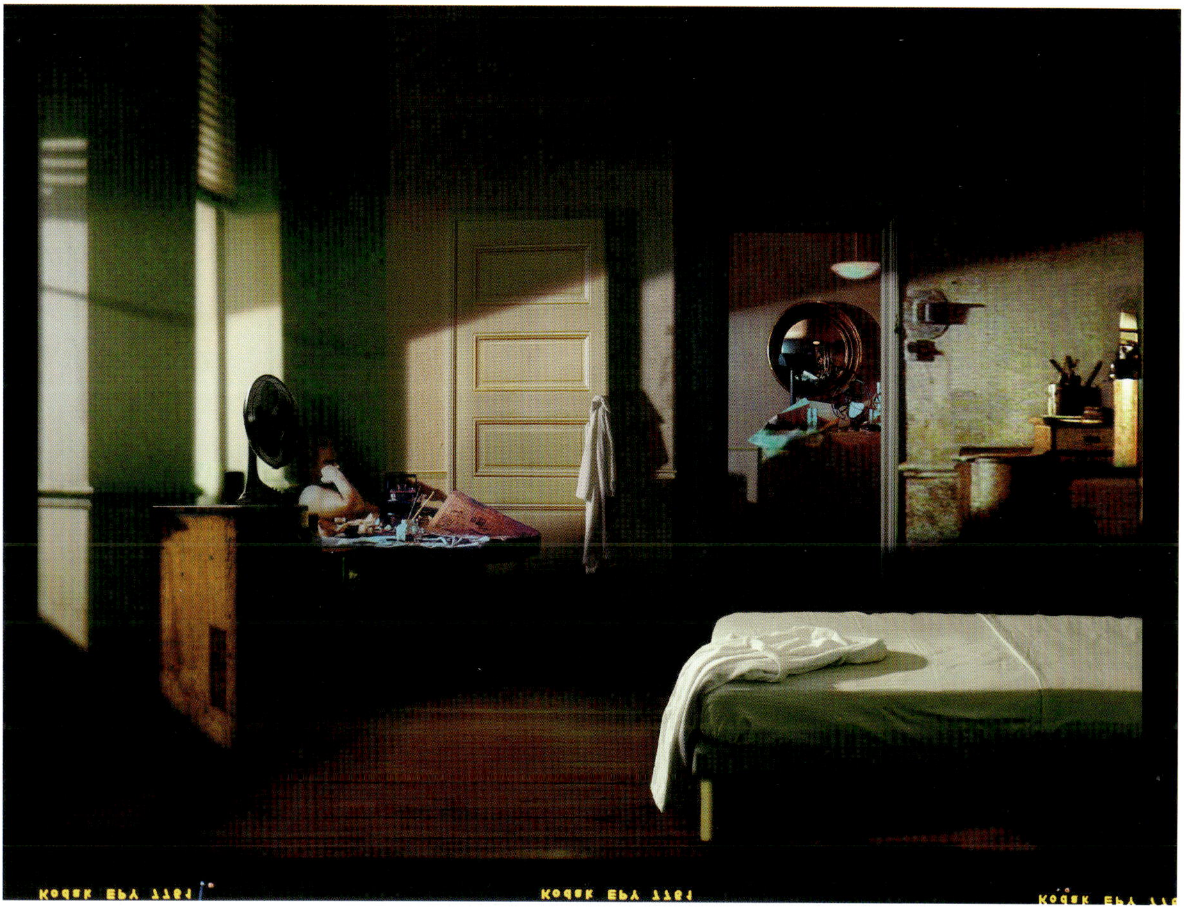

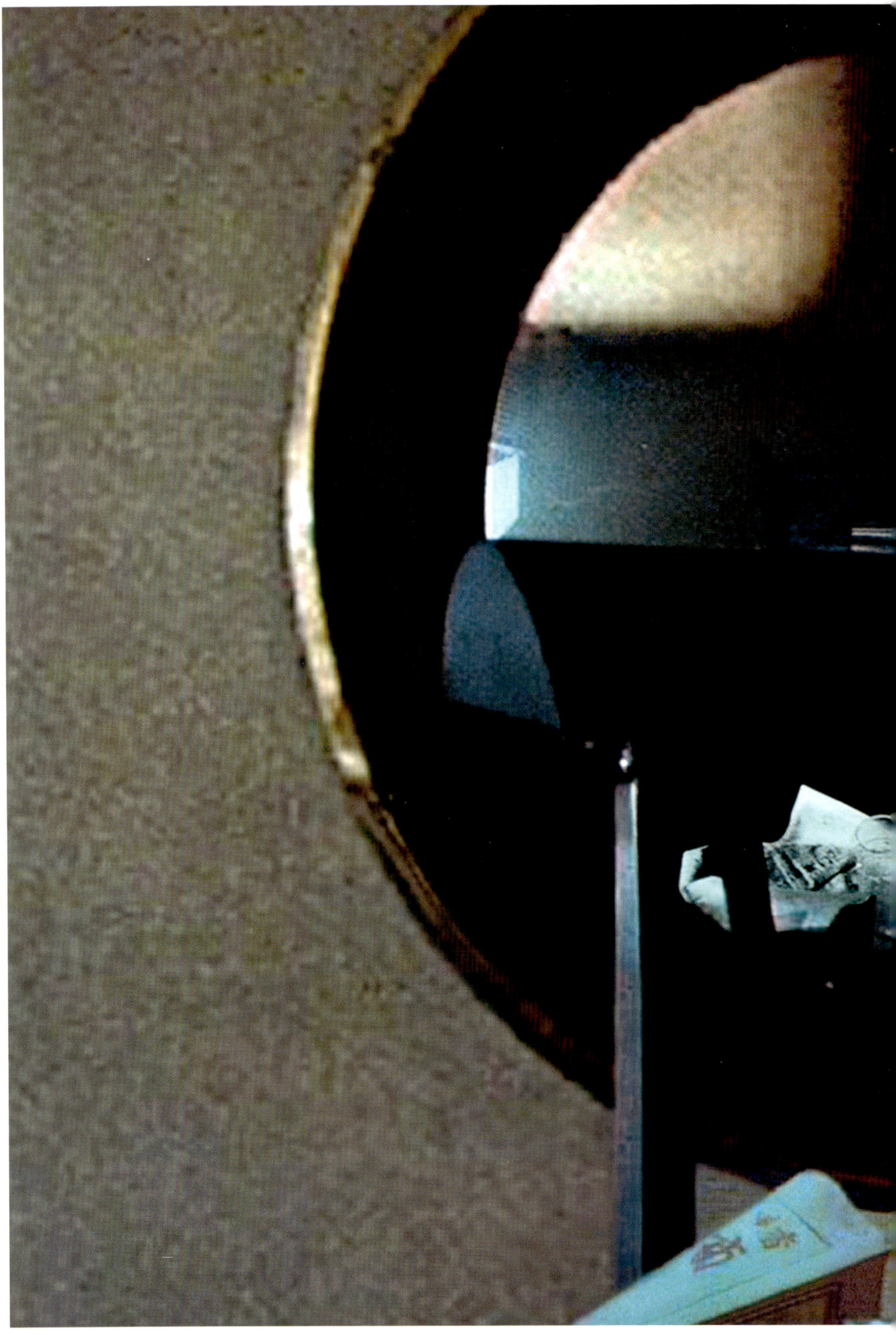

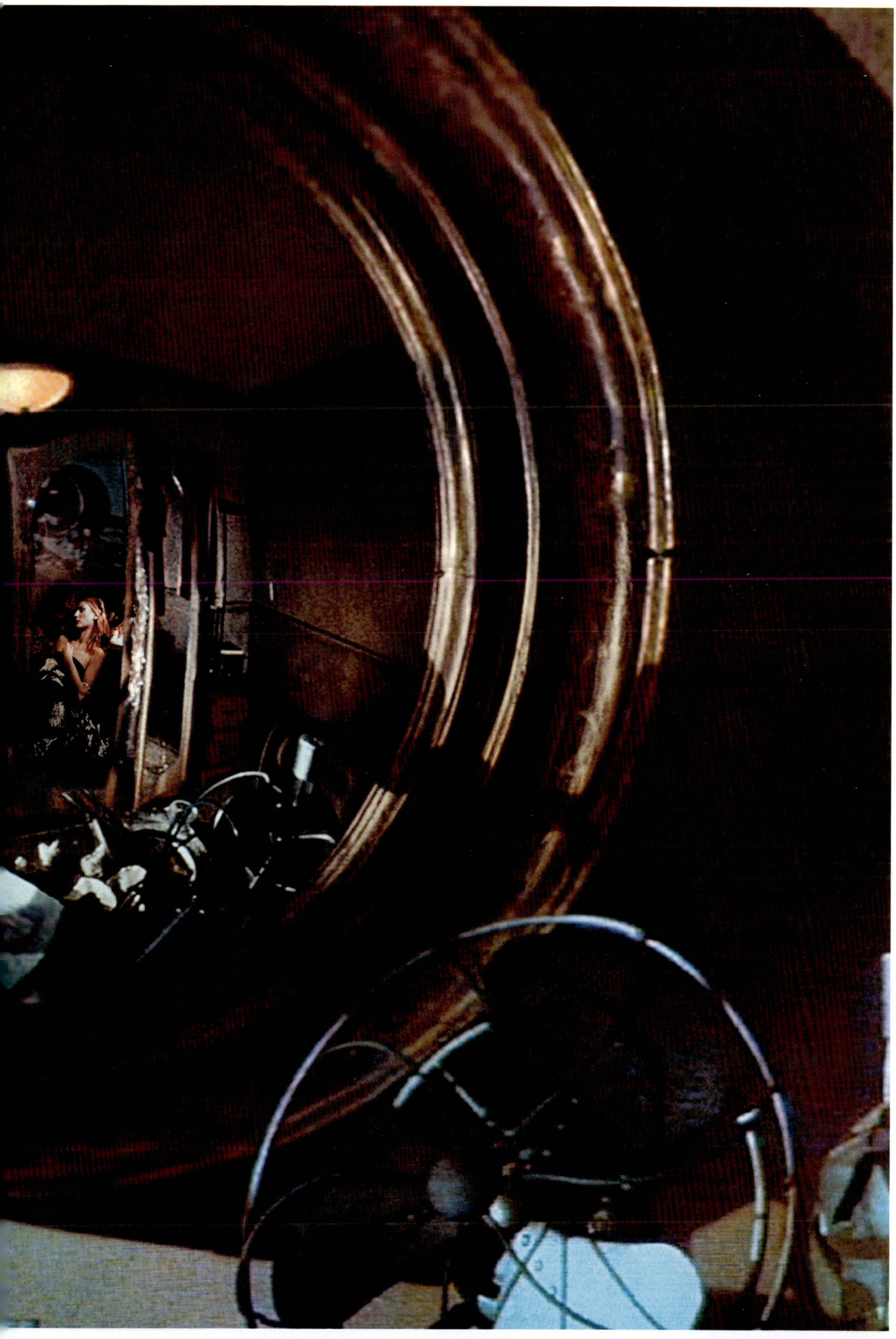

Royal Albert Hall, 2005
Tirage Lambda / Lambda print, 57 × 200 cm

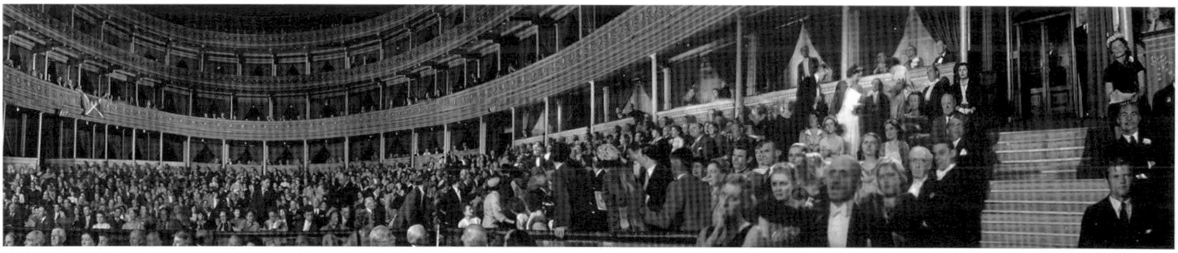

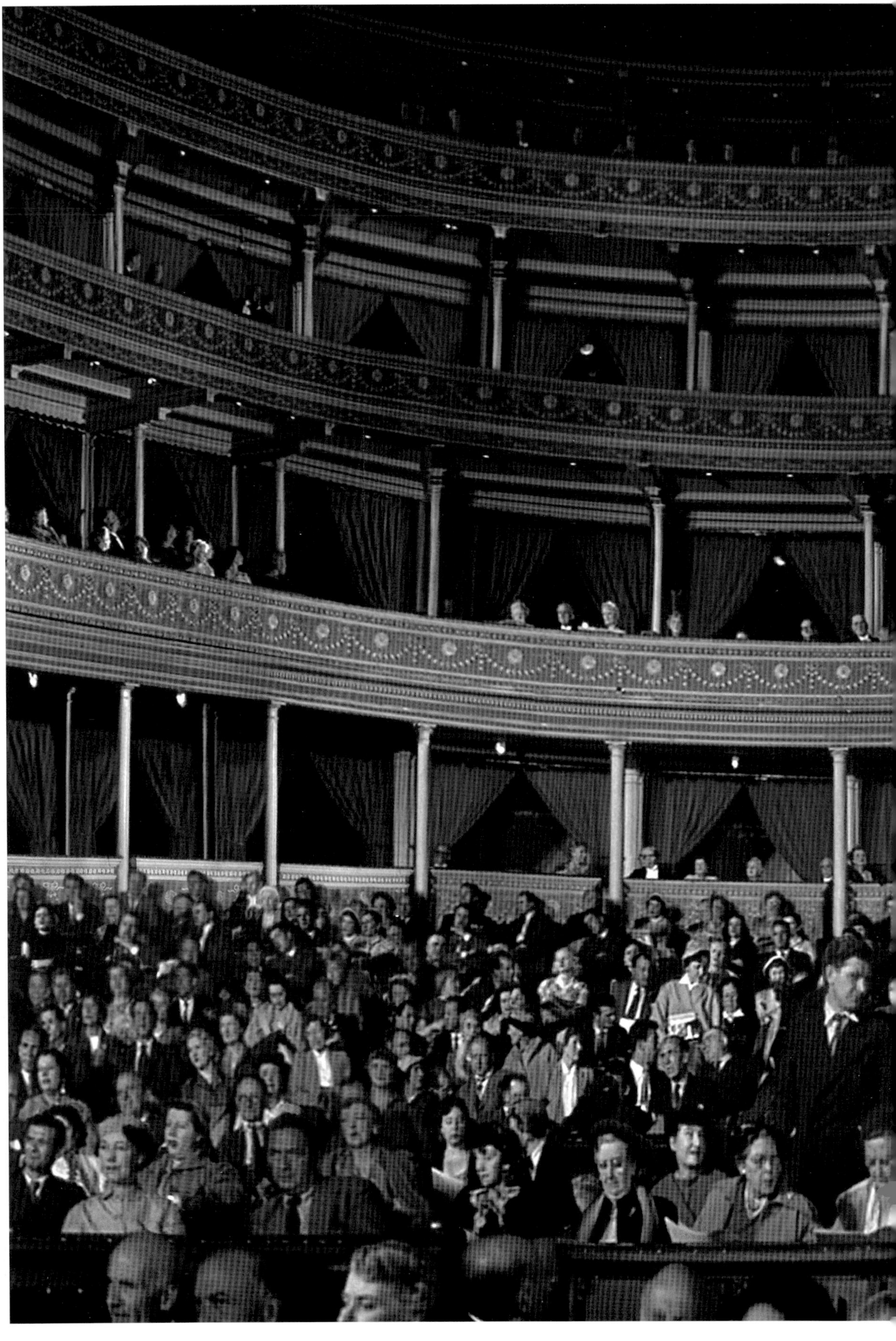

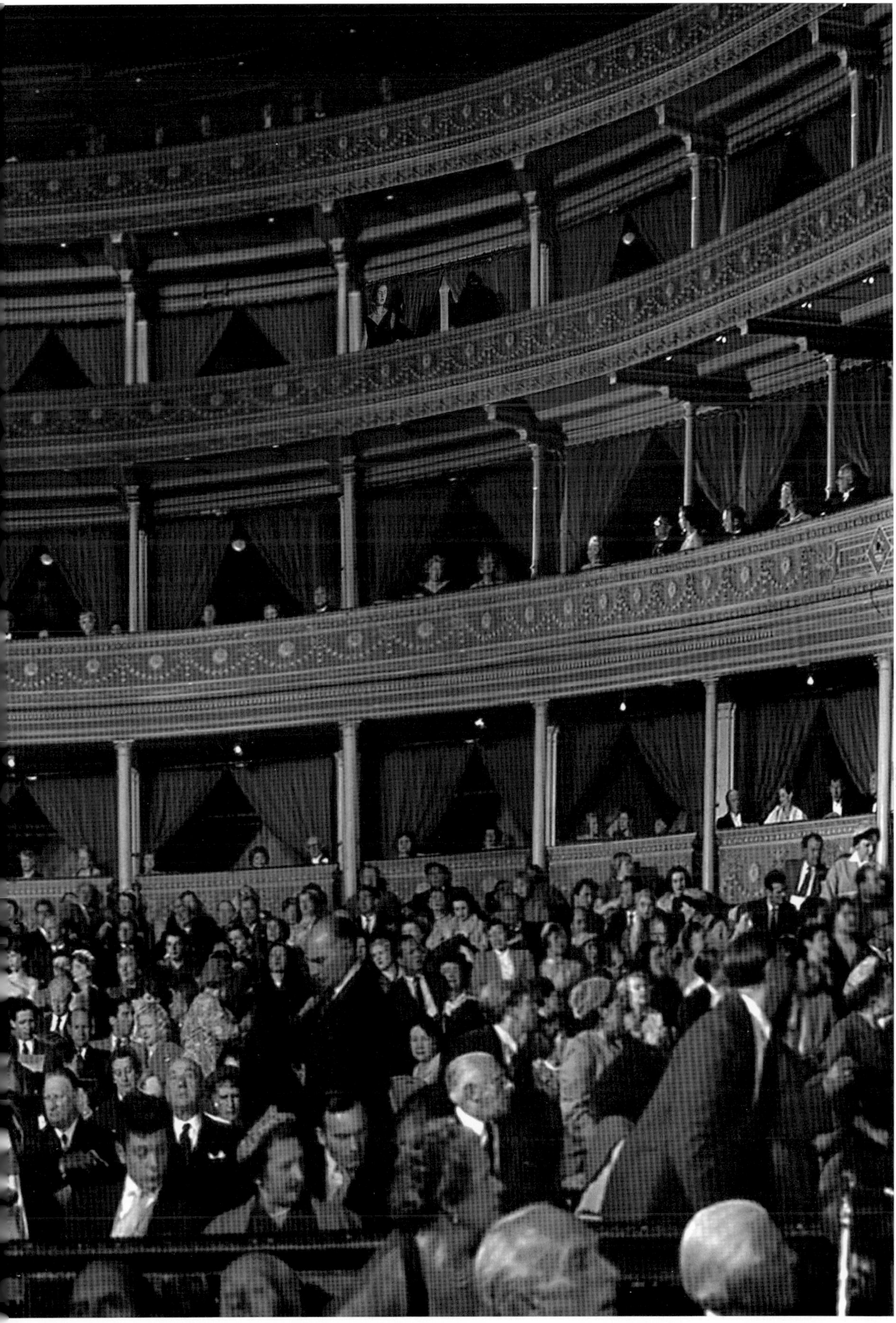

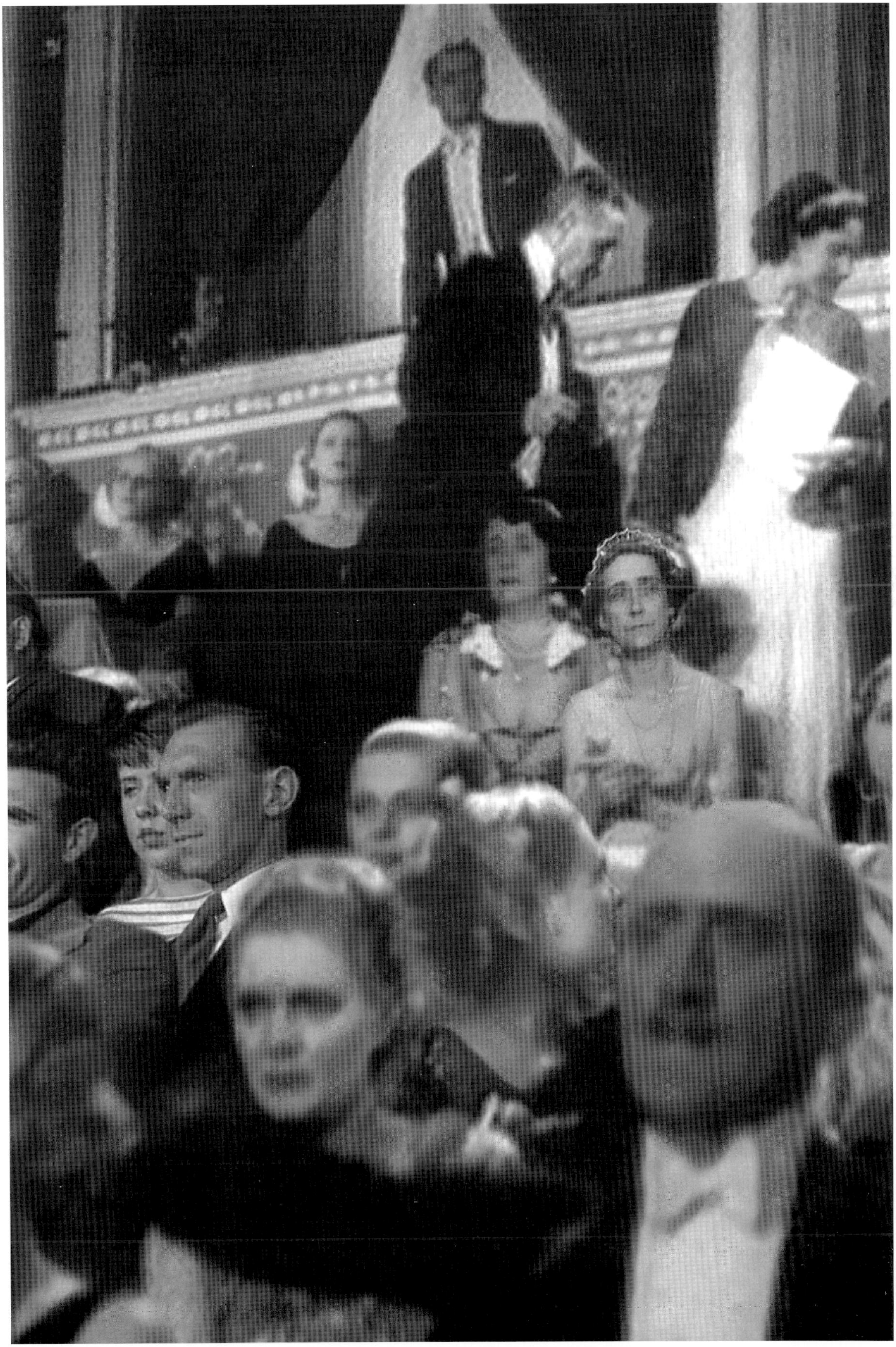

60 *Narcisse/Echo*, 2009
Carte postale imprimée sur maille drapeau, projecteur de diapositives, diapositive / Postcard print on flag mesh, slide projector, slide, dimensions variables / dimensions variable

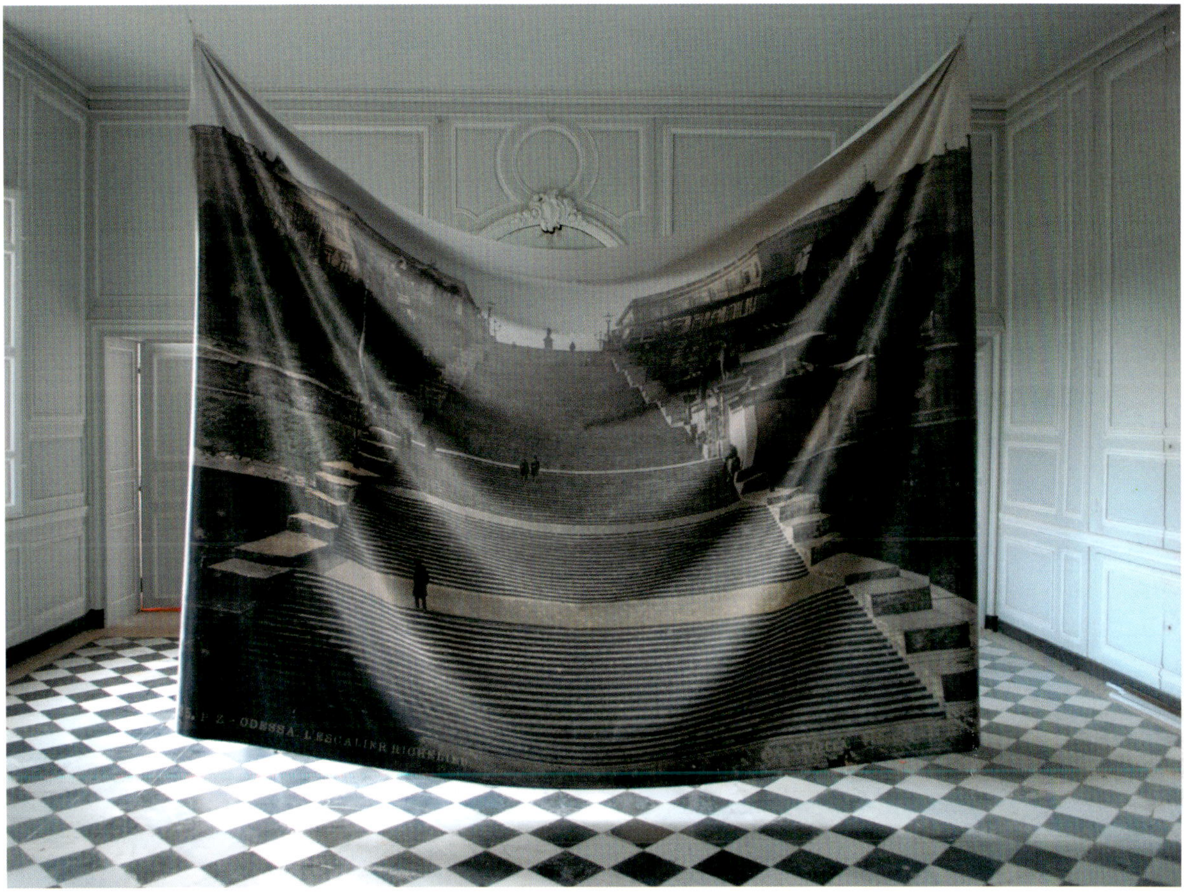
ODESSA. L'ESCALIER

Studio, 2006
Tirage Lambda / Lambda print, 90 × 190 cm

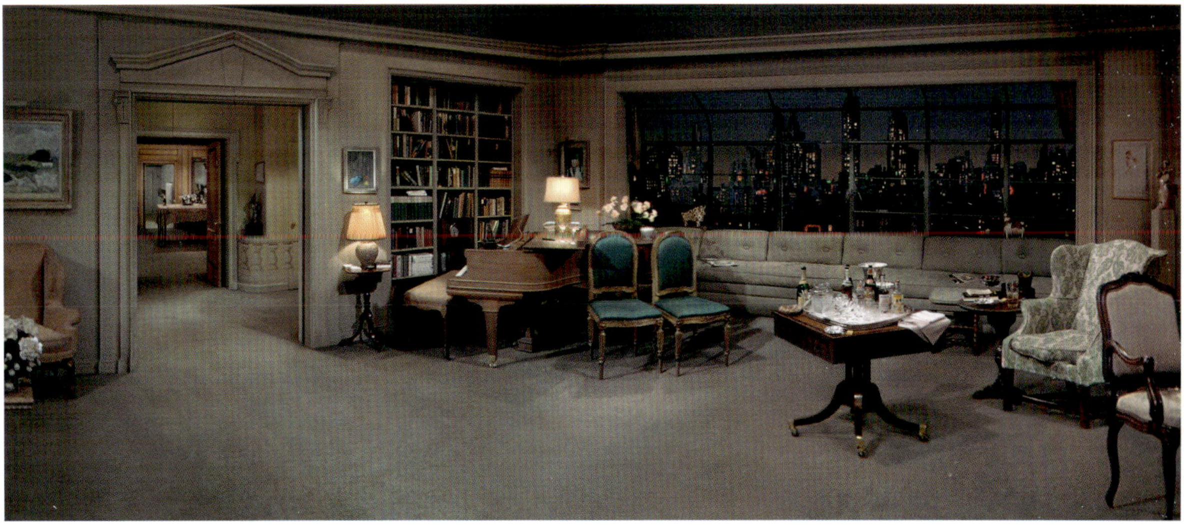

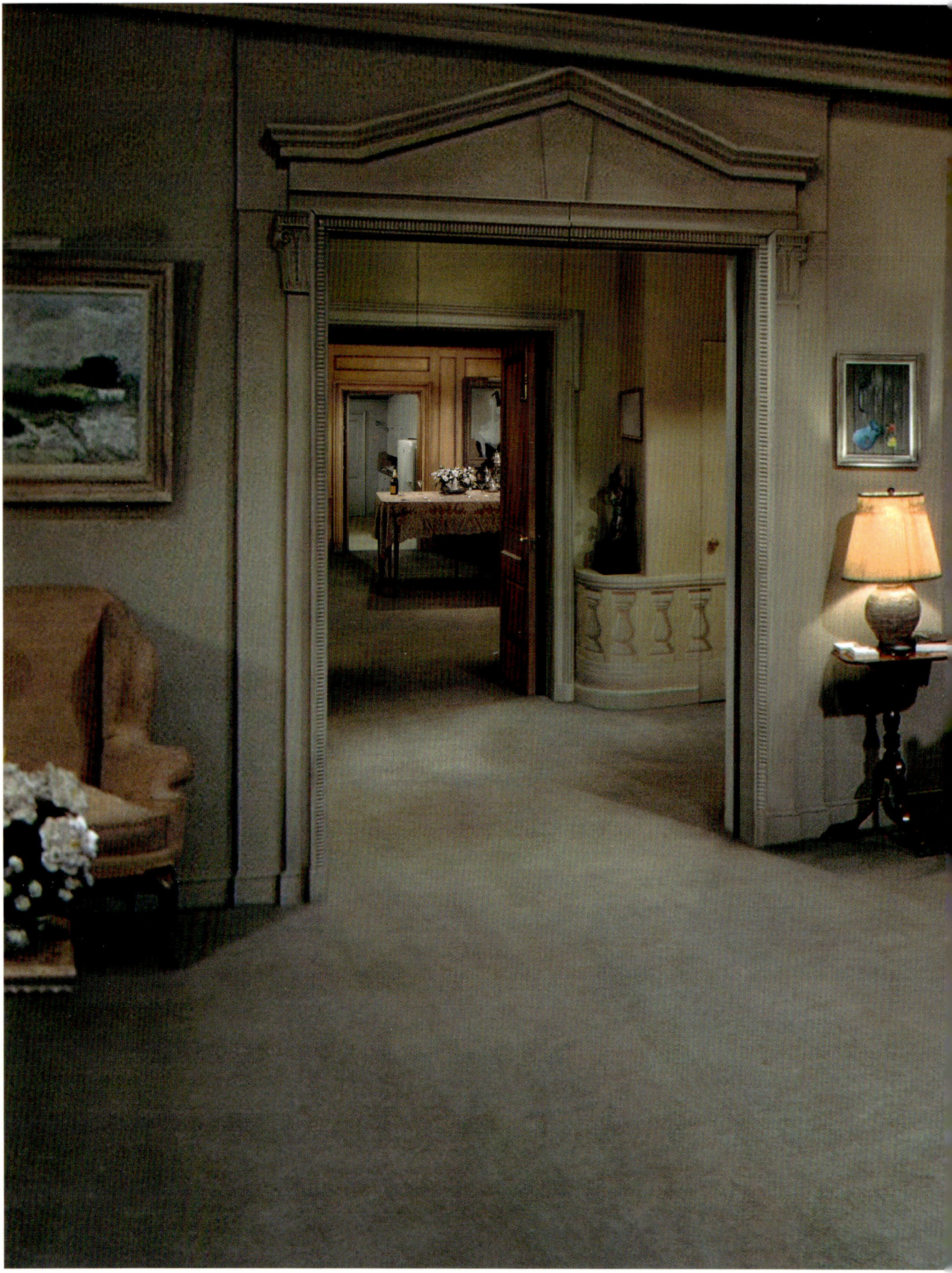

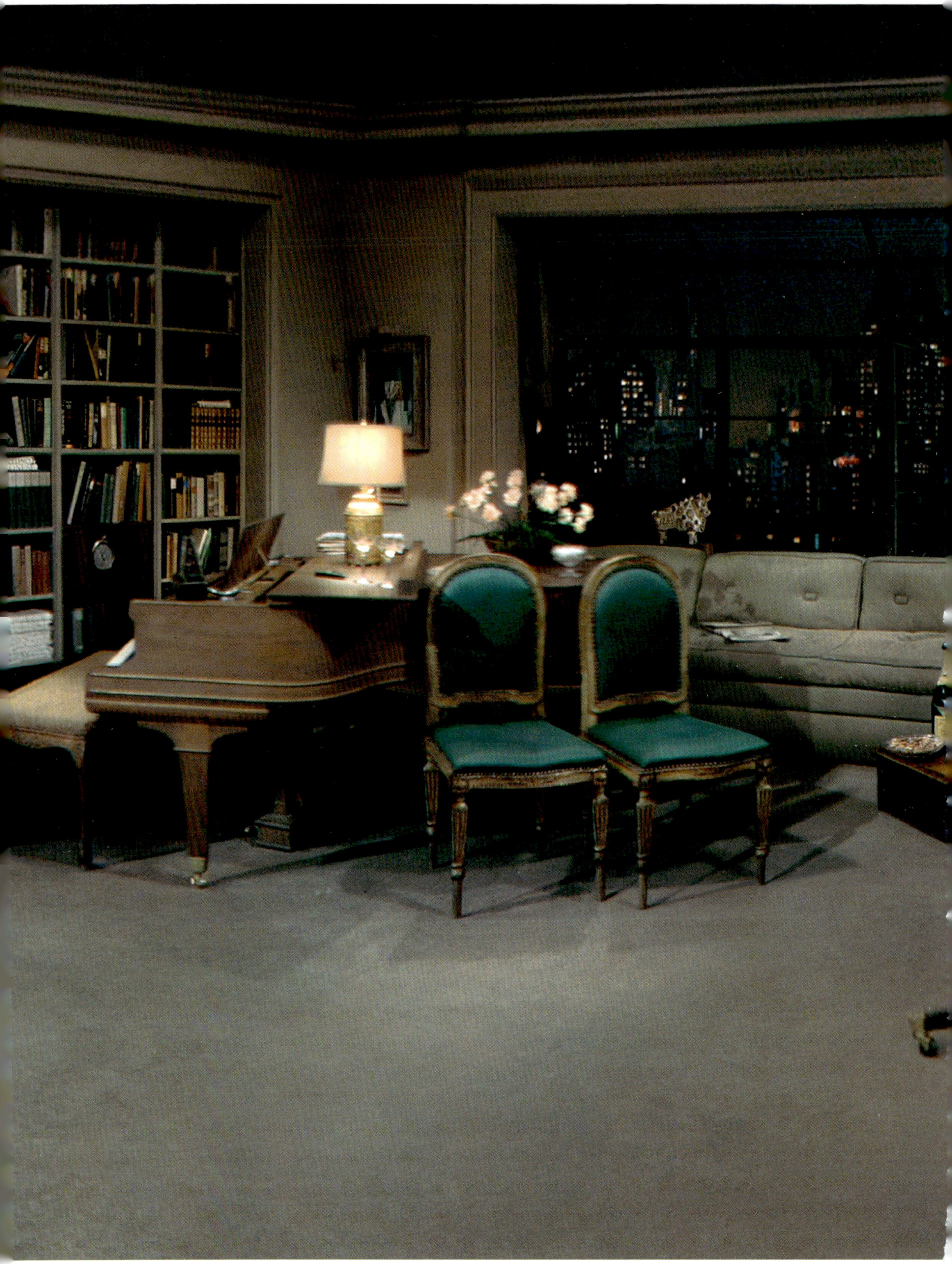

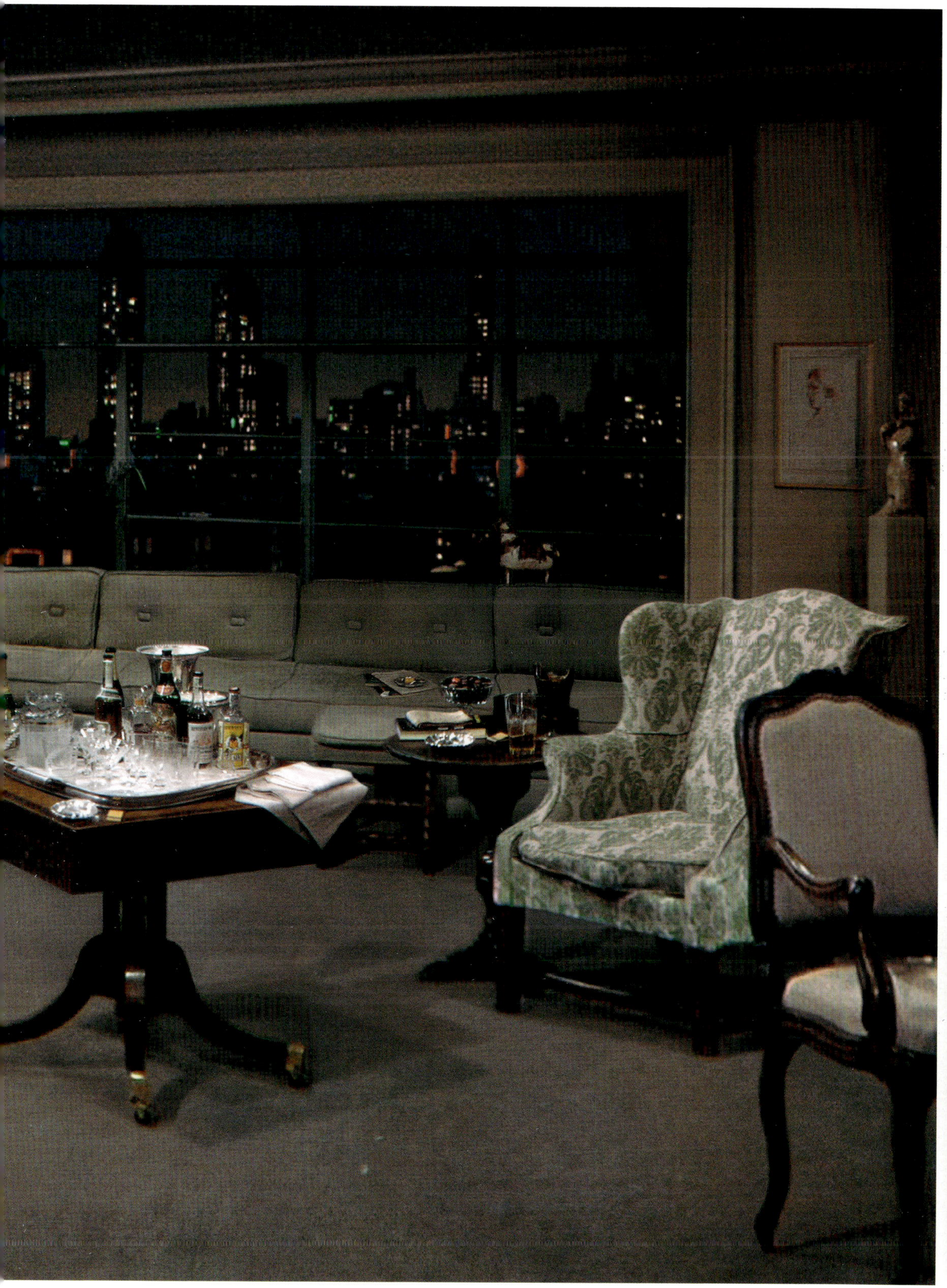

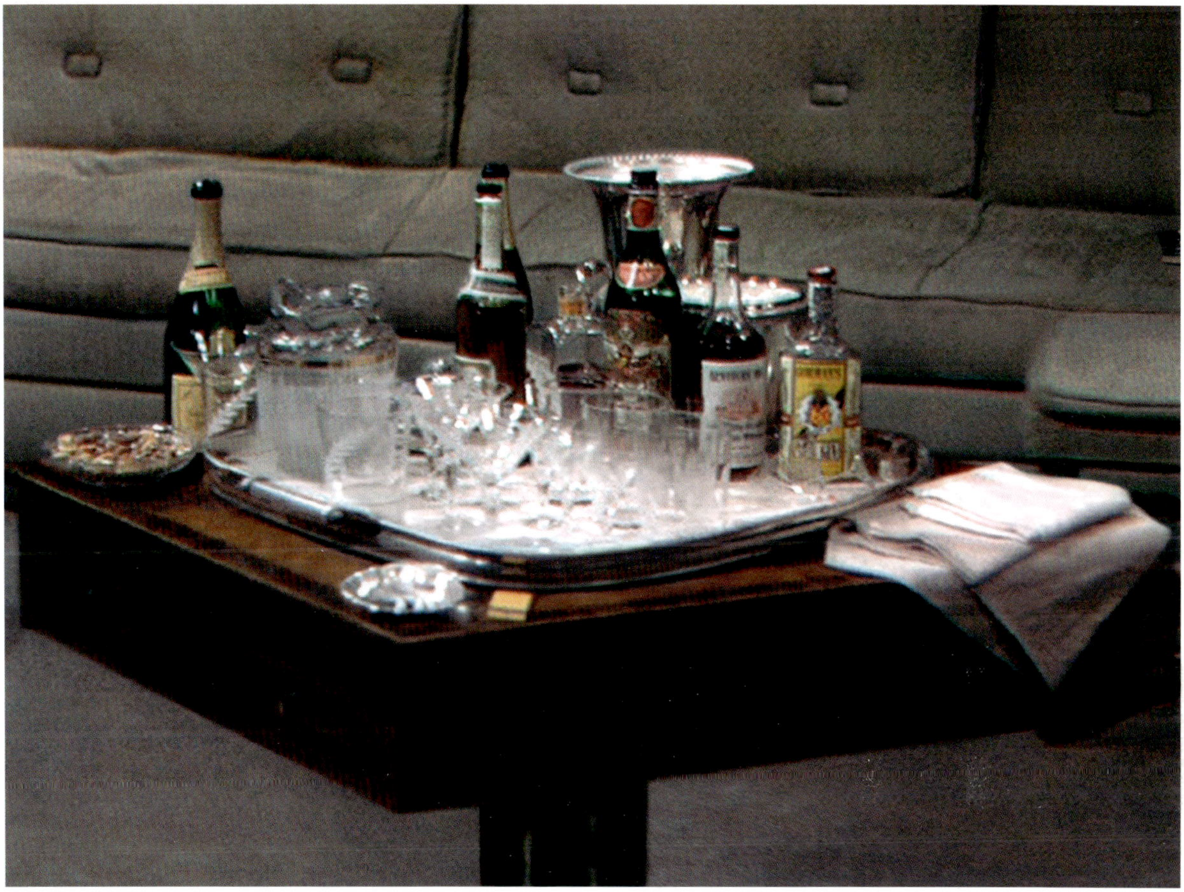

69-71
Inclusion -1798

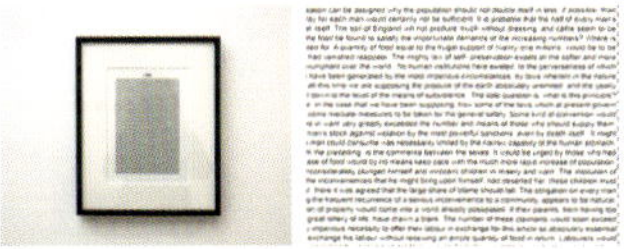

72-73
Est/Ouest

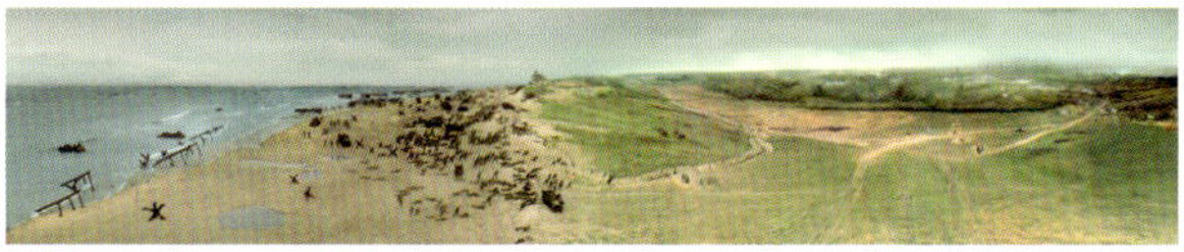

75-79
Danse américaine

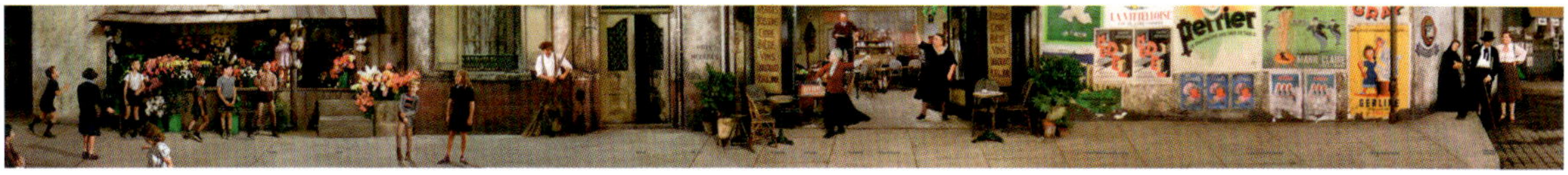

81-83
La Règle du jeu

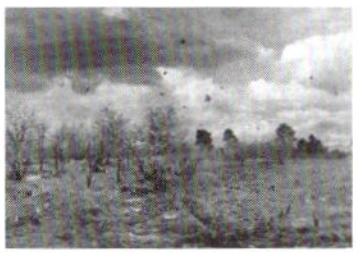

85-87
Sandbagwal

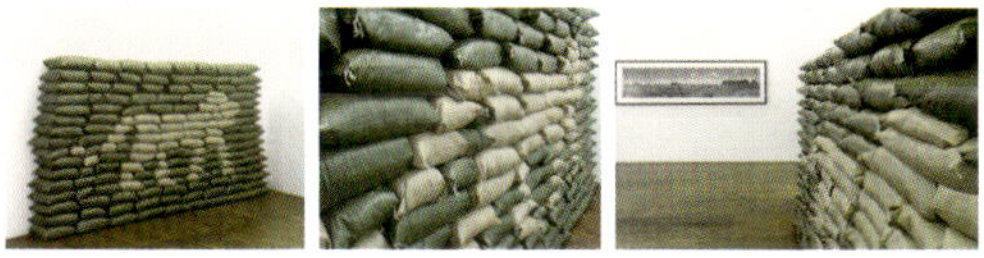

89-91
Summit

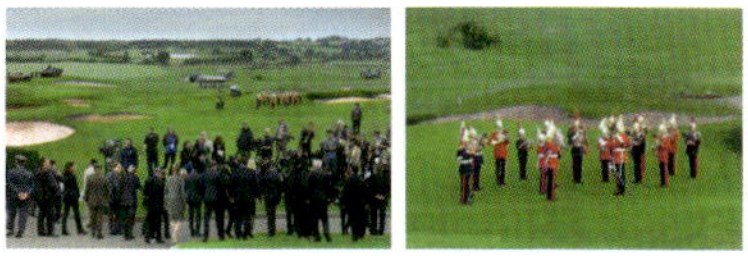

93
BPM

95-97
Odyssée

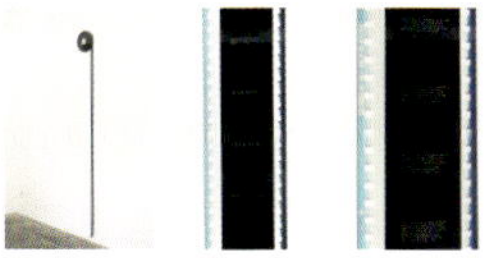

99
La main invisible

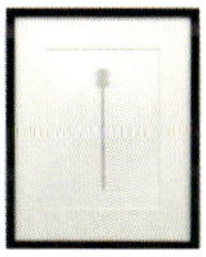

101-103
Nocturne (été)

105-109
Obsidionales

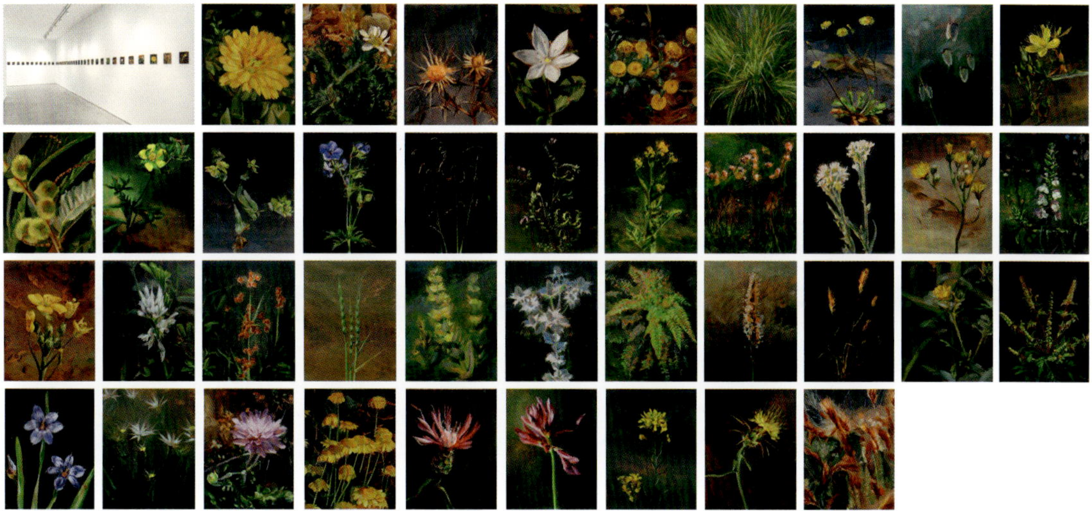

Le Tribut

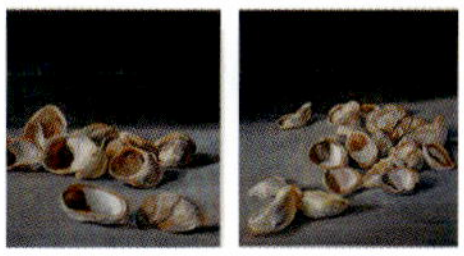

Inclusion -1798, 2020
Tirage photographique par contact sur papier baryté / Contact printing on baryta paper, 17 × 12 cm

1798

England and Wales.) For five years, ending in 1777, the proportion of births to burials in the kingdom of Naples was 144 to 100, but there is reason to suppose that this proportion would indicate an increase much greater than would be really found to have taken place in that kingdom during a pe
ce thinks that the registers in the former period are not to be depended upon, but, probably, in this instance they do not give incorrect proportions. At least there are many reasons for expecting to find a greater excess of births above the burials in the former period than in the latter. In the natura
s have great influence in exciting and directing this spirit.) And a greater proportional yearly increase of produce will almost invariably be followed by a greater proportional increase of population. But, besides this great cause, which would naturally give the excess of births above burials greater at
f the population. For some few years after the great plague in 1666, it is probable that there was a more than usual excess of births above burials, particularly if Dr Price's opinion be founded, that England was more populous at the revolution (which happened only twenty-two years afterwards) th
l has accommodated itself very nearly to the average produce of each country. The discouragements to marriage, the consequent vicious habits, war, luxury, the silent though certain depopulation of large towns, and the close habitations, and insufficient food of many of the poor, prevent populati
ntry at present. In New Jersey, the proportion of births to deaths on an average of seven years, ending in 1743, was as 300 to 100. In France and England, taking the highest proportion, it is as 117 to 100. Great and astonishing as this difference is, we ought not to be so wonder-struck at it as to
. And since the world began, the causes of population and depopulation have probably been as constant as any of the laws of nature with which we are acquainted. The passion between the sexes has appeared in every age to be so nearly the same that it may always be considered, in algebra
regular, but though we cannot always predict the mode we may with certainty predict the fact. If the proportion of births to deaths for a few years indicate an increase of numbers much beyond the proportional increased or acquired produce of the country, we may be perfectly certain that unless
subject to some slight variations which are, however, completely open to our view and observations. In some countries population appears to have been forced, that is, the people have been habituated by degrees to live almost upon the smallest possible quantity of food. There must have been p
ipally thus to force the population. A nation in this state must necessarily be subject to famines. Where a country is so populous in proportion to the means of subsistence that the average produce of it is but barely sufficient to support the lives of the inhabitants, any deficiency from the badness o
ill in time be much less liberally rewarded. The numbers will in this case permanently increase without a proportional increase in the means of subsistence. In the different states of Europe there must be some variations in the proportion between the number of inhabitants and the quantity of food c
ulation. But to effect this must always be a most difficult, and, every friend to humanity will hope, an abortive attempt. Nothing is so common as to hear of encouragements that ought to be given to population. If the tendency of mankind to increase be so great as I have represented it to be, it may
attempt to effect this purpose in any other way is vicious, cruel, and tyrannical, and in any state of tolerable freedom cannot therefore succeed. It may appear to be the interest of the rulers, and the rich of a state, to force population, and thereby lower the price of labour, and consequently the expe
ne has above three. I confess, that before the bill was brought into Parliament, and for some time after, I thought that such a regulation would be highly beneficial, but further reflection on the subject has convinced me that if its object be to better the condition of the poor, it is calculated to defeat th
cases where population may permanently increase without a proportional increase in the means of subsistence. But it is evident that the variation in different states, between the food and the numbers supported by it, is restricted to a limit beyond which it cannot pass. In every country, the popula
populous than corn countries. The lands in England are not suited to rice, but they would all bear potatoes; and Dr Adam Smith observes that if potatoes were to become the favourite vegetable food of the common people, and if the same quantity of land was employed in their culture as is now
rmation is always the nearest in new colonies, where the knowledge and industry of an old state operate on the fertile unappropriated land of a new one. In other cases, the youth or the age of a state is not in this respect of very great importance. It is probable that the food of Great Britain is divid
might be considered as an unit, to the time that it might be considered as a million, during the lapse of many hundred years, there would not be a single period when the mass of the people could be said to be free from distress, either directly or indirectly, for want of food. In every state in Europe,
e and able ministers of depopulation. They are the precursors in the great army of destruction; and often finish the dreadful work themselves. But should they fail in this war of extermination, sickly seasons, epidemics, pestilence, and plague, advance in terrific array, and sweep off their thousan
e means of subsistence increase. And that the superior power of population it repressed, and the actual population kept equal to the means of subsistence, by misery and vice? CHAPTER 8. Mr Wallace - Error of supposing that the difficulty arising from population is at a great distance - Mr Cond
variably represent the difficulties arising from it as at a great and almost immeasurable distance. Even Mr Wallace, who thought the argument itself of so much weight as to destroy his whole system of equality, did not seem to be aware that any difficulty would occur from this cause till the whol
being remote, would be imminent and immediate. At every period during the progress of cultivation, from the present moment to the time when the whole earth was become like a garden, the distress for want of food would be constantly pressing on all mankind, if they were equal. Though the pr
singular instance of the attachment of a man to principles, which every day's experience was so fatally for himself contradicting. To see the human mind in one of the most enlightened nations of the world, and after a lapse of some thousand years, debased by such a fermentation of disgusting
executed. It necessarily, therefore, wants that detail and application which can alone prove the truth of any theory. A few observations will be sufficient to shew how completely the theory is contradicted when it is applied to the real, and not to an imaginary, state of things. In the last division of th
upplying their wants than their industry. Having allowed the necessity of such a class of men, and adverting afterwards to the precarious revenue of those families that would depend so entirely on the life and health of their chief, he says, very justly: 'There exists then, a necessary cause of ineq
found inefficacious. By the application of calculations to the probabilities of life and the interest of money, he proposes that a fund should be established which should assure to the old an assistance, produced, in part, by their own former savings, and, in part, by the savings of individuals who in
neans might be found of more completely preserving a state of equality, by preventing credit from being the exclusive privilege of great fortunes, and yet giving it a basis equally solid, and by rendering the progress of industry, and the activity of commerce, less dependent on great capitalists. S
if by establishments of this kind of spur to industry be removed, if the idle and the negligent are placed upon the same footing with regard to their credit, and the future support of their wives and families, as the active and industrious, can we expect to see men exert that animated activity in better
on to these establishments, and supposing for a moment that they would give no check to productive industry, by far the greatest difficulty remains yet behind. Were every man sure of a comfortable provision for his family, almost every man would have one, and were the rising generation free t
counteract each other? When the increase of the number of men surpassing their means of subsistence, the necessary result must be either a continual diminution of happiness and population, a movement truly retrograde, or, at least, a kind of oscillation between good and evil? In societies arri
e realization of an event which cannot take place but at an era when the human race will have attained improvements, of which we can at present scarcely form a conception.' Mr Condorcet's picture of what may be expected to happen when the number of men shall surpass the means of their s
ny degree near the truth, it will appear, on the contrary, that the period when the number of men surpass their means of subsistence has long since arrived, and that this necessity oscillation, this constantly subsisting cause of periodical misery, has existed ever since we have had any histories
prejudices of superstition would by that time have ceased to throw over morals a corrupt and degrading austerity, he alludes, either to a promiscuous concubinage, which would prevent breeding, or to something else as unnatural. To remove the difficulty in this way will, surely, in the opinion of m
vation of plants. THE LAST QUESTION WHICH MR CONDORCET PROPOSES for examination is the organic perfectibility of man. He observes that if the proofs which have been already given and which, in their development will receive greater force in the work itself, are sufficient to establis
ss, from the destruction of the two great causes of the degradation of man, misery, and too great riches, from the gradual removal of transmissible and contagious disorders by the improvement of physical knowledge, rendered more efficacious by the progress of reason and of social order, he in
of these senses to the duration of human life is in the highest degree unphilosophical and totally unwarranted by any appearances in the laws of nature. Variations from different causes are essentially distinct from a regular and unretrograde increase. The average duration of human life will to a
me measure tend to prove that there has been no marked advance in an opposite direction. It may perhaps be said that the world is yet so young, so completely in its infancy, that it ought not to be expected that any difference should appear so soon. If this be the case, there is at once an end of
facts. The grand and consistent theory of Newton will be placed upon the same footing as the wild and eccentric hypotheses of Descartes. In short, if the laws of nature are thus fickle and inconstant, if it can be affirmed and be believed that they will change, when for ages and ages they have ap
nay undoubtedly happen. All that I mean to say is that it is impossible to infer it from reasoning. If without any previous observable symptoms or indications of a change, we can infer that a change will take place, we may as well make any assertion whatever and think it as unreasonable to be co
xtension, and the sandy foundation on which the argument rests is that because the limit of human life is undefined; because you cannot mark its precise term, and say so far exactly shall it go and no further; that therefore its extent may increase for ever, and be properly termed indefinite or un
the desirable qualities of the parents in a greater degree. In the famous Leicestershire breed of sheep, the object is to procure them with small heads and small legs. Proceeding upon these breeding maxims, it is evident that we might go on till the heads and legs were evanescent quantities,
h further improvement will stop, I can very easily mention a point at which it will not arrive. I should not scruple to assert that were the breeding to continue for ever, the head and legs of these sheep would never be so small as the head and legs of a rat. It cannot be true, therefore, that among an
n gradually larger by cultivation. If the progress were really unlimited it might be increased ad infinitum, but this is so gross an absurdity that we may be quite sure that among plants as well as among animals there is a limit to improvement, though we do not exactly know where it is. It is probable
antities much greater than a cabbage. No man can say that he has seen the largest ear of wheat, or the largest oak that could ever grow, but he might easily, and with perfect certainty, name a point of magnitude at which they would not arrive. In all these cases therefore, a careful distinction sh
but I only know this from my experience of the weakness and want of tenacity in the materials of a carnation stalk. There are many substances in nature of the same size that would support as large a head as a cabbage. The reasons of the mortality of plants are at present perfectly unknown to
tality of man on earth, till it can be clearly proved that the human race has made, and is making, a decided progress towards an illimitable extent of life. And the chief reason why I adduced the two particular instances from animals and plants was to expose and illustrate, if I could, the fallacy of th
s from different causes, it may be doubted whether, since the world began, any organic improvement whatever in the human frame can be clearly ascertained. The foundations, therefore, on which the arguments for the organic perfectibility of man rest, are unusually weak, and can only be consi
ting between a small improvement, the limit of which is undefined, and an improvement really unlimited. As the human race, however, could not be improved in this way, without condemning all the bad specimens to celibacy, it is not probable that an attention to breed should ever become gen
ch in man towards immortality on earth, to urge the very great additional weight that an increase in the duration of life would give to the argument of population. Many, I doubt not, will think that the attempting gravely to controvert so absurd a paradox as the immortality of man on earth, or inde
iews, they will look upon this neglect merely as an indication of poverty, and narrowness, in the mental exertions of their contemporaries, and only think that the world is not yet prepared to receive their sublime truths. On the contrary, a candid investigation of these subjects, accompanied with a
which science has of late made such rapid advances. The present rage for wide and unrestrained speculation seems to be a kind of mental intoxication, arising, perhaps, from the great and unexpected discoveries which have been made of late years, in various branches of science. To men ela
t assertions for patient investigation, and well authenticated proofs. Mr Condorcet's book may be considered not only as a sketch of the opinions of a celebrated individual, but of many of the literary men in France at the beginning of the Revolution. As such, though merely a sketch, it seems wort
ruck with the spirit and energy of his style, the force and precision of some of his reasonings, the ardent tone of his thoughts, and particularly with that impressive earnestness of manner which gives an air of truth to the whole. At the same time, it must be confessed that he has not proceeded in
at has yet appeared. An amelioration of society to be produced merely by reason and conviction wears much more the promise of permanence than any change effected and maintained by force. The unlimited exercise of private judgement is a doctrine inexpressibly grand and captivating and ha
hole is little better than a dream, a beautiful phantom of the imagination. These 'gorgeous palaces' of happiness and immortality, these 'solemn temples' of truth and virtue will dissolve, 'like the baseless fabric of a vision', when we awaken to real life and contemplate the true and genuine situatio
ysterious and occult cause and which he does not attempt to investigate, will be found to be the grinding law of necessity, misery, and the fear of misery. The great error under which Mr Godwin labours throughout his whole work is the attributing almost all the vices and misery that are seen in c
d obtrusive causes of much mischief to mankind, yet in reality they are light and superficial, they are mere feathers that float on the surface, in comparison with those deeper seated causes of impurity that corrupt the springs and render turbid the whole stream of human life. Mr Godwin, in his ch
expire. The narrow principle of selfishness would vanish. No man being obliged to guard his little store or provide with anxiety and pain for his restless wants, each would lose his individual existence in the thought of the general good. No man would be an enemy to his neighbour, for they woul
cannot live in the midst of plenty. All cannot share alike the bounties of nature. Were there no established administration of property, every man would be obliged to guard with force his little store. Selfishness would be triumphant. The subjects of contention would be perpetual. Every individual m
ee fourths of the habitable globe is now uncultivated.' The parts already cultivated are capable of immeasurable improvement. Myriads of centuries of still increasing population may pass away, and the earth be still found sufficient for the subsistence of its inhabitants.' I have already pointed out

emoved. War and
cessary labours of
edom. Mr Godwin
k VIII, ch. 8, in the
nd every cause of
s, if possible, than
alf of every man's
cattle seem to be
umbers? Where is
hs, would be to be
e softer and more
erseness of which
erent in the nature
ed, and the yearly
at is this principle?
al present govern
convention would
ould supply them,
ath itself. It might
e human stomach,
by those who had
ase of population.
The institution of
ese children must
tion on every man
ears to be natural,
s, from having too
ould soon exceed
solutely essential
Labourers would
ture, and not from
een years, instead
land, it must have
CHAPTER 11 Mr
x thousand years
pleasures of pure
Intemperance in
neral expediency
of the pleasures of
er, the affectionate
tellectual, reason,
es, no observable
nts of the species
on any indications
examine a few of
ccasions the most
equal strength, or

The Alien and Sedition Acts of July 14, 1798. An Act in addition to the act, entitled «An act for the punishment of certain crimes against the United States.» SEC. 1 Be it enacted by the Senate and House of Representatives of the United States of America in Congress assembled. That if any persons shall unlawfully combine or conspire together, with intent to oppose any measure or measures of the government of the United States, which are or shall be directed by proper authority, or to impede the operation of any law of the United States, or to intimidate or prevent any person holding a place or office in or under the government of the United States, from undertaking, performing or executing his trust or duty, and if any person or persons, with intent as aforesaid, shall counsel, advise or attempt to procure any insurrection, riot, unlawful assembly, or combination, whether such conspiracy, threatening, counsel, advice, or attempt shall have the proposed effect or not, he or they shall be deemed guilty of a high misdemeanor, and on conviction, before any court of the United States having jurisdiction thereof, shall be punished by a fine not exceeding five thousand dollars, and by imprisonment during a term not less than six months nor exceeding five years, and further, at the discretion of the court may be holden to find sureties for his good behaviour in such sum, and for such time, as the said court may direct. SEC. 2 And be it further enacted. That if any person shall write, print, utter or publish, or shall cause or procure to be written, printed, uttered or publishing, or shall knowingly and willingly assist or aid in writing, printing, uttering or publishing any false, scandalous and malicious writing or writings against the government of the United States, or either house of the Congress of the United States, or the President of the United States, with intent to defame the said government, or either house of the said Congress, or the said President, or to bring them, or either of them, into contempt or disrepute, or to excite against them, or either or any of them, the hatred of the good people of the United States, or to excite any unlawful combinations therein, for opposing or resisting any law of the United States, or any act of the President of the United States, done in pursuance of any such law, or of the powers in him vested by the constitution of the United States, or to resist, oppose, or defeat any such law or act, or to aid, encourage or abet any hostile designs of any foreign nation against the United States, their people or government, then such person, being thereof convicted before any court of the United States having jurisdiction thereof, shall be punished by a fine not exceeding two thousand dollars, and by imprisonment not exceeding two years. SEC. 3 And be it further enacted, and declared. That if any person shall be prosecuted under this act, for the writing or publishing any libel aforesaid, it shall be lawful for the defendant, upon the trial of the cause, to give in evidence in his defense, the truth of the matter contained in the publication charged as a libel. And the jury who shall try the cause, shall have a right to determine the law and the fact, under the direction of the court, as in other cases. SEC. 4 And be it further enacted. That this act shall continue and be in force until the third day of March, one thousand eight hundred and one, and no longer. Provided. That the expiration of the act shall not prevent or defeat a prosecution and punishment of any offense against the law, during the time it shall be in force. JONATHAN DAYTON, Speaker of the House of Representatives. THEODORE SEDGWICK, President of the Senate, pro tempore. APPROVED, July 14, 1798. JOHN ADAMS, President of the United States. Source: The Laws of the United States of America, printed by Richard Folwell, Philadelphia, 1796-1798.

contention cease. Unwholesome trades and manufactories do not exist. Crowds no longer collect together in great and pestilent cities for purposes of court intrigue, of commerce, and vicious
agriculture are shared amicably among all. The number of persons, and the produce of the island, we suppose to be the same as at present. The spirit of benevolence, guided by impartial jus
does not think himself that this freedom would lead to a promiscuous intercourse, and in this I perfectly agree with him. The love of variety is a vicious, corrupt, and unnatural taste and cou
third edition, Vol II, p. 512) And every man would be ready to furnish instruction to the rising generation according to his capacity. I cannot conceive a form of society so favourable upon the w
depopulation, as we have supposed, removed, the numbers would necessarily increase faster than in any society that has ever yet been known. I have mentioned, on the authority of a pamphle
fifteen years. But to be quite sure that we do not go beyond the truth, we will only suppose the period of doubling to be twenty-five years, a ratio of increase which is well known to have taker
time must be employed for this purpose. Yet with such, or much greater exertions, a person who is acquainted with the nature of the soil in this country, and who reflects on the fertility of the
necessary to make that species of manure which best suits the land. In China it is said that the soil in some of the provinces is so fertile as to produce two crops of rice in the year without dres
the fresh land to turn up? Where is the dressing necessary to improve that which is already in cultivation? There is no person with the smallest knowledge of land but would say that it was imp
divided among twenty-eight millions. Alas! what becomes of the picture where men lived in the midst of plenty, where no man was obliged to provide with anxiety and pain for his restless want
exalted emotions of the soul. The temptations to evil are too strong for human nature to resist. The corn is plucked before it is ripe, or secreted in unfair proportions, and the whole black train
Mr Godwin ascribes the original sin of the worst men. (Bk VIII, ch. 3, in the third edition, Vol. II, p. 462) No opposition had been produced by them between public and private good. No mor
of man, and absolutely independent of it human regulations. If we are not yet too well convinced of the reality of this melancholy picture, let us but look for a moment into the next period of t
increase greater than the boldest speculator can imagine. This is undoubtedly a very different view of the difficulty arising from population from that which Mr Godwin gives, when he says, 'M
is it some obscure and occult cause? Is it some mysterious interference of heaven which, at a certain period, strikes the men with impotence, and the women with barrenness? Or is it a caus
civilized society, would be successively dictated by the most imperious necessity. As man, according to Mr Godwin, is the creature of the impressions to which he is subject, the goadings of
then be called, and the dangerous situation of the country stated in the strongest terms. It would be observed, that while they lived in the midst of plenty, it was of little consequence who lab
that these pressing wants, which from the state of the produce of the country could not all be gratified, had occasioned some flagrant violations of justice, that these violations had already che
be urged perhaps by some objectors that, as the fertility of the land increased, and various accidents occurred, the share of some men might be much more than sufficient for their support, a
that it was not certainly probable that he should throw away the rest, but that even if he exchanged his surplus food for the labour of others, and made them in some degree dependent on hi
turned their attention to the true cause of the difficulties under which the community laboured, that while every man felt secure that all his children would be well provided for by general benev
that some check to population therefore was imperiously called for, that the most natural and obvious check seemed to be to make every man provide for his own children, that this would c
marriage, or at least, of some express or implied obligation on every man to support his own children, seems to be the natural result of these reasonings in a community under the difficulties t
necessarily fall for support upon the society, or starve. And to prevent the frequent recurrence of such an inconvenience, as it would be highly unjust to punish so natural a fault by personal r
to maintain his children, the society would enforce, if there were occasion, and the greater degree of inconvenience or labour, to which a family would necessarily subject him, added to some
though not perhaps perfectly justifiable. This origin, however, is now lost in the new train of ideas which the custom has since generated. What at first might be dictated by state necessity is
large a family, could not give them sufficient for their support, what are they to do in a world where everything is appropriated? We have seen the fatal effects that would result to a society, if
the ability of the surplus produce to supply. Moral merit is a very difficult distinguishing criterion, except in extreme cases. The owners of surplus produce would in general seek some more ob
to existence. The fund appropriated to the maintenance of labour would be the aggregate quantity of food possessed by the owners of land beyond their own consumption. When the deman
live in ease and comfort, and would consequently be able to rear a numerous and vigorous offspring. On the state of this fund, the happiness, or the degree of misery, prevailing among the lo
any original depravity of man, in a very short period degenerate into a society constructed upon a plan not essentially different from that which prevails in every known state at present. I mea
of twenty-five years, and reflect upon the labour necessary to double the produce in so short a time, even if we allow it possible, we may venture to pronounce with certainty that if Mr Godwir
degenerated strangely from its original purity, and administer but a very small portion of the happiness it proposed, in short, its essential principle must be completely destroyed, before any c
Godwin's conjecture concerning the future extinction of the passion between the sexes - Little apparent grounds for such a conjecture - Passion of love not inconsistent either with reason or v
that the world has existed. Men in the decline of life have in all ages declaimed against a passion which they have ceased to feel, but with as little reason as success. Those who from coldne
love will bear the contemplation of the most improved reason, and the most exalted virtue. Perhaps there is scarcely a man who has once experienced the genuine delight of virtuous love, hc
every enjoyment defeats its own purpose. A walk in the finest day through the most beautiful country, if pursued too far, ends in pain and fatigue. The most wholesome and invigorating food, -
According to either of these definitions, a sensual pleasure not attended with the probability of unhappy consequences does not offend against the laws of morality, and if it be pursued with
sense. Strip the commerce of the sexes of all its attendant circumstances, and it would be generally despised. (Bk. I, ch. 5, in the third edition, Vol. I, pp. 71-72) He might as well say to a m
kindness of feelings, the imagination and the wit of a woman that excite the passion of love, and not the mere distinction of her being female. Urged by the passion of love, men have been driv
that faculty which enables us to calculate consequences, is the proper corrective and guide. It is probable therefore that improved reason will always tend to prevent the abuse of sensual p
progress whatever has hitherto been made. To suppose such an extinction, therefore, is merely to offer an unfounded conjecture, unsupported by any philosophical probabilities. It is a truth,
at present before any difference can take place sufficient sensibly to affect population. I would by no means suppose that the mass of mankind has reached its term of improvement, but the
in the past not to be considered as philosophical conjectures - Mr Godwin's and Mr Condorcet's conjecture respecting the approach of man towards immortality on earth, a curious instance c
the appearances from which the probable immortality of man is inferred. To prove the power of the mind over the body, Mr Godwin observes: 'How often do we find a piece of good news dissi
extraordinary revolutions in our frame, accelerates the circulation, causes the heart to palpitate, the tongue to refuse its office, and has been known to occasion death by extreme anguish or ex
if they could be so applied, for a time, that they would not exhaust and wear out the subject. In some of the cases here noticed, the strength of the stimulus depends upon its novelty and une

f frame which fix the attention of a man who has nothing else to think of, but this does not tend to prove that activity of mind will enable a man to disregard a high fever, the smallpox, or the plague. The man who walks twenty miles with a motive that engrosses his soul does not attend to his sligh
but it would not make him walk a hundred miles in twenty-four hours. This statement of the case shews the fallacy of supposing that the person was really not at all tired in his first walk of twenty miles, because he did not appear to be so, or, perhaps, scarcely felt any fatigue himself. The mind c
the proper management of the bit, he may be put so much upon his mettle, that he would appear to a standerby, as fresh and as high spirited as if he had not gone a mile. Nay, probably, the horse himself, while in the heat and passion occasioned by this stimulus, would not feel any fatigue, but
s fatigue would have its full weight and effect, and make them tire sooner. When I have taken a long walk with my gun, and met with no success, I have frequently returned home feeling a considerable degree of uncomfortableness from fatigue. Another day, perhaps, going over nearly the same
from the bodily fatigue, than by really and truly counteracting it. If the energy of my mind had really counteracted the fatigue of my body, why should I feel tired the next morning? if the stimulus of the hounds had as completely overcome the fatigue of the journey in reality, as it did in appearance,
rations. The multiplicity of vibrations of another kind may perhaps prevent their admission, or overcome them for a time when admitted, till a shoot of extraordinary energy puts all other vibration to the rout, destroys the vividness of my argumentative conceptions, and rides triumphant in the brair
aps, upon a comparison, the body has more effect upon the mind than the mind upon the body. The first object of the mind is to act as purveyor to the wants of the body. When these wants are completely satisfied, an active mind is indeed apt to wander further, to range over the fields of science,
ls of hunger, or sink with the exhausted body in sleep. It seems as if one might say with certainty that if a medicine could be found to immortalize the body there would be no fear of its [not] being accompanied by the immortality of the mind. But the immortality of the mind by no means seems to
f this latter description, and could such stimulants be continually applied, instead of tending to immortalize, they would tend very rapidly to destroy the human frame. The probable increase of the voluntary power of man over his animal frame comes next under Mr Godwin's consideration, and he
ptible progress in the regular correction of the disorders of their frames and the consequent prolongation of their lives. Mr Godwin says, 'Nothing can be more unphilosophical than to conclude, that, because a certain species of power is beyond the train of our present observation, that it is beyon
oment we leave past experience as the foundation of our conjectures concerning the future, and, still more, if our conjectures absolutely contradict past experience, we are thrown upon a wide field of uncertainty, and any one supposition is then just as good as another. If a person were to tell m
ine indications that man will become immortal upon earth than that he will have four eyes and four hands, or that trees will grow horizontally instead of perpendicularly. It will be said, perhaps, that many discoveries have already taken place in the world that were totally unforeseen and unexpec
I am far from saying, that we are at present by any means fully acquainted with the powers of the human mind, but we certainly know more of this instrument than was known four thousand years ago; and therefore, though not to be called competent judges, we are certainly much better able t
nk, that as long as the size of the specula and the length of the tubes could be increased, the powers and advantages of the instrument would increase; but experience has since taught us, that the smallness of the field, the deficiency of light, and the circumstance of the atmosphere being magr
to expect in future, at least of what we are not to expect, which, though negative, is a very useful piece of information. As the necessity of sleep seems rather to depend upon the body than the mind, it does not appear how the improvement of the mind can tend very greatly to supersede this 'c
have some knowledge, relative to the energies of their minds, their benevolent pursuits, etc., to enable us to judge whether the operations of intellect have any decided effect in prolonging the duration of human life. It is certain that no decided effect of this kind has yet been observed. Though n
se bodily cravings. The citizen who has retired, and whose ideas, perhaps, scarcely soar above or extend beyond his little garden, puddling all the morning about his borders of box, will, perhaps, live as long as the philosopher whose range of intellect is the most extensive, and whose views are
great diversity of characters that have existed during some thousand years, no decided difference has been observed in the duration of human life from the operation of intellect, the mortality of man on earth seems to be as completely established, and exactly upon the same grounds, as any on
ly rise instead of fall or that the earth will fly off at a certain period to some more genial and warmer sun. The conclusion of this chapter presents us, undoubtedly, with a very beautiful and desirable picture, but like some of the landscapes drawn from fancy and not imagined with truth, it fails of t
ects in all ages has indicated the future existence of the soul. Yet so congenial is the idea of immortality to the mind of man that they cannot consent entirely to throw it out of their systems. After all their fastidious scepticisms concerning the only probable mode of immortality, they introduce a spe
uch a tenet been advanced as a tenet of revelation I am very sure that all the enemies of religion, and probably Mr Godwin and Mr Condorcet among the rest, would have exhausted the whole force of their ridicule upon it, as the most puerile, the most absurd, the poorest, the most pitiful, the mc
bservation and knowledge. So diversified are the natural objects around us, so many instances of mighty power daily offer themselves to our view, that we may fairly presume, that there are many forms and operations of nature which we have not yet observed, or which, perhaps, we are not ca
him two little pieces of matter, a grain of wheat, and an acorn, to desire him to examine them, to analyse them if he pleased, and endeavour to find out their properties and essences; and then to tell him, that however trifling these little bits of matter might appear to him, that they possessed suc
ittle doubt that the imaginary being which I have supposed would hesitate more, would require better authority, and stronger proofs, before he believed these strange assertions, than if he had been told, that a being of mighty power, who had been the cause of all that he saw around him, and of t
ous difference, but surely no man can hesitate a moment in saying that, putting Revelation out of the question, the resurrection of a spiritual body from a natural body, which may be merely one among the many operations of nature which we cannot see, is an event indefinitely more probable thar
espect to contradict what I said before, when I observed that it was unphilosophical to expect any specifick event that was not indicated by some kind of analogy in the past. In ranging beyond the bourne from which no traveller returns, we must necessarily quit this rule; but with regard to events
, and transmutation, which every seed shews, are truly miraculous. Who can imagine that these wonderful faculties are contained in these little bits of matter? To me it appears much more philosophical to suppose that the mighty God of nature is present in full energy in all these operations
s a mighty process for the creation and formation of mind. Many vessels will necessarily come out of this great furnace in wrong shapes. These will be broken and thrown aside as useless, while those vessels whose forms are full of truth, grace, and loveliness, will be wafted into happier situation
en, seems at least to deserve investigation. For my own part I feel no disinclination whatever to give that degree of credit to the opinion of the probable immortality of man on earth, which the appearances that can be brought in support of it deserve. Before we decide upon the utter improbability
ption favour the supposition, he must certainly intend that these appearances should be examined and this is all that I have meant to do. CHAPTER 13. Error of Mr Godwin is considering man too much in the light of a being merely rational - In the compound being, man, the passions will alway
d of myriads of centuries, it is really not thirty years, or even thirty days, distant from us. The supposition of the approach of man to immortality on earth is certainly not of a kind to soften the difficulty. The only argument, therefore, in the chapter which has any tendency to remove the objection is t
er point of view the little hope that we can reasonably entertain of those vast improvements in the nature of man and of society which he holds up to our admiring gaze in his Political Justice. Mr Godwin considers man too much in the light of a being merely intellectual. This error, at least such I
Such is the appearance which this proposition assumes, when examined in a loose and practical view. In strict consideration it will not admit of debate. Man is a rational being, etc.' (Bk. I, ch. 5, in the third edition Vol. I, p. 88). So far from calling this a strict consideration of the subject, I own I s
erse ratio of the squares of the distances. To make the general theory just in application to the revolutions of these bodies, it was necessary to calculate accurately the disturbing force of the sun upon the moon, and of the moon upon the earth; and till these disturbing forces were properly estima
not merely depend upon whether a man may be made to understand a distinct proposition or be convinced by an unanswerable argument. A truth may be brought home to his conviction as a rational being, though he may determine to act contrary to it, as a compound being. The cravings of hun
ll the circumstances of their situation with these bodily cravings, the decision of the compound being is different from the conviction of the rational being. If this be the just view of the subject, and both theory and experience unite to prove that it is, almost all Mr Godwin's reasonings on the subject
will hardly think this intended for conviction, at least it does not appear how the individual or the society could reap much future benefit from an understanding enlightened in this manner. The principal objects which human punishments have in view are undoubtedly restraint and example, restrai
the most successful, and, indeed, almost the only attempt towards the moral amelioration of offenders. He talks of the selfish passions that are fostered by solitude and of the virtues generated in society. But surely these virtues are not generated in the society of a prison. Were the offender con
The indefatigable pains taken in this country to find out a murder, and the certainty of its punishment, has powerfully contributed to generate that sentiment which is frequent in the mouths of the common people, that a murder will sooner or later come to light; and the habitual horror in which mur
variably punished, the use of the stiletto in transports of passion would have been comparatively but little known. That human laws either do, or can, proportion the punishment accurately to the offence, no person will have the folly to assert. From the inscrutability of motives the thing is absolutel
find fault with human institutions; nothing so difficult as to suggest adequate practical improvements. It is to be lamented, that more men of talents employ their time in the former occupation than in the latter. The frequency of crime among men, who, as the common saying is, know better, suffic
this truth to a person who has scarcely ever felt intellectual pleasure? I may as well attempt to explain the nature and beauty of colours to a blind man. If I am ever so laborious, patient, and clear, and have the most repeated opportunities of expostulation, any real progress toward the accomplist
ed with tedium and disgust; but that intellectual pleasures appeared to me ever fresh and young, filled up all my hours satisfactorily, gave a new zest to life, and diffused a lasting serenity over my mind. If he believe me, it can only be from respect and veneration for my authority. It is credulity, an
a pretty woman, I feel alive, and in spirits, and truly enjoy my existence. Under such circumstances, reasoning and arguments are not instruments from which success can be expected. At some future time perhaps, real satiety of sensual pleasures, or some accidental impressions that awake
Mr Godwin uses the term, not applicable to man - Nature of the real perfectibility of man illustrated. IF THE REASONINGS OF THE PRECEDING CHAPTER ARE JUST, the corollaries respecting political truth, which Mr Godwin draws from the proposition that the voluntary actions of men origi
by adequately communicated, be meant such a conviction as to produce an adequate effect upon the conduct, the major may be allowed and the minor denied. The consequent, or the omnipotence of truth, of course falls to the ground. If by 'adequately communicated' be meant merely the convic
d moral weakness of man can never be wholly overcome in this world. Man, according to Mr Godwin, is a creature formed what he is by the successive impressions which he has received, from the first moment that the germ from which he sprung was animated. Could he be placed in a situatior
or no temptation in the world to evil. As it has been clearly proved, however, (at least as I think) that this is entirely a false conception, and that, independent of any political or social institutions whatever, the greater part of mankind, from the fixed and unalterable laws of nature, must ever be subjec
f combinations upon the dice in a repeated succession of throws appears to me not inaptly to represent the great variety of character that must necessarily exist in the world, supposing every individual to be formed what he is by that combination of impressions which he has received since his fir

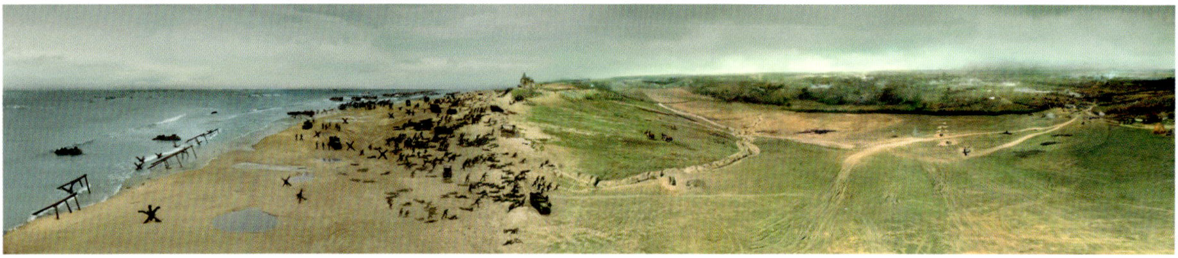

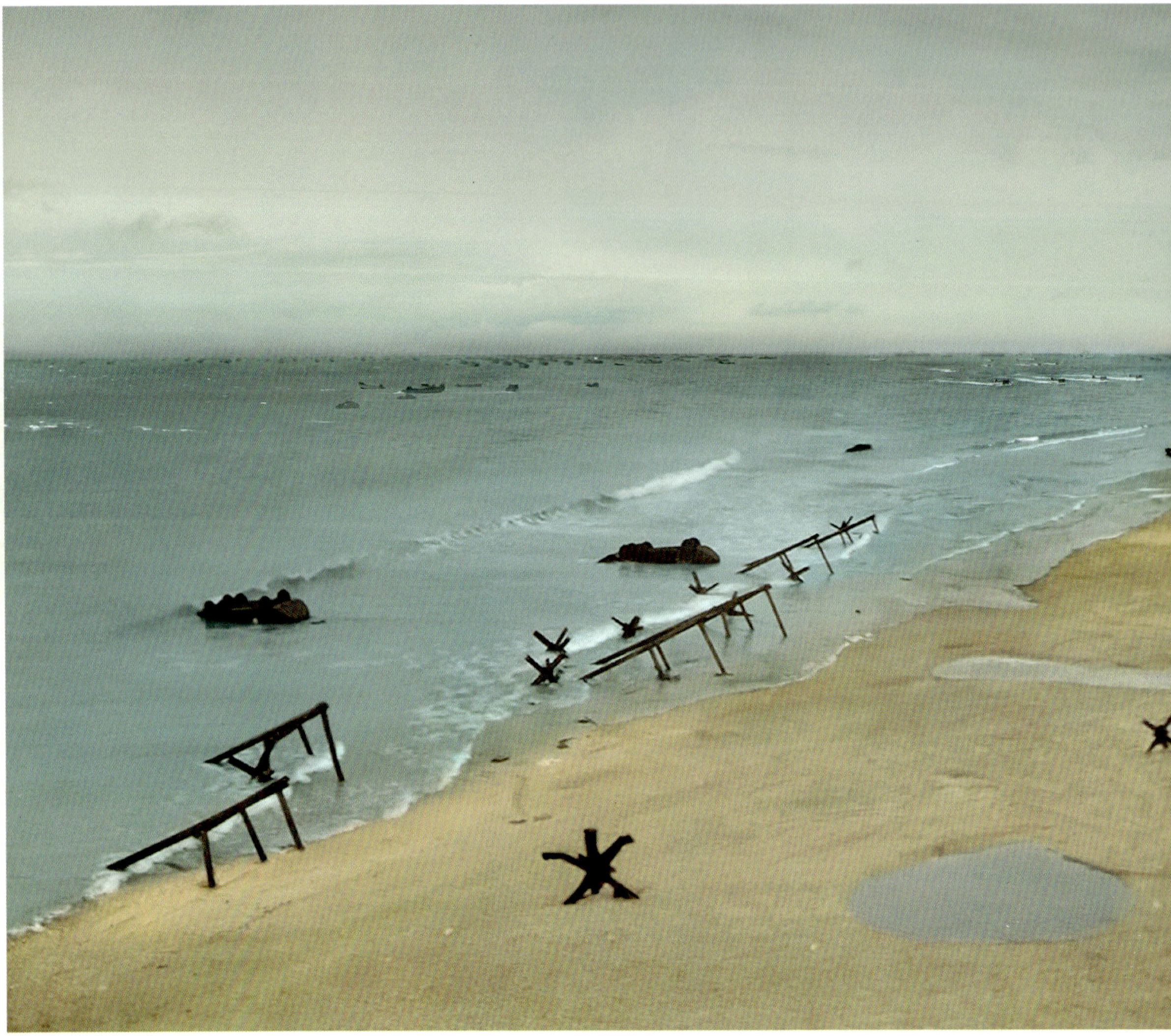

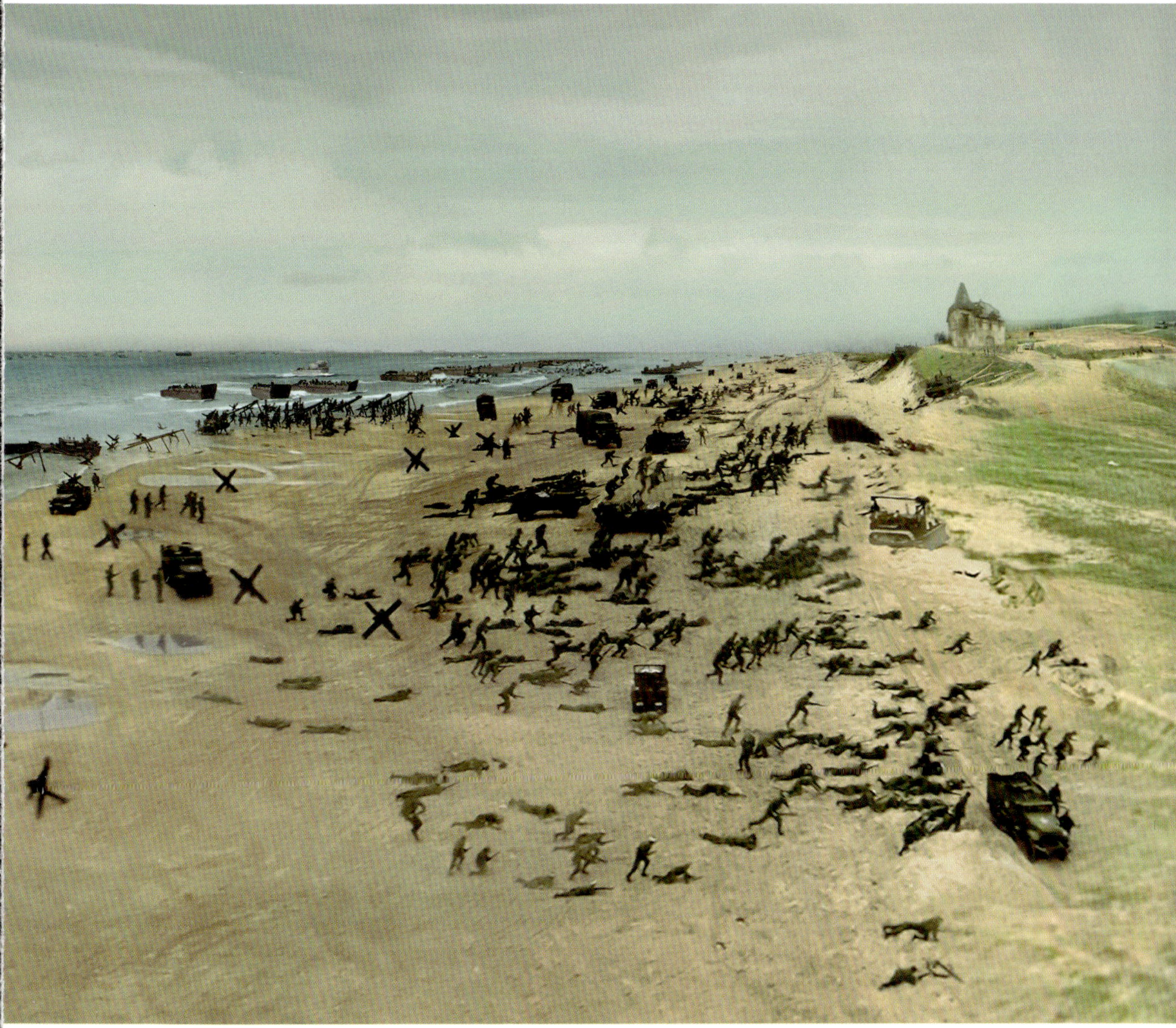

Est/Ouest, 2012
Tirage Lambda / Lambda print, 111 × 396 cm

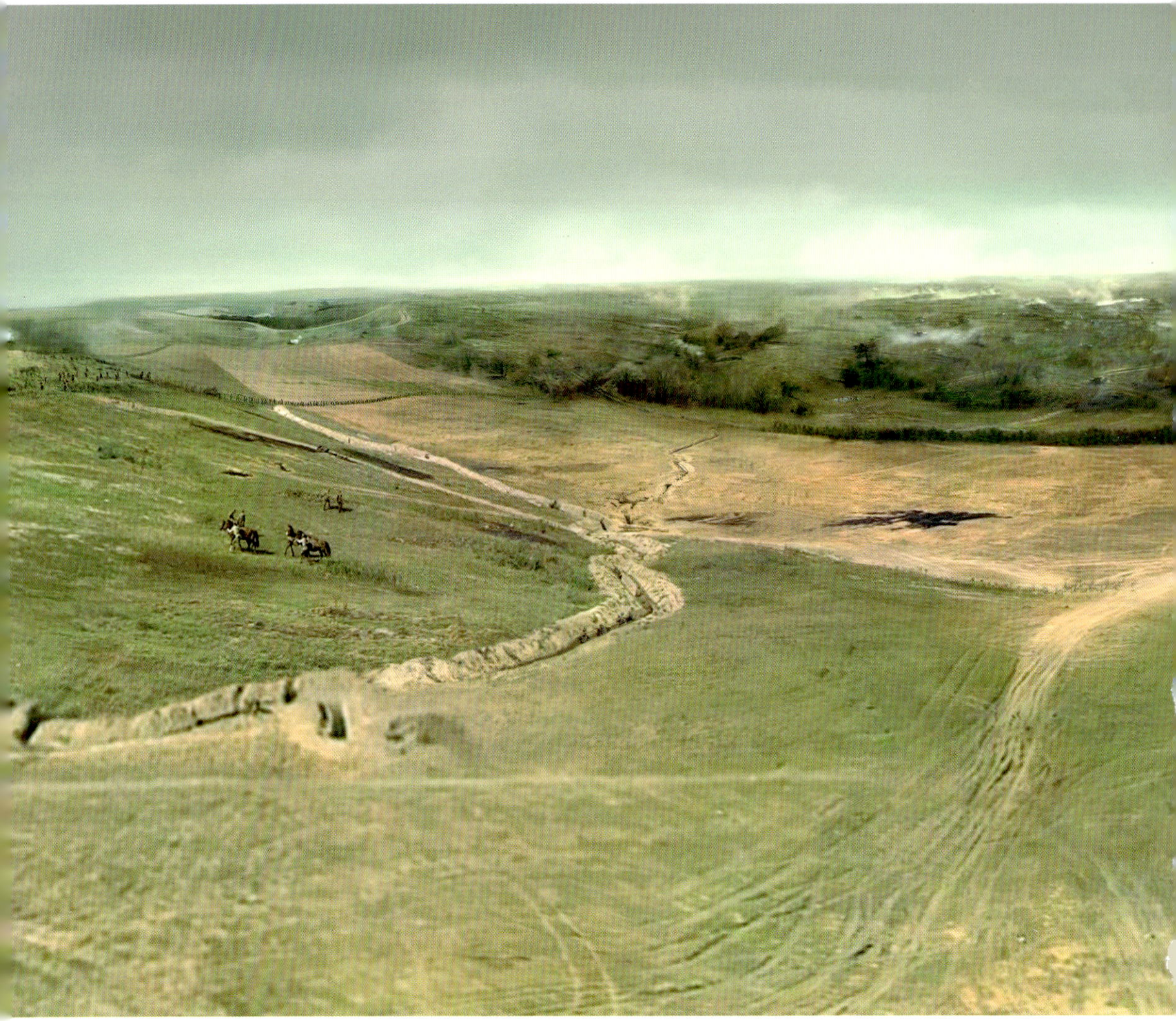

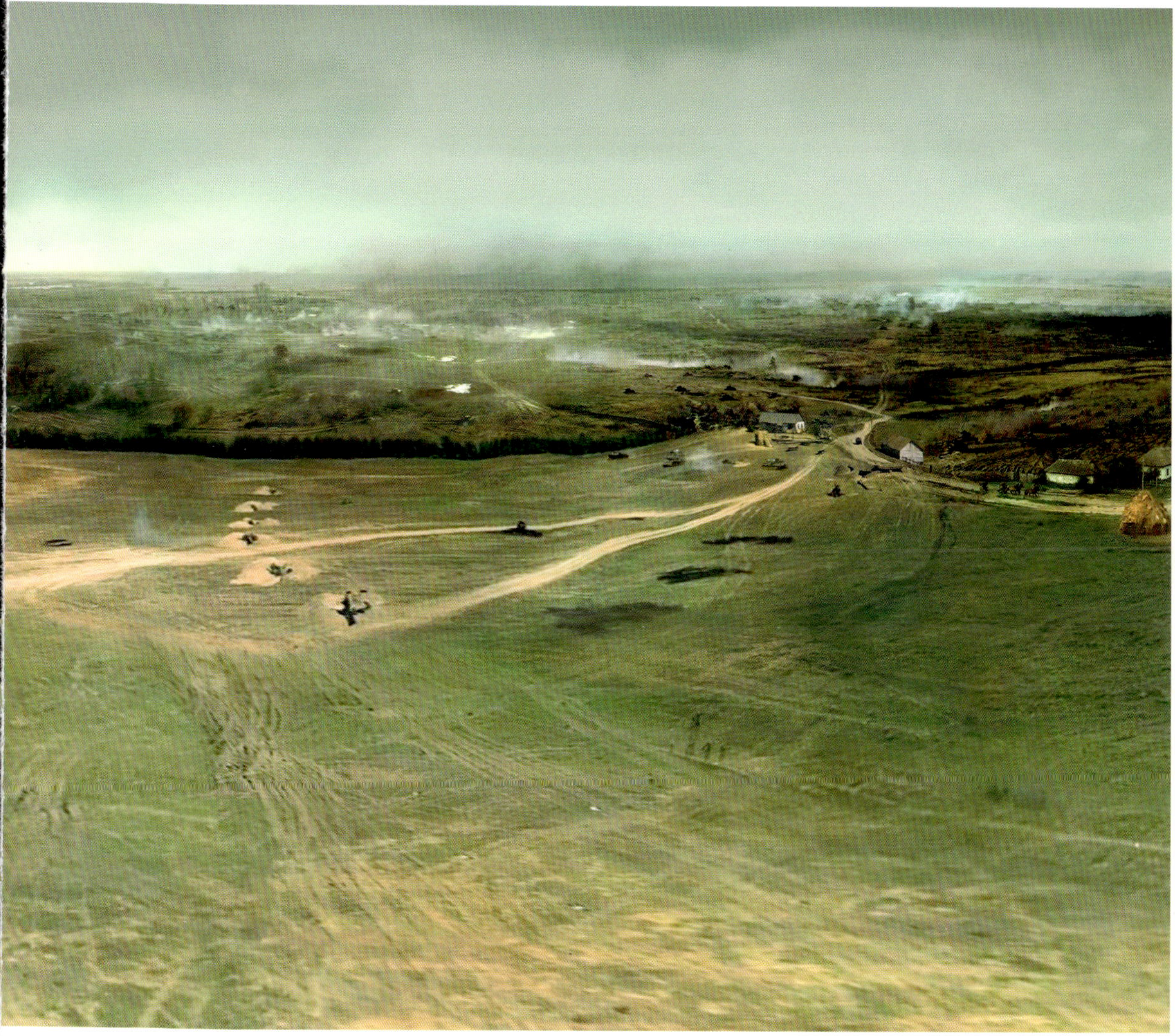

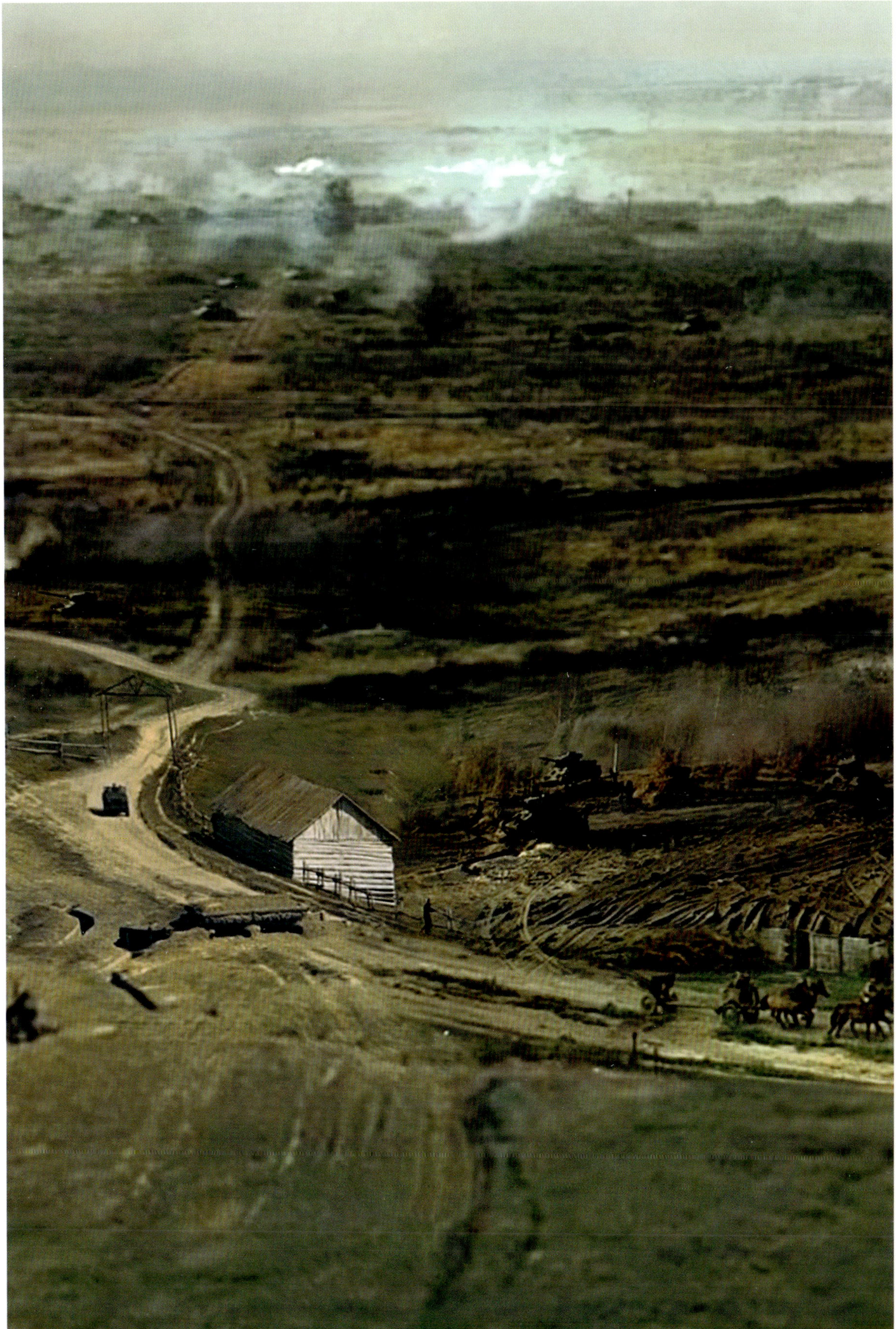

Danse américaine, 2015
Tirage Lambda / Lambda print, 35 × 216 cm

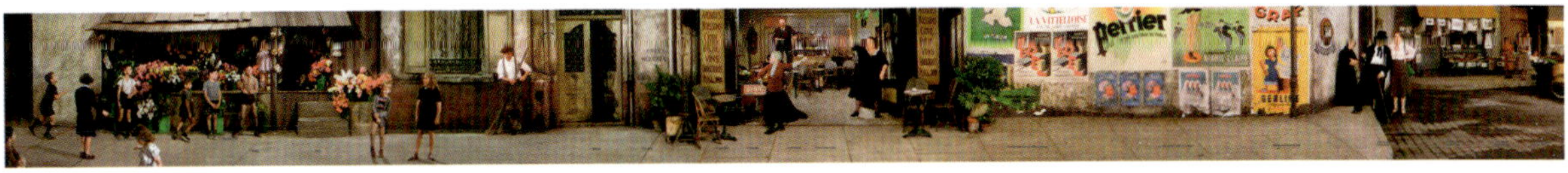
perrier

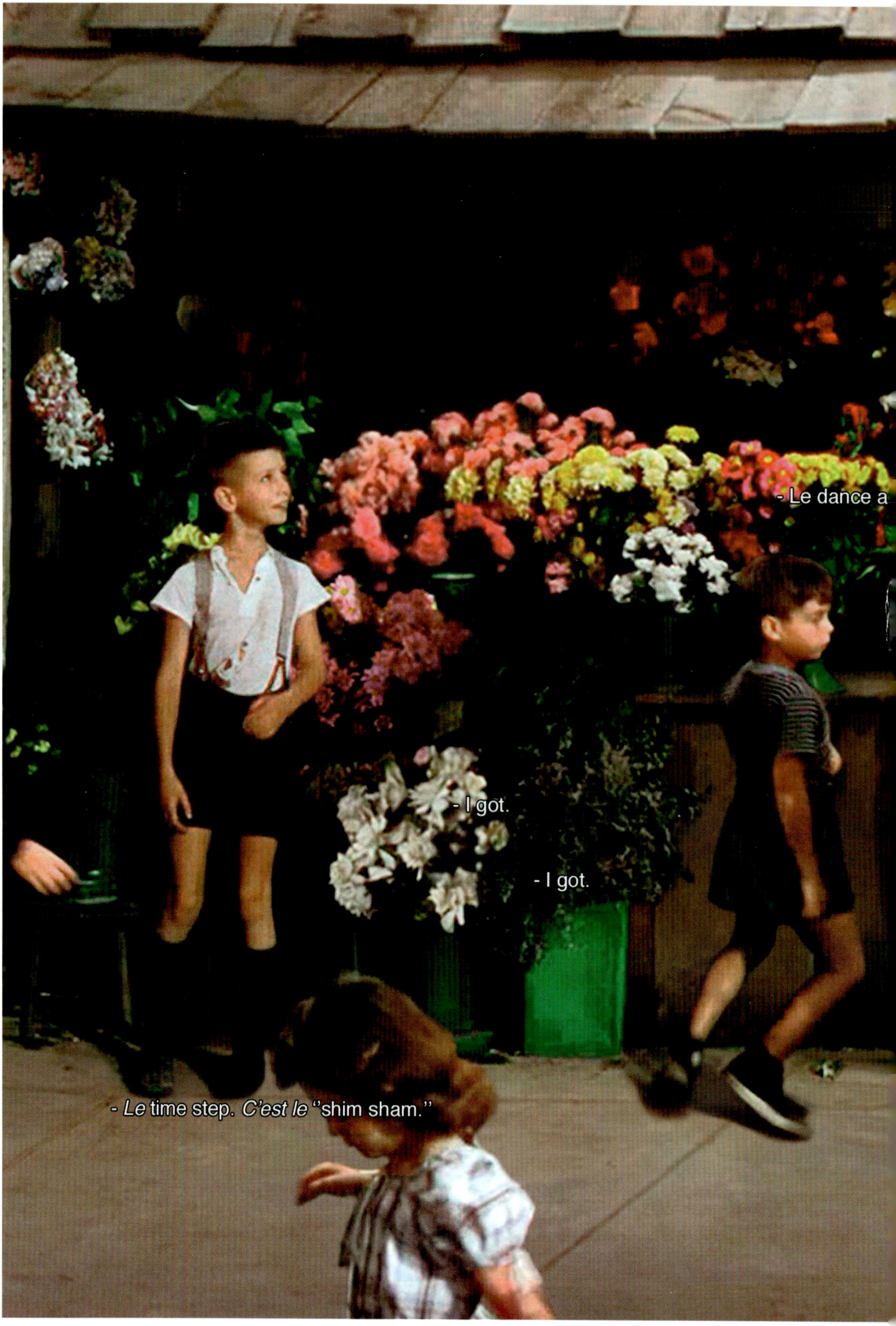
- Le dance a
- I got.
- I got.
- *Le* time step. *C'est le* "shim sham."

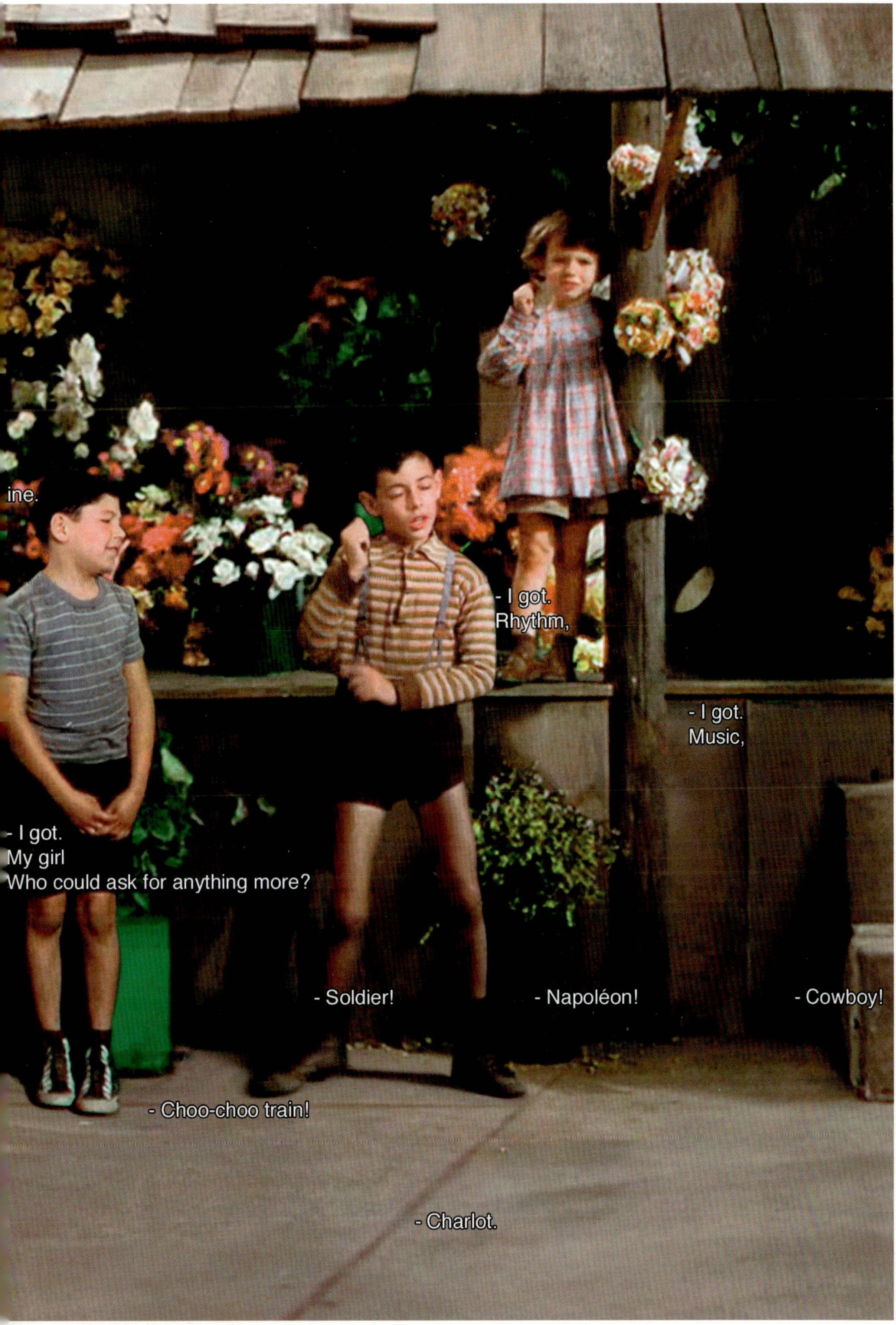
ine.
- I got.
Rhythm,
- I got.
Music,
- I got.
My girl
Who could ask for anything more?
- Soldier!
- Napoléon!
- Cowboy!
- Choo-choo train!
- Charlot.

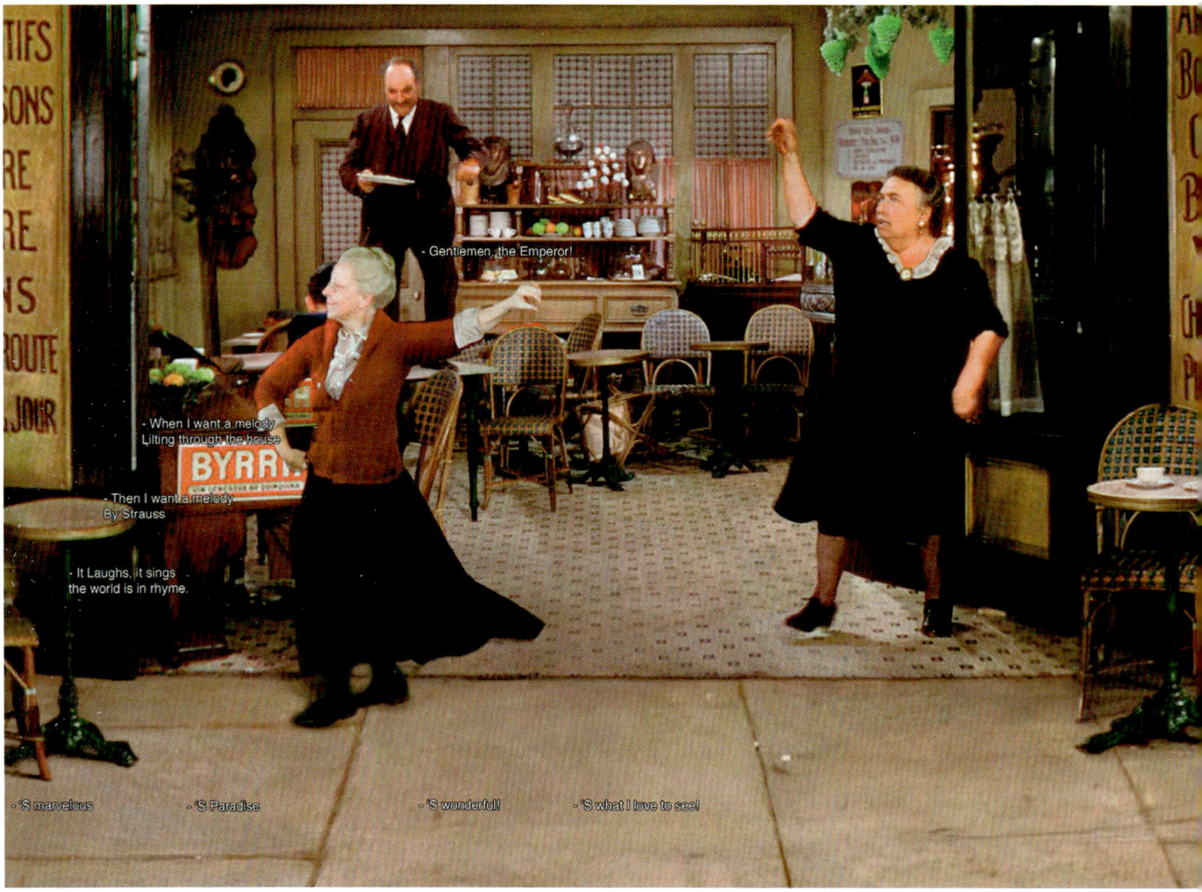
- Gentlemen, the Emperor!
- When I want a melody
Lilting through the house
- Then I want a melody
By Strauss
- It Laughs, it sings
the world is in rhyme.
- 'S marvelous
- 'S Paradise
- 'S wonderful!
- 'S what I love to see!

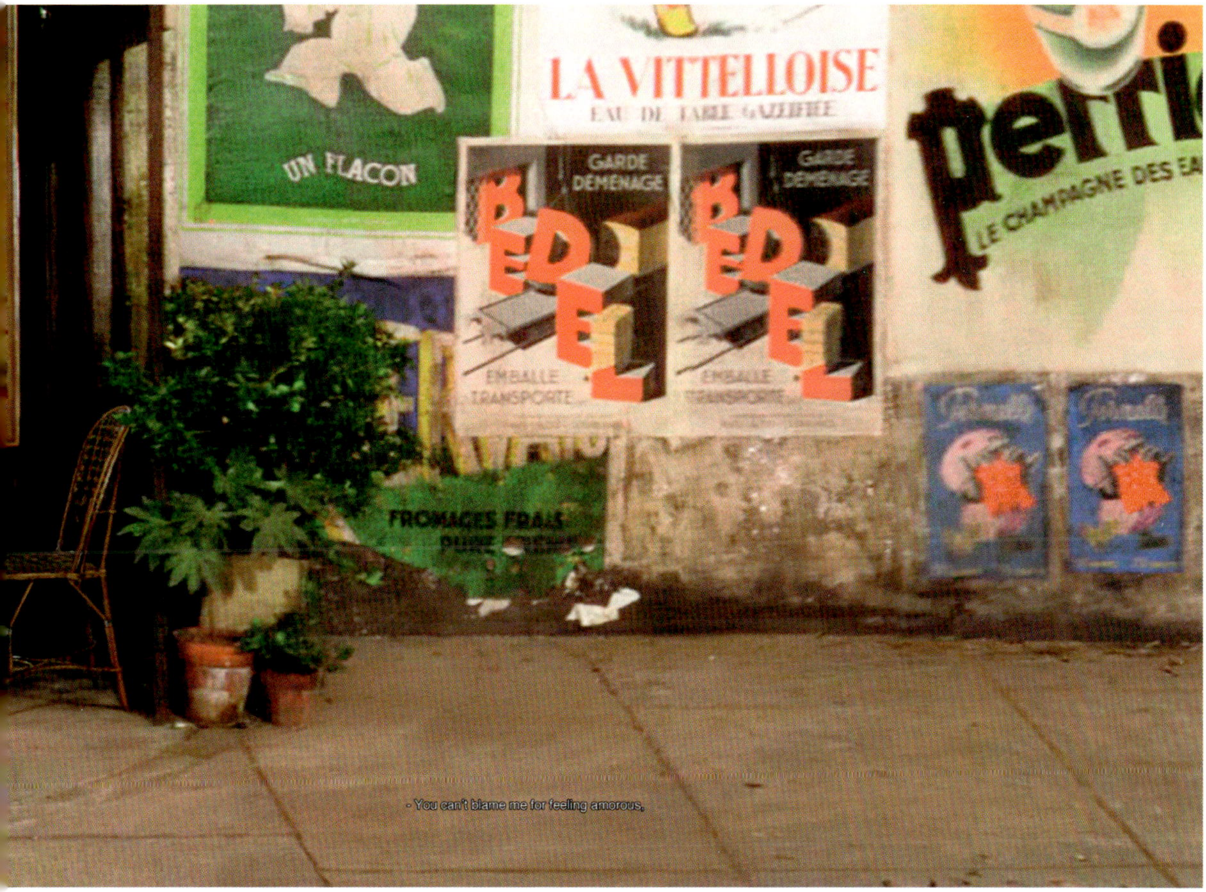
LA VITTELLOISE
EAU DE TABLE GAZEIFIEE
UN FLACON
GARDE DÉMÉNAGE
EMBALLE TRANSPORTE
FROMAGES FRAIS
LE CHAMPAGNE DES EA
- You can't blame me for feeling amorous,

La Règle du jeu, 2007
Tirage Lambda / Lambda print, 57 × 77 cm

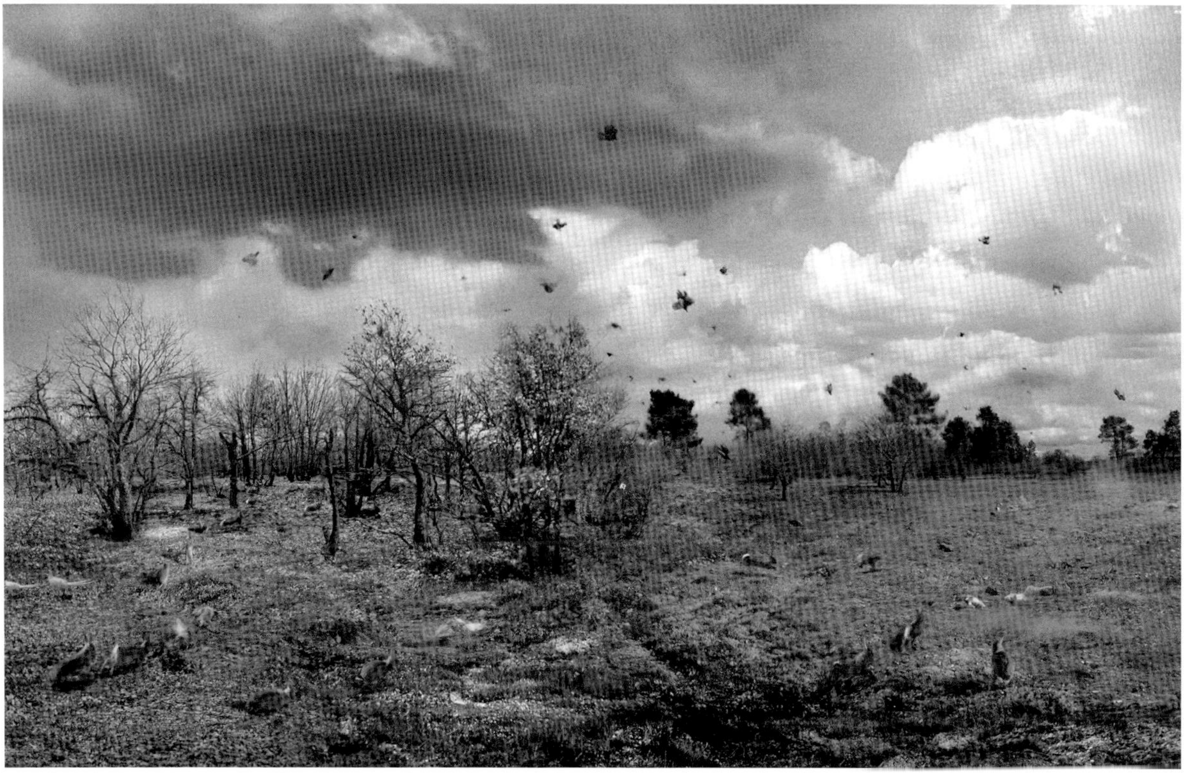

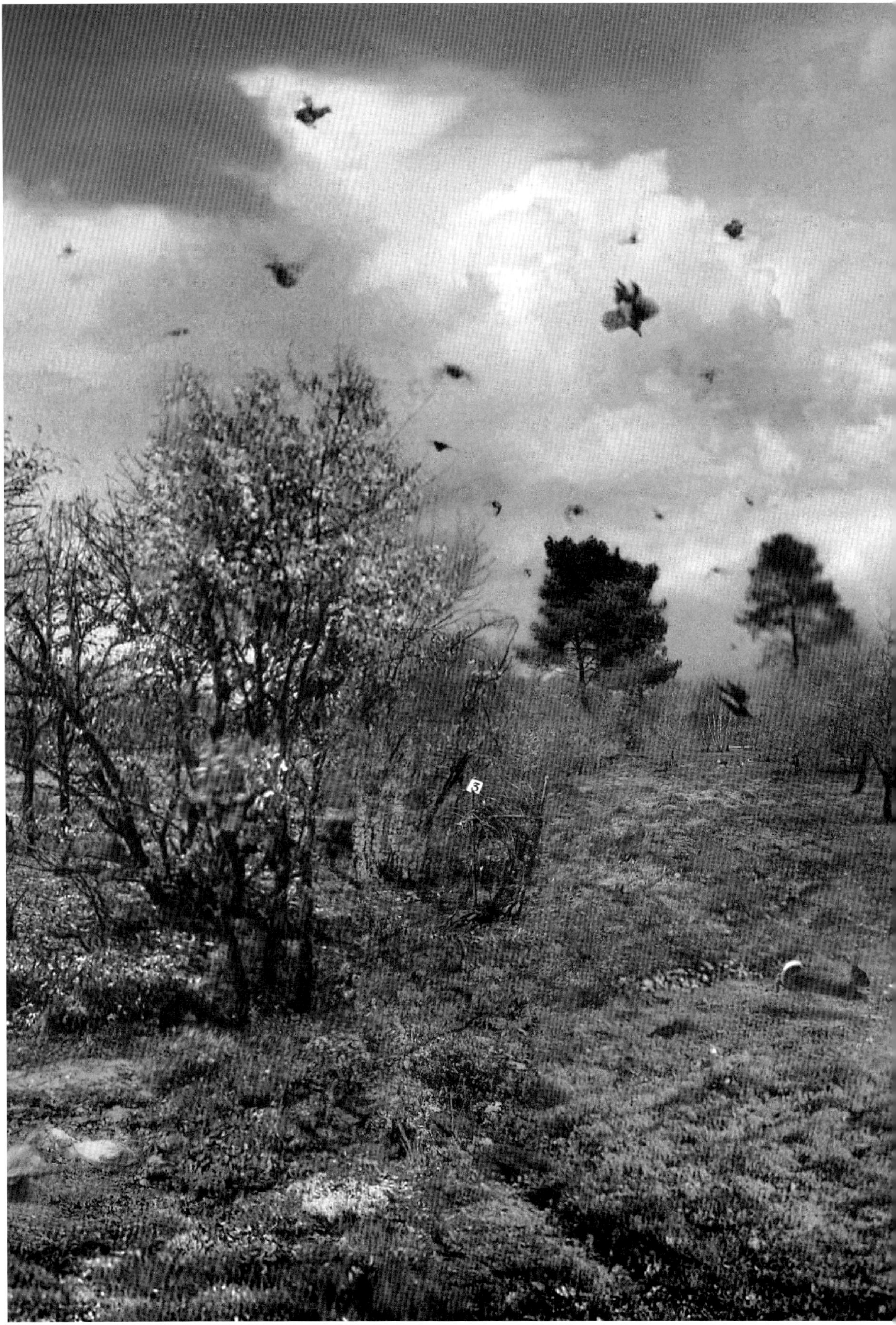
3

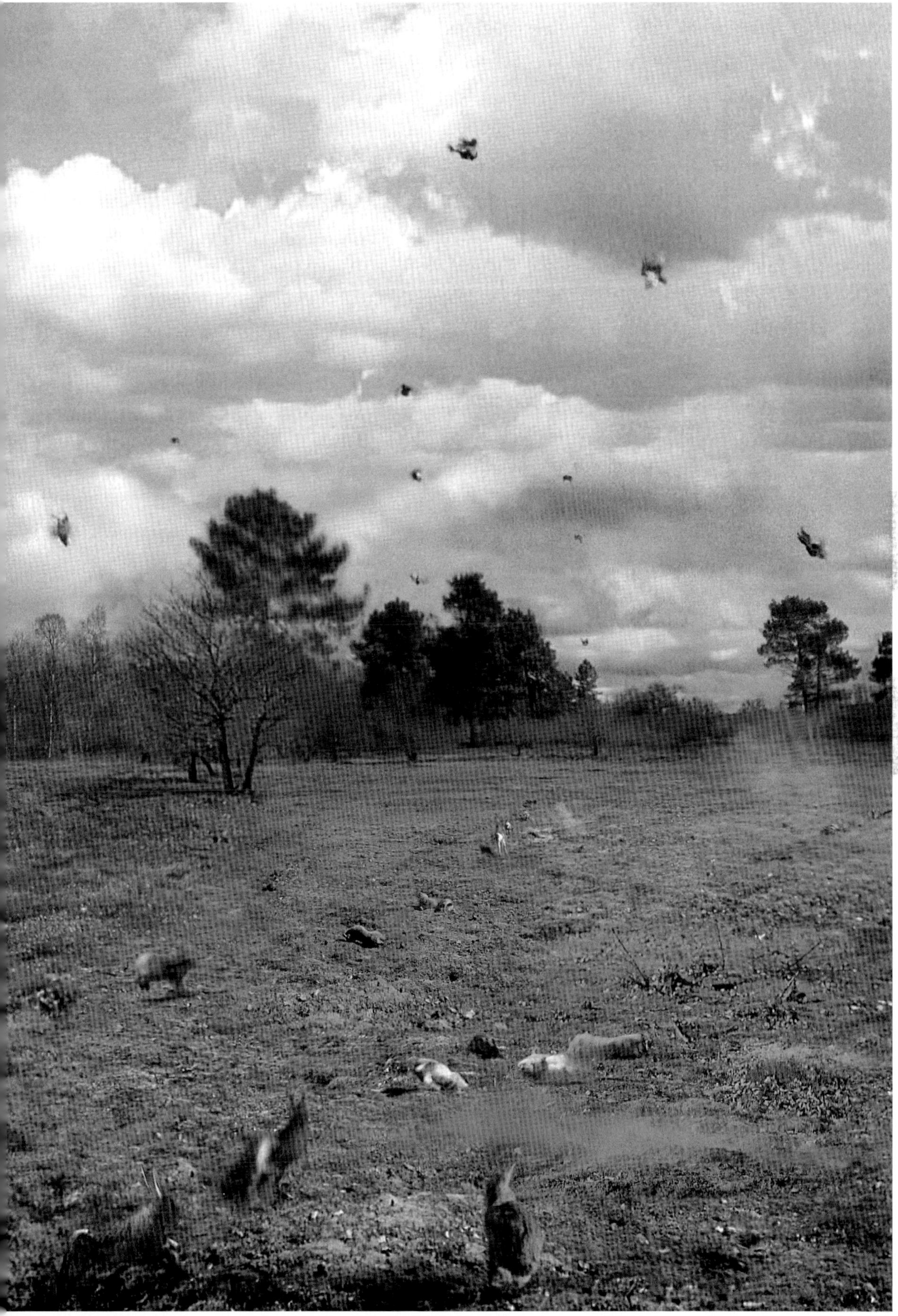

Sandbagwal, 2011
Sacs militaires remplis de sable / Military sandbags filled with sand, 160 × 325 × 35 cm

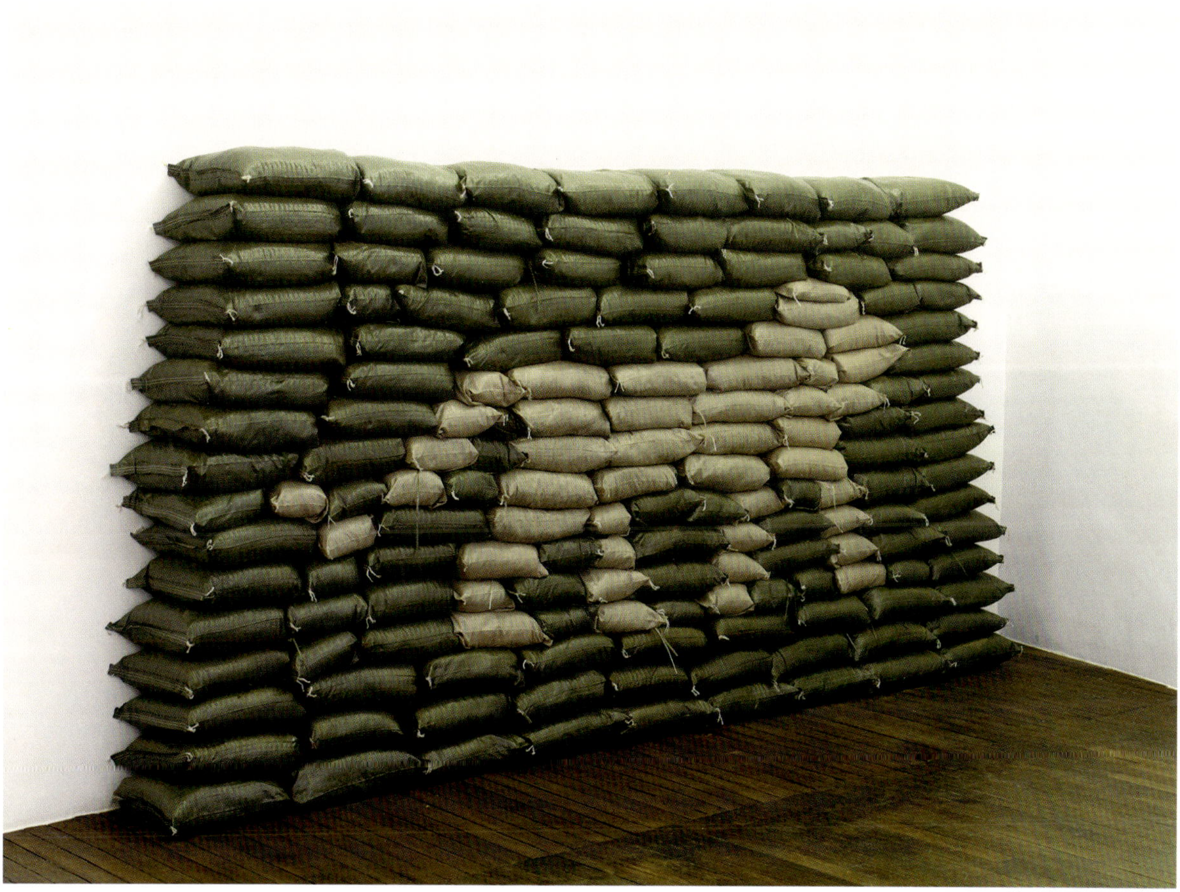

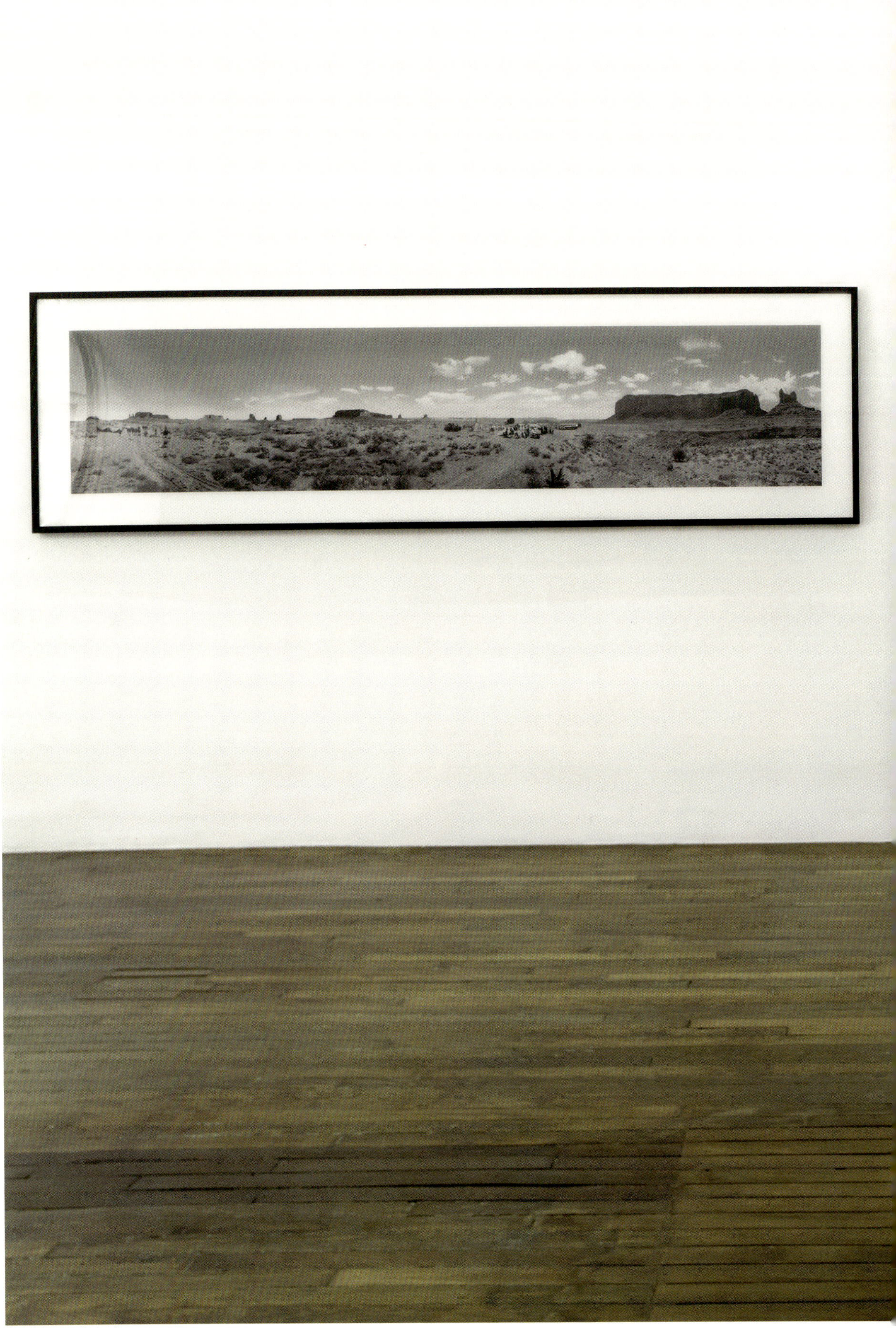

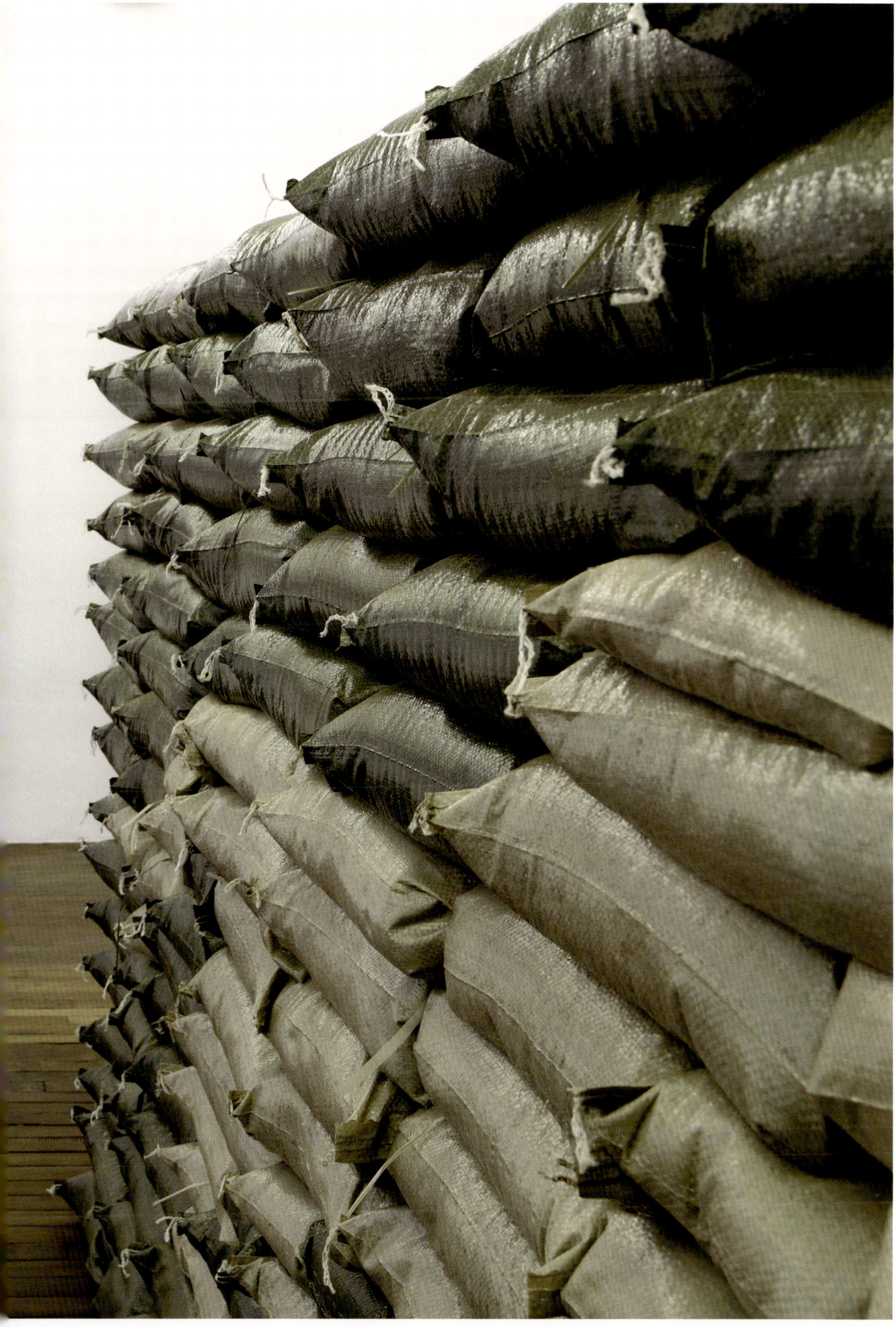

Summit, 2016
Tirage Lambda / Lambda print, 46.3 × 80.4 × 4 cm

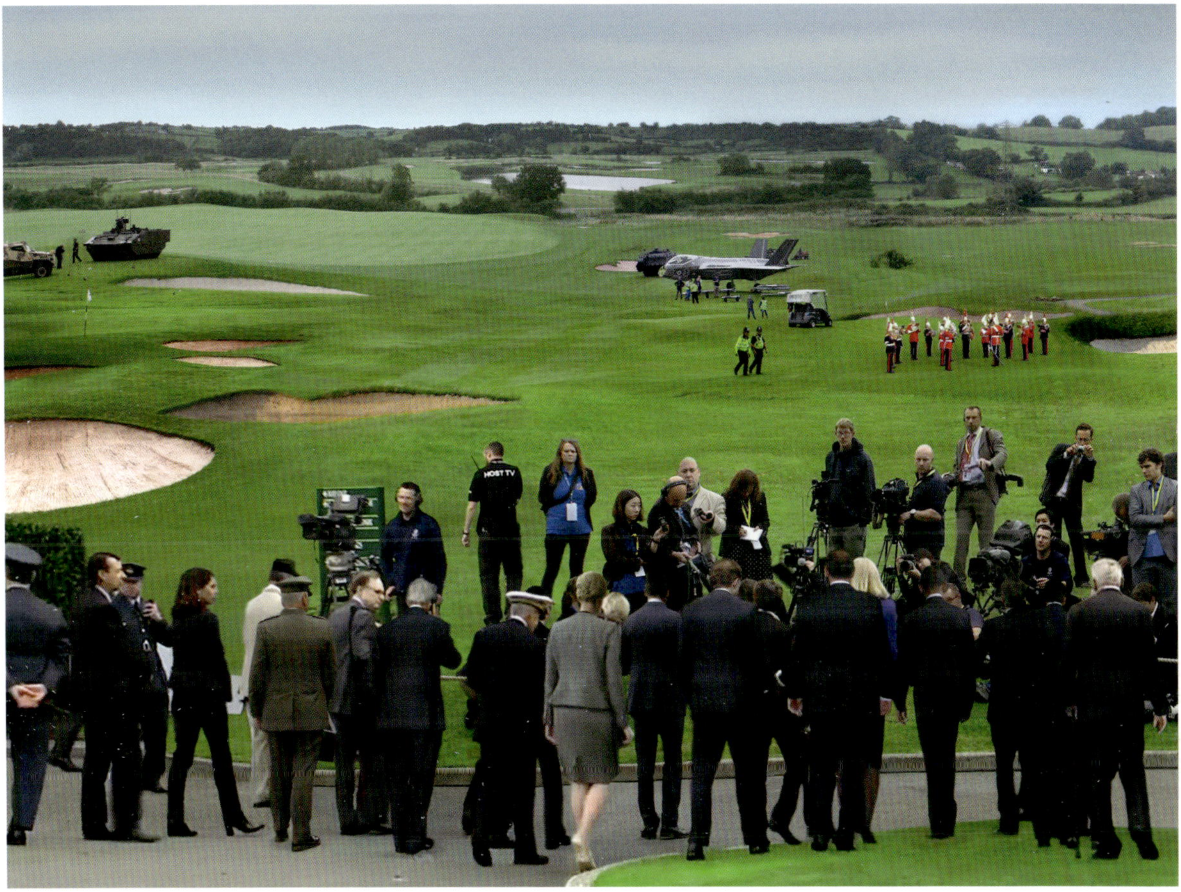
HOST TV

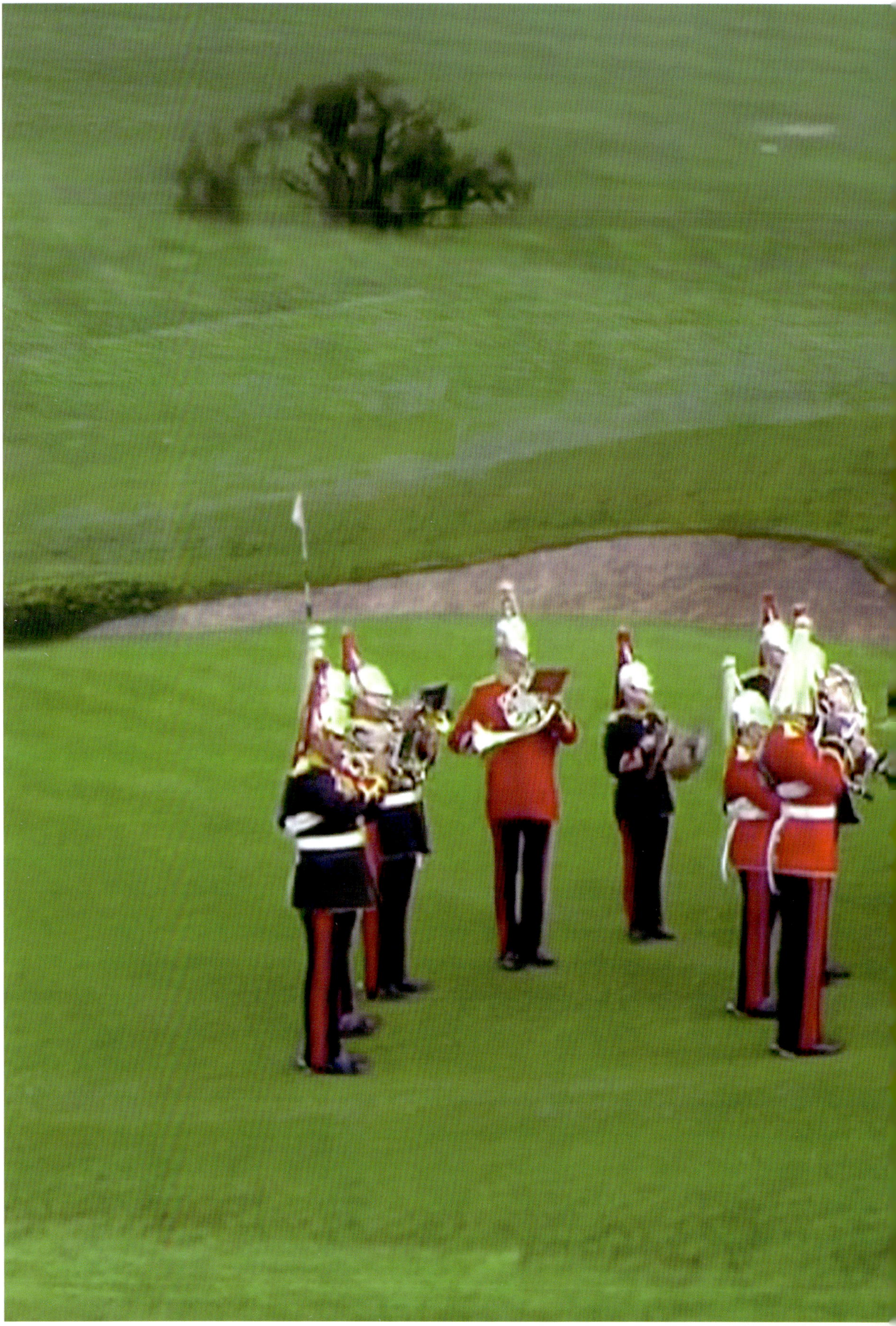

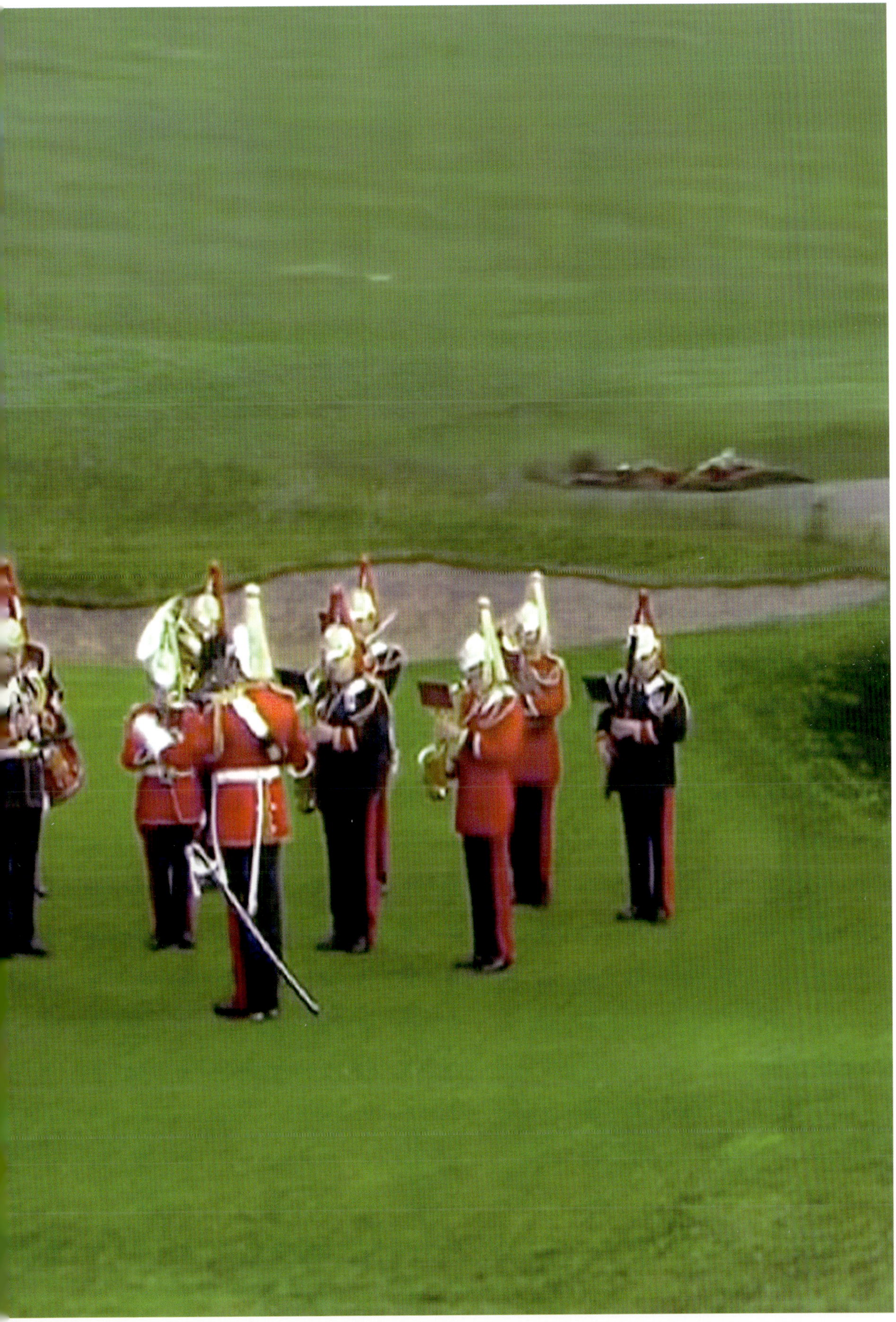

BPM, 2003
Tirage photographique par contact sur bromure d'argent / Contact print on silver bromide, 47 × 85 cm

Odyssée, 2006
Texte d'Homère kinéscopé sur film 35 mm / Homer's text transferred to 35 mm film, longueur / length: 307 m

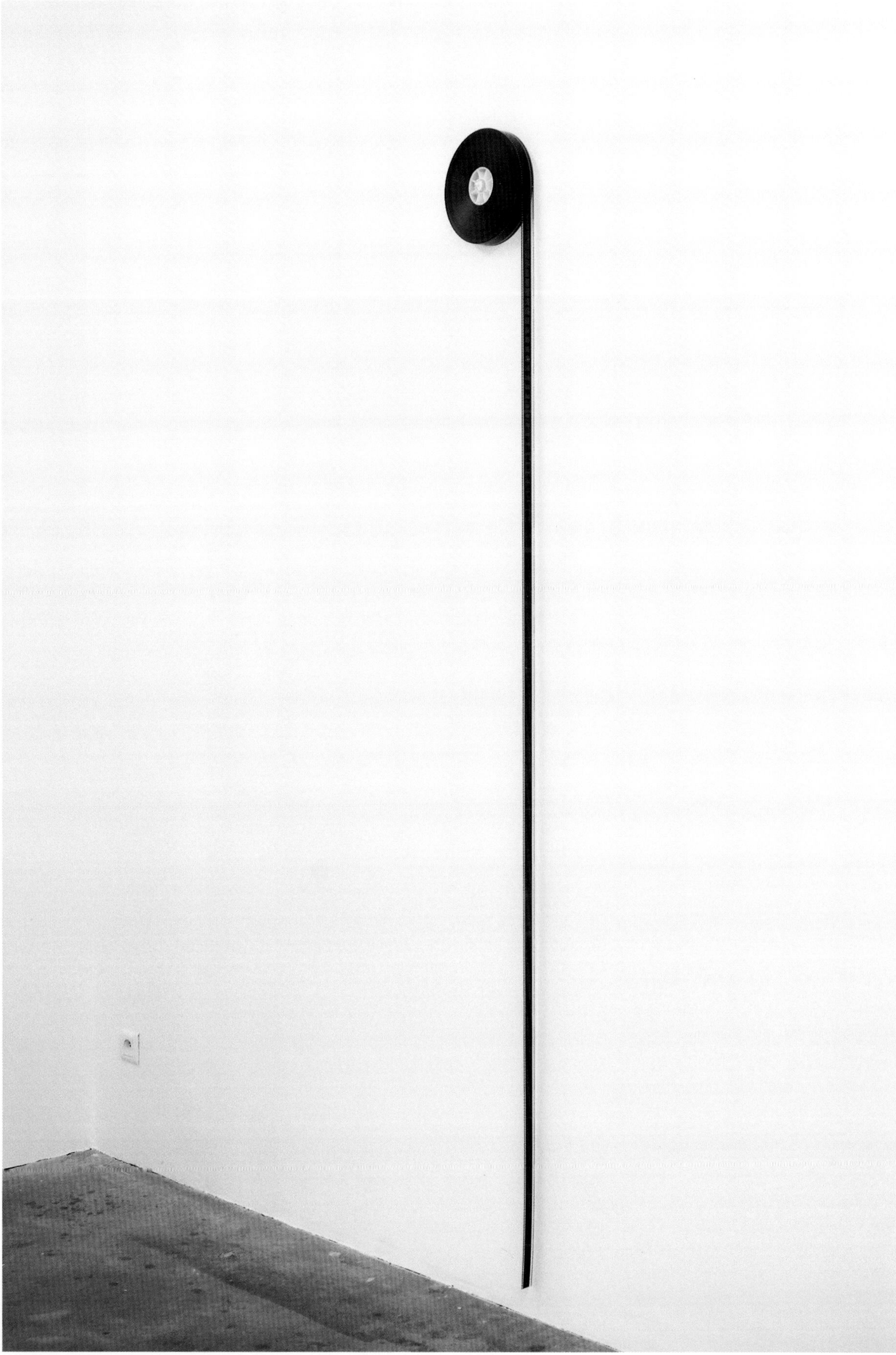

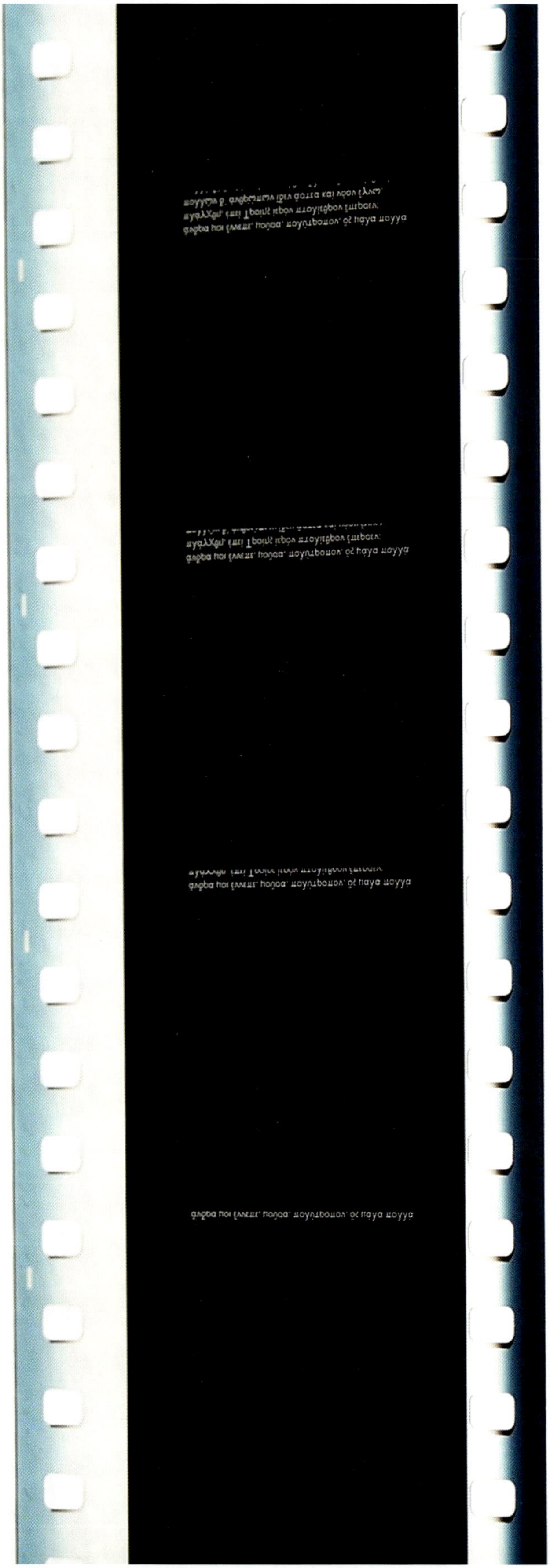

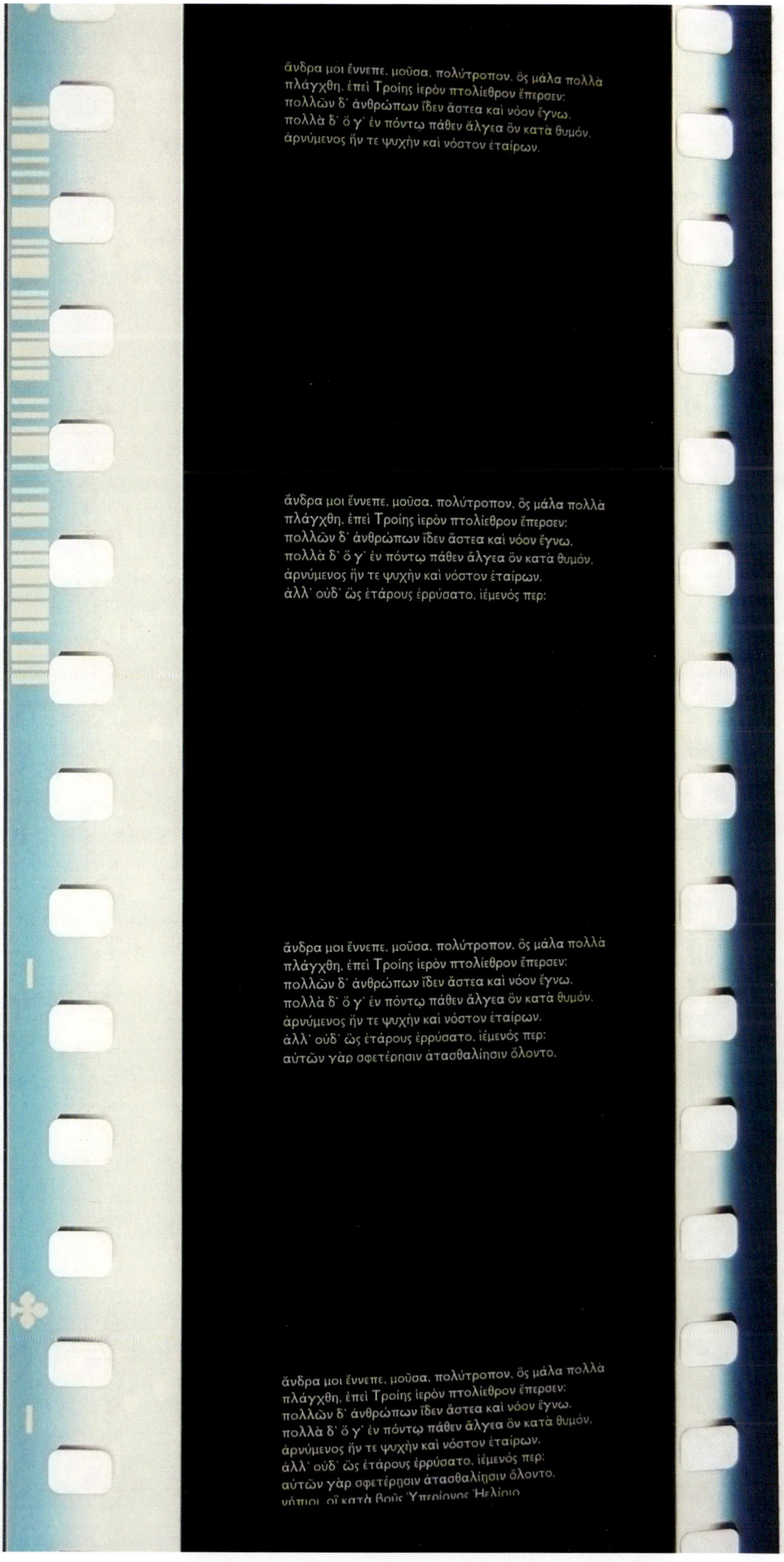
ἄνδρα μοι ἔννεπε, μοῦσα, πολύτροπον, ὃς μάλα πολλὰ
πλάγχθη, ἐπεὶ Τροίης ἱερὸν πτολίεθρον ἔπερσεν·
πολλῶν δ᾽ ἀνθρώπων ἴδεν ἄστεα καὶ νόον ἔγνω,
πολλὰ δ᾽ ὅ γ᾽ ἐν πόντῳ πάθεν ἄλγεα ὃν κατὰ θυμόν,
ἀρνύμενος ἥν τε ψυχὴν καὶ νόστον ἑταίρων.

ἄνδρα μοι ἔννεπε, μοῦσα, πολύτροπον, ὃς μάλα πολλὰ
πλάγχθη, ἐπεὶ Τροίης ἱερὸν πτολίεθρον ἔπερσεν·
πολλῶν δ᾽ ἀνθρώπων ἴδεν ἄστεα καὶ νόον ἔγνω,
πολλὰ δ᾽ ὅ γ᾽ ἐν πόντῳ πάθεν ἄλγεα ὃν κατὰ θυμόν,
ἀρνύμενος ἥν τε ψυχὴν καὶ νόστον ἑταίρων.
ἀλλ᾽ οὐδ᾽ ὣς ἑτάρους ἐρρύσατο, ἱέμενός περ·

ἄνδρα μοι ἔννεπε, μοῦσα, πολύτροπον, ὃς μάλα πολλὰ
πλάγχθη, ἐπεὶ Τροίης ἱερὸν πτολίεθρον ἔπερσεν·
πολλῶν δ᾽ ἀνθρώπων ἴδεν ἄστεα καὶ νόον ἔγνω,
πολλὰ δ᾽ ὅ γ᾽ ἐν πόντῳ πάθεν ἄλγεα ὃν κατὰ θυμόν,
ἀρνύμενος ἥν τε ψυχὴν καὶ νόστον ἑταίρων.
ἀλλ᾽ οὐδ᾽ ὣς ἑτάρους ἐρρύσατο, ἱέμενός περ·
αὐτῶν γὰρ σφετέρῃσιν ἀτασθαλίῃσιν ὄλοντο,

ἄνδρα μοι ἔννεπε, μοῦσα, πολύτροπον, ὃς μάλα πολλὰ
πλάγχθη, ἐπεὶ Τροίης ἱερὸν πτολίεθρον ἔπερσεν·
πολλῶν δ᾽ ἀνθρώπων ἴδεν ἄστεα καὶ νόον ἔγνω,
πολλὰ δ᾽ ὅ γ᾽ ἐν πόντῳ πάθεν ἄλγεα ὃν κατὰ θυμόν,
ἀρνύμενος ἥν τε ψυχὴν καὶ νόστον ἑταίρων.
ἀλλ᾽ οὐδ᾽ ὣς ἑτάρους ἐρρύσατο, ἱέμενός περ·
αὐτῶν γὰρ σφετέρῃσιν ἀτασθαλίῃσιν ὄλοντο,

La main invisible, 2020
Tirage photographique par contact sur papier baryté / Contact printing on baryta paper, 33 × 41 cm

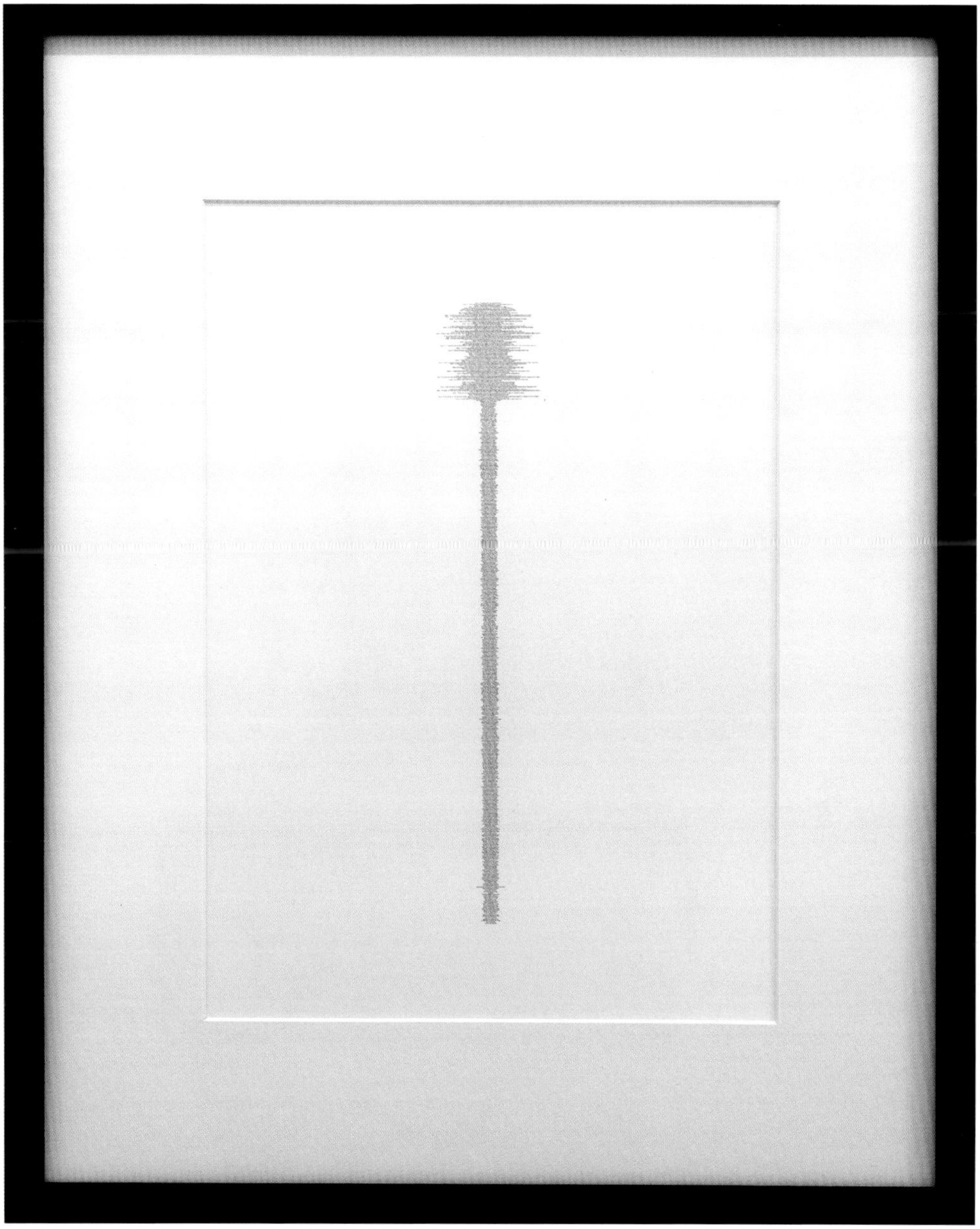

Nocturne (été), 2015
Impression pigmentaire / Pigment print, 78 × 298 × 5 cm

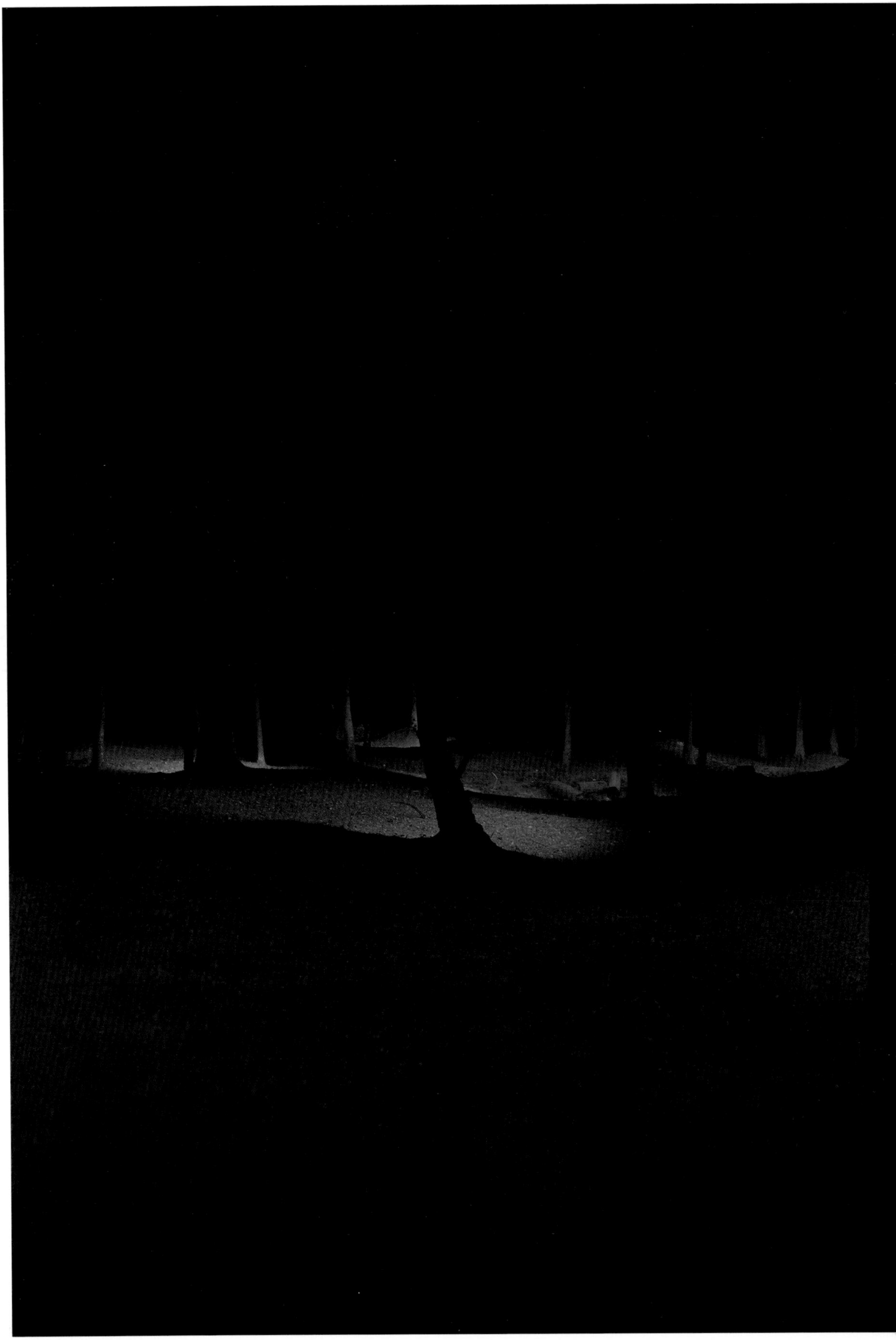

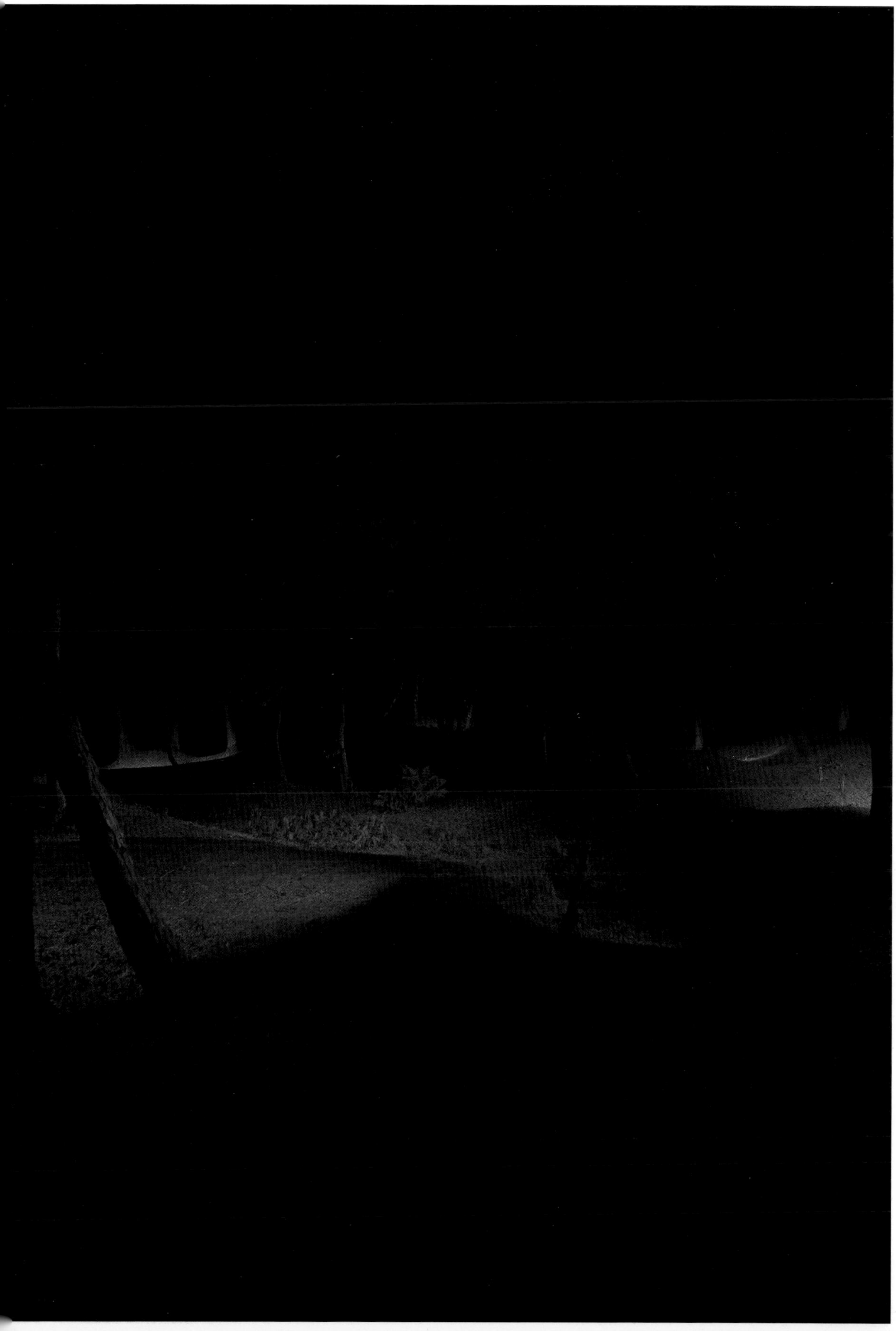

Obsidionales, 2019
Huile sur cuivre / Oil on copper, 18 × 15 cm

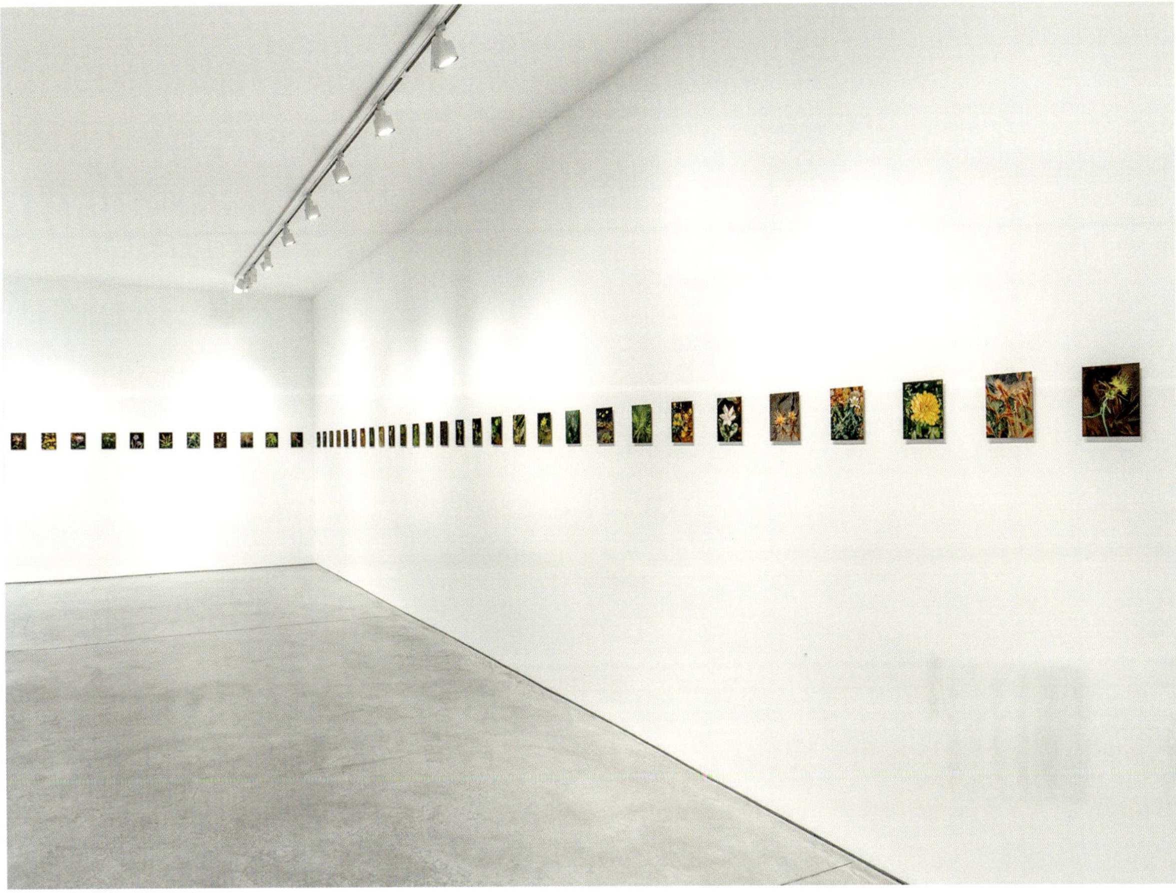

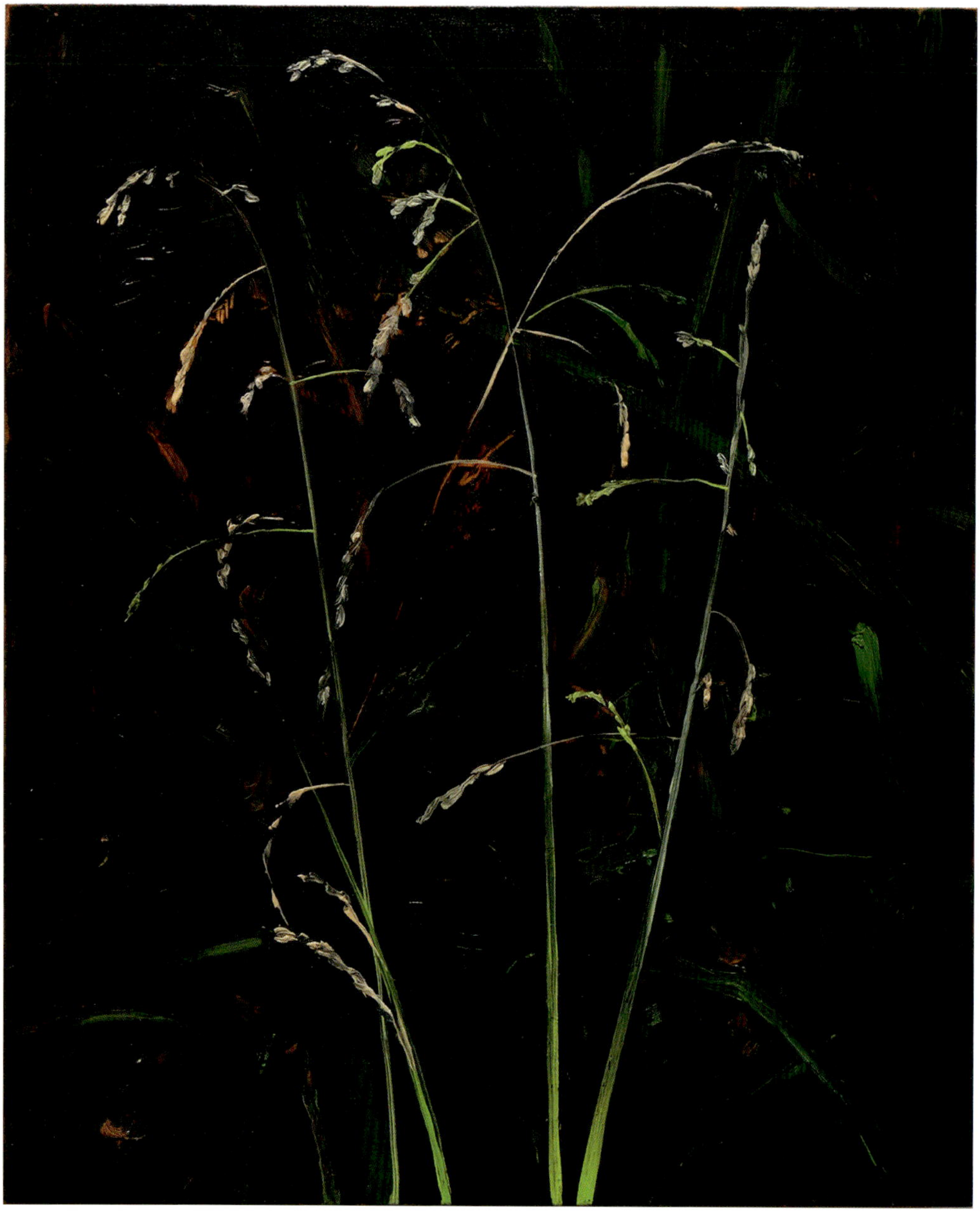

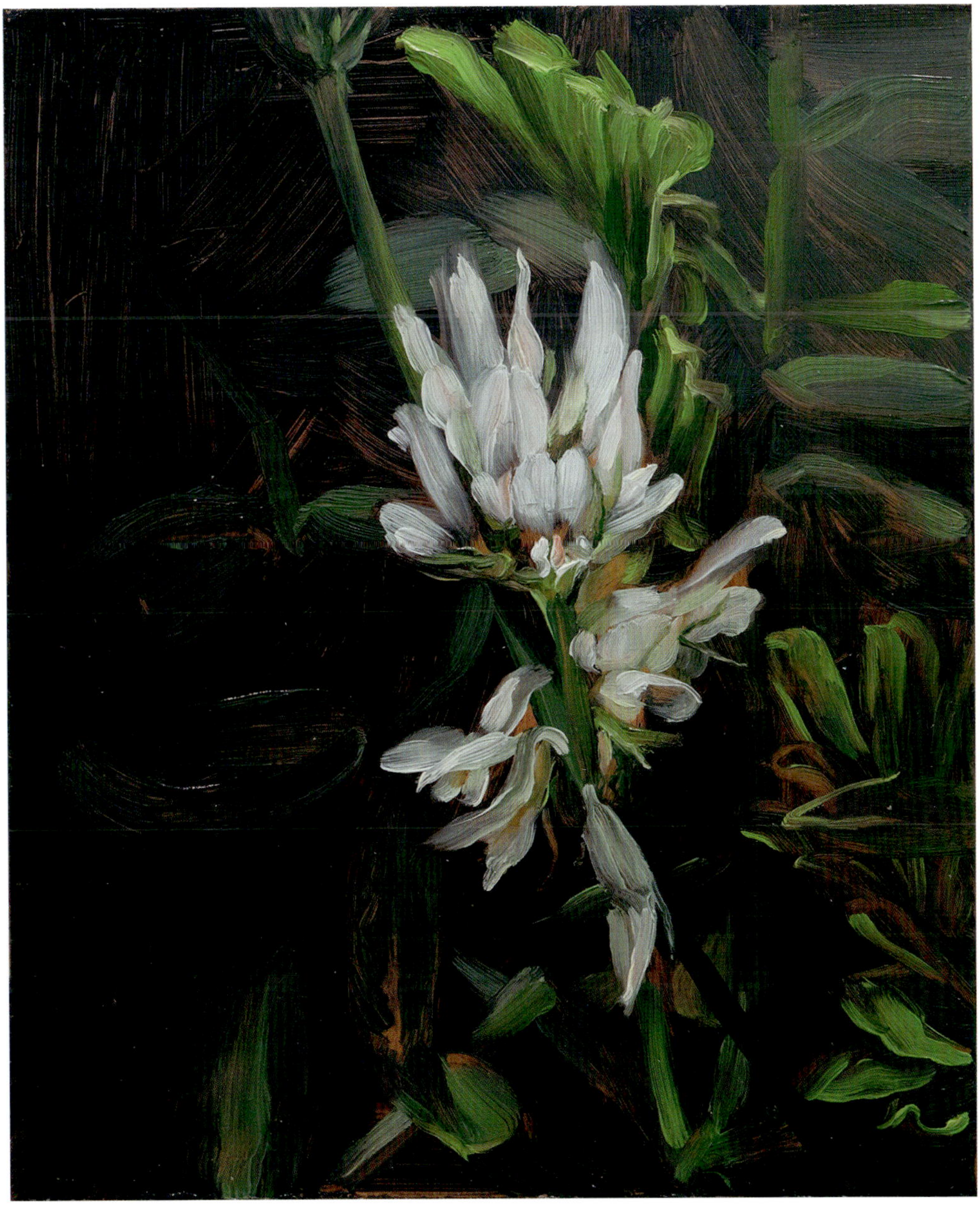

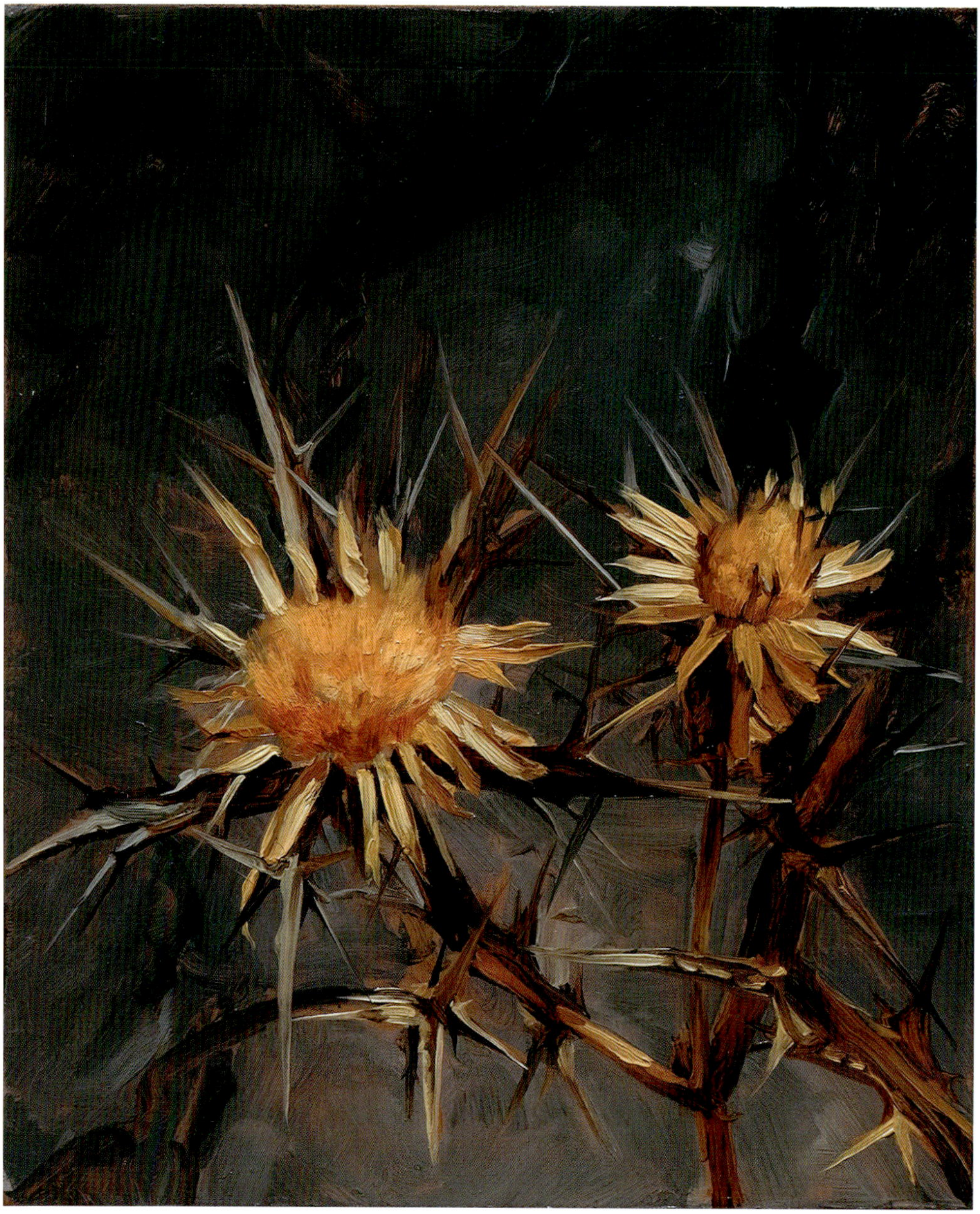

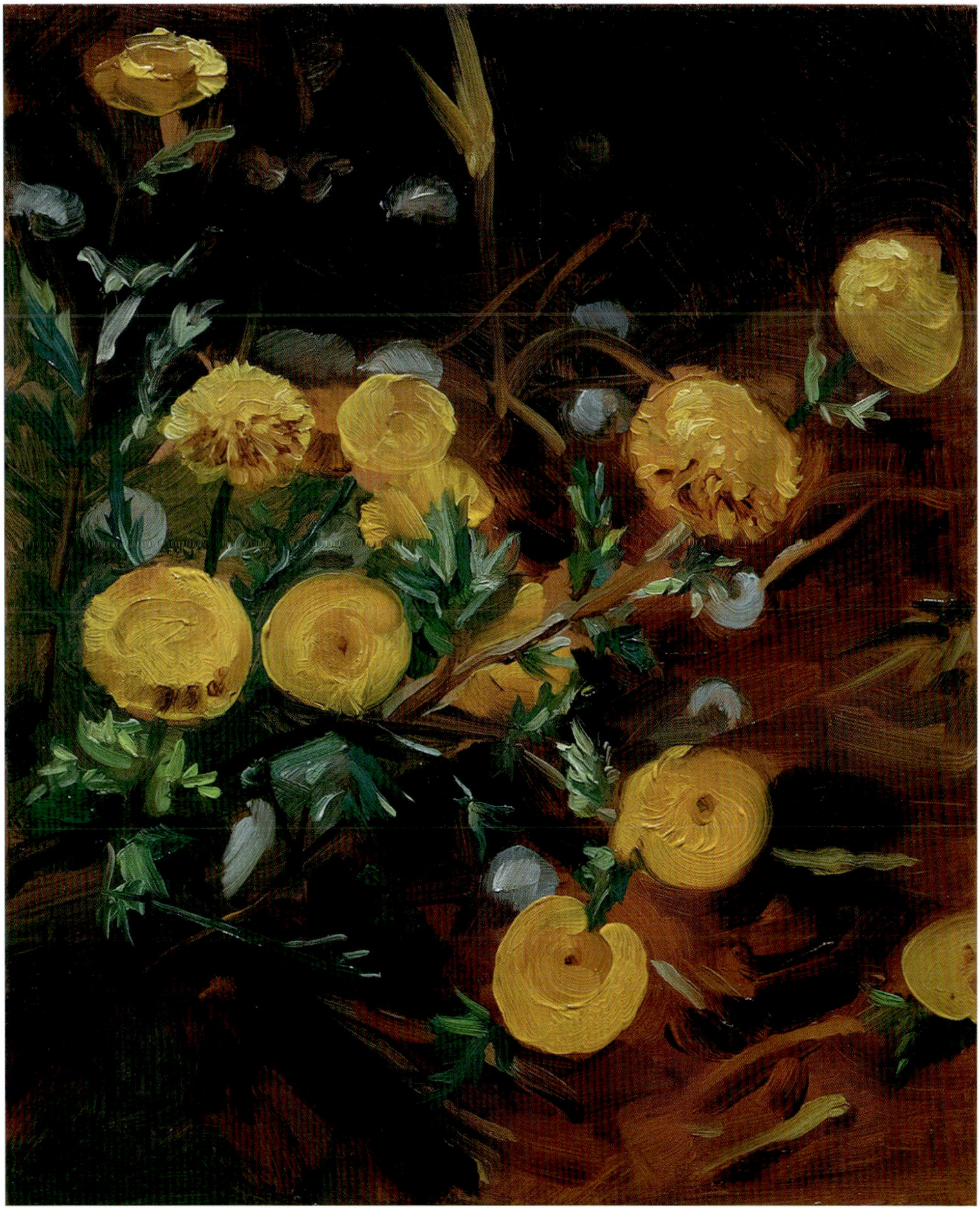

129-131
Mars et Vénus, phases d'opposition

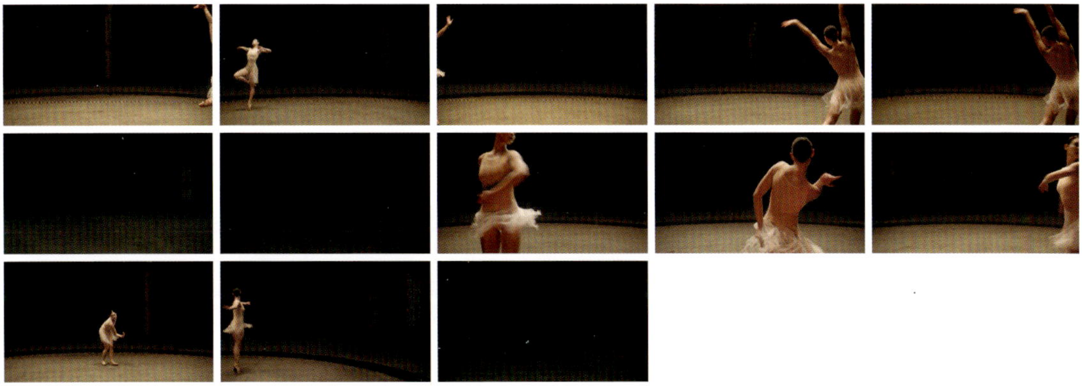

133-135
Chant 23

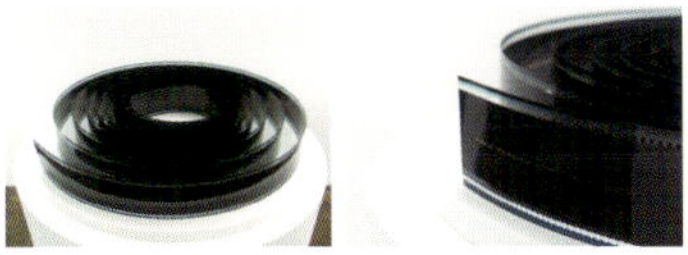

137-141
1925-1964

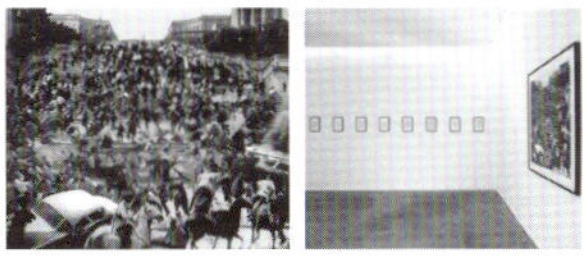

143
L'oeuvre d'art à l'époque de sa reproduction mécanisée (pour W. Benjamin)

144-145
Le Chariot de Mars

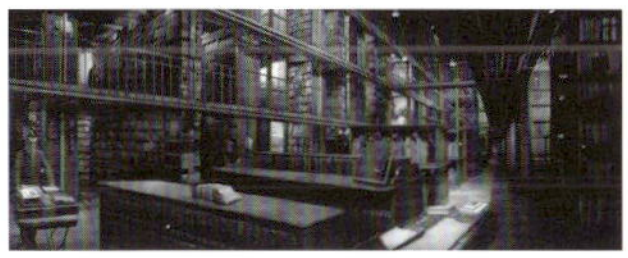

147
L'Éternité par les astres

L'Histoire retournée

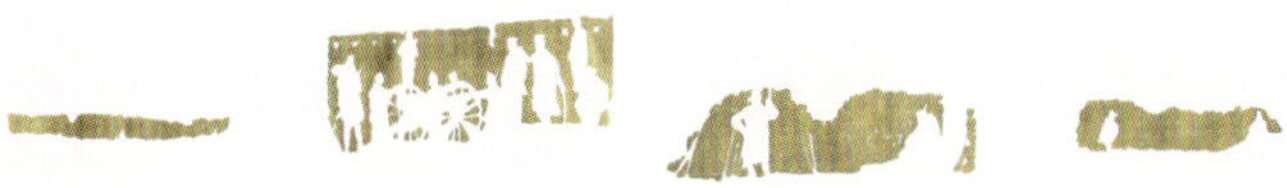

Screenshot sequence

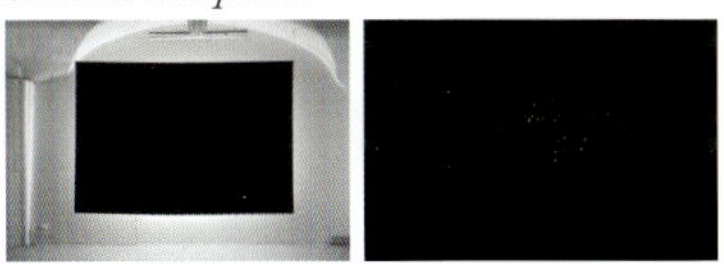

Dans un vaste hangar, violemment éclairé en son centre et autrement plongé dans l'ombre, une danseuse évolue au son d'un métronome sur une trajectoire circulaire, exécutant périodiquement des voltes sans dévier de son axe. À la périphérie, sur un cercle plus large, une caméra montée sur un travelling et contrôlée à distance suit les mouvements de la danseuse qui sort parfois du cadre avant d'y entrer à nouveau. Le cercle sur lequel évolue la caméra est légèrement décentré par rapport à l'axe de celui sur lequel évolue la danseuse, de sorte que la courbe dessinée par la double révolution des deux mobiles forme non pas un cercle, mais une ellipse. La danseuse et la caméra n'évoluent pas à la même vitesse, et si le mouvement de la caméra est uniforme, celui de la danseuse est marqué d'accélérations et de retards qui régulièrement se résolvent, fugitivement, au moment où les deux mobiles se trouvent strictement alignés.
En dehors de la figure de la danseuse, le seul élément apparaissant par intermittence à l'image est le rail du travelling qui circonscrit au sol l'espace de la représentation et marque le partage entre l'ombre et la lumière. À trois reprises, à la faveur d'un panoramique, la caméra se perd dans les ténèbres du hangar, à l'extérieur du champ éclairé, au-delà de la limite circonscrite par le travelling circulaire. La double trajectoire qui règle le mouvement de la caméra et de la danseuse représentent respectivement celle de Mars et de Vénus, inspirée d'une illustration de l'*Astronomia Nova* de Johannes Kepler, publiée à Prague en 1609, représentant le système des épicycles de Mars, calculé avec l'aide d'une équipe d'astronomes de l'Observatoire de Paris. C'est ce schéma, contraction en une dizaine de minutes d'un phénomène qui se déroule sur plusieurs mois et observé d'un point de vue impossible, que Julien Audebert a demandé à Alice Renavand, une étoile de l'Opéra de Paris, de danser. Il s'agit donc d'une fiction. Mais alors de quoi *Mars et Vénus, phases d'opposition* est-il la fiction ?

Mysterium Cosmographicum Philippe-Alain Michaud

Dans une célèbre étude de 1954, *Galilée critique d'art*, où il entreprend de montrer la concordance rigoureuse entre l'attitude esthétique et l'attitude scientifique de Galilée, Erwin Panofsky s'attarde sur la question des relations du mathématicien astronome avec Johannes Kepler. Selon l'historien de l'art, Galilée a complètement ignoré la découverte astronomique fondamentale de Kepler, à savoir que les orbites des planètes ne sont pas des cercles, mais des ellipses, découverte qui apportait des réponses aux questions restées sans solution par la théorie héliocentrique de Copernic qui ne permettait pas de rendre compte de la rétrogradation apparente des planètes ni de la variation d'intensité de leur brillance. Or, selon Panofsky, ce n'est pas par manque d'information mais de propos délibéré que Galilée a ignoré l'hypothèse elliptique keplérienne, et « il faut se demander pourquoi[1]. »

Au commencement du *Dialogue sur les deux grands systèmes du monde* (1632), Galilée expose la perfection du mouvement circulaire « qui part toujours d'un terme naturel et se meut vers un terme naturel ; dans lequel la répugnance et l'inclination sont toujours de force égale » qui, de ce fait n'est ni retardé, ni accéléré, mais uniforme et, par conséquent, capable d'une continuation perpétuelle, laquelle ne peut avoir lieu dans un mouvement rectiligne continuellement retardé ou accéléré[2]. Le caractère privilégié du mouvement rectiligne pour le monde matériel est l'une des thèses les plus fondamentales de la physique d'Aristote. Si pour celui-ci le mouvement circulaire est naturel dans les cieux, c'est justement que les sphères et les astres ne sont pas matériels ou du moins que leur nature est différente de celle du monde sublunaire. Le mouvement rectiligne exprime donc la finitude et l'imperfection relative du monde créé. L'adoption de l'ellipse introduit une simplification dans le système des mouvements planétaires ; une trajectoire elliptique s'accorde bien mieux avec une conception dynamique de ces mouvements qu'une trajectoire composée de mouvements circulaires. Une telle trajectoire, dans son imperfection, convient mieux au monde mobile, temporel et changeant que la suprême perfection de la sphère. Mais il était impossible à Galilée de visualiser le système solaire comme une combinaison d'ellipses parce qu'il ne pouvait pas ne pas sentir que l'ellipse est un cercle déformé, une forme dans laquelle l'ordre parfait a été troublé par l'intrusion de la rectilinéarité ; une forme qui, peut-on ajouter, « fut aussi énergiquement rejetée par l'art de la haute Renaissance à son âge d'or qu'elle fut chérie par le maniérisme[3]. »

L'astronomie keplérienne était donc pour Galilée une astronomie maniériste. Mais pour Kepler comme pour Galilée, l'univers a toujours gardé la forme d'une sphère finie et bien centrée. Aussi pour obliger les planètes à décrire des ellipses dans le ciel, a-t-il été contraint de leur attribuer une libration sur leurs rayons vecteurs et des moteurs propres qui le leur font accomplir. Sous l'influence de l'action du soleil, les planètes décriraient des cercles : c'est l'action de leurs moteurs propres qui les détourne de leur chemin[4]. Galilée voit le propre du mouvement animal et humain dans la rotation de ses membres autour de leurs points d'attache « concaves ou convexes » et le réduit ainsi à un système de cercles et d'épicycles tandis que Kepler affirme, au contraire, que tous les muscles opèrent selon le principe du mouvement rectiligne, alignant ainsi le mouvement des planètes sur celui du corps humain[5].

L'identification par Kepler de la physique terrestre à la physique céleste repose sur la destruction par Copernic de la division du monde en sublunaire et astral. Mais elle repose tout autant sur sa fidélité à la conception aristotélicienne du mouvement, processus dans lequel tout mouvement continu implique nécessairement l'action également continue d'un moteur. Là où l'empirisme progressiste

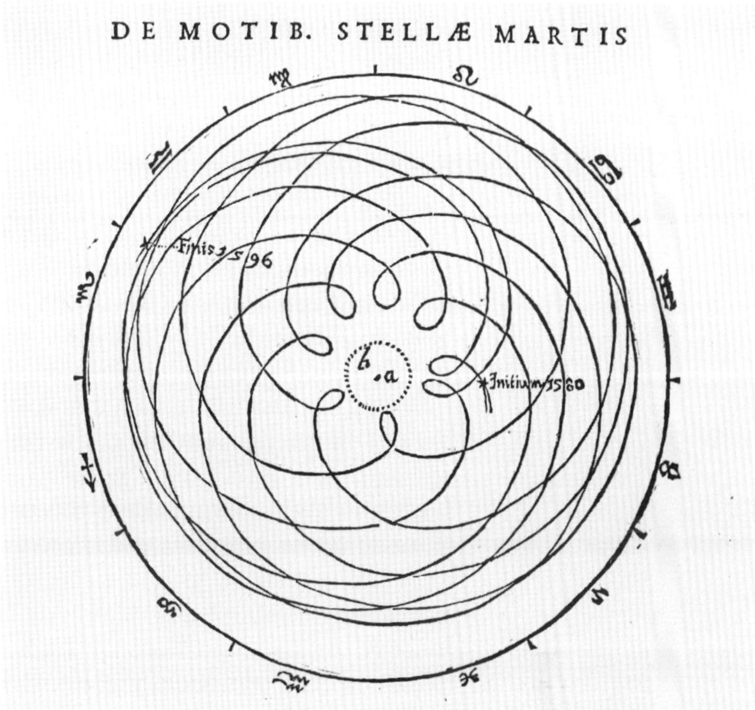

Représentation des mouvements géocentriques de Mars par / Representation of the geocentric movements of Mars by Johannes Kepler (*Astronomia Nova*, 1609)

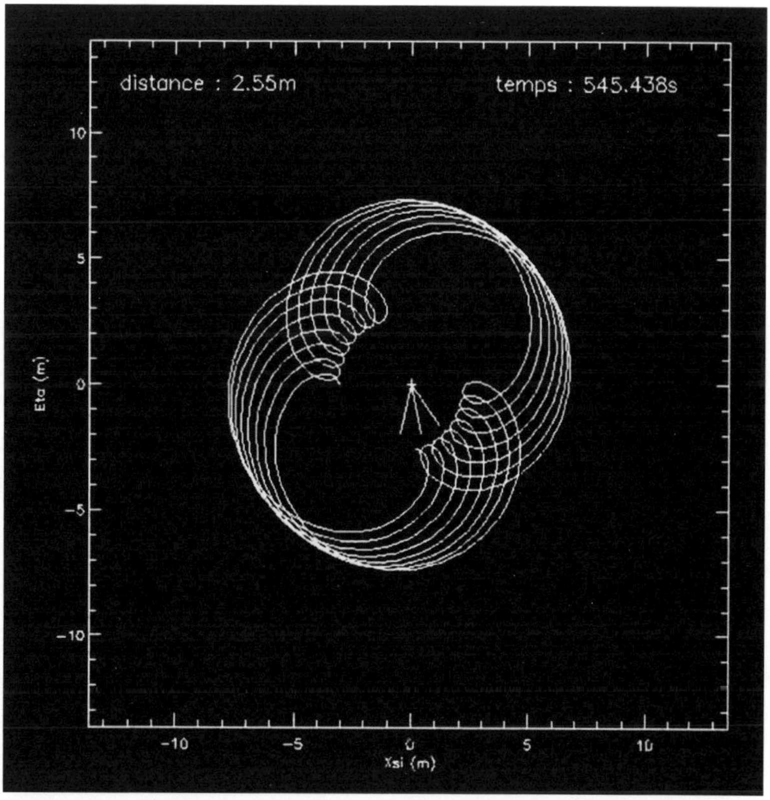

Représentation du mouvement relatif perçu par le spectateur de / Representation of the relative movement perceived by the viewer of *Mars et Vénus, phases d'opposition* (Julien Audebert et / and Pascal Descamps, Observatoire de Paris)

de Galilée l'empêcha de distinguer entre la forme idéale du cercle et l'action mécanique et par là même contribua à maintenir sa théorie du mouvement sous l'égide de la circularité, l'idéalisme conservateur de Kepler lui permit de faire cette distinction. L'acceptation des trajectoires elliptiques permit à Kepler de maintenir l'identité matérielle du monde, c'est-à-dire l'assimilation de la terre aux planètes et donc des planètes à la terre. Mais l'unification de la physique terrestre et de la physique céleste s'appuyait sur un animisme astral, animisme qui devait apparaître à Galilée comme un retour à des conceptions magiques, mais désormais libérée, selon les mots d'Alexandre Koyré, de « la hantise de la circularité[6]. »

La Renaissance avait assimilé la doctrine antique selon laquelle les lois du mouvement règlent le cosmos de manière eurythmique autour d'un point central. C'est ainsi que Bernardo Buontalenti représente en 1589 dans une série d'*Intermezzi*, spectacles complexes associant danse, musique et théâtre présentés à Florence au Palazzo Pitti à l'occasion du mariage de Ferdinando de Médicis et de Christine de Lorraine, l'harmonie des sphères de l'univers en suivant strictement la lettre du *Timée* de Platon : « Le Soleil, la Lune et les cinq autres astres, ceux qu'on appelle errants, sont nés pour définir les nombres du temps et en assurer la conservation. Ayant façonné le corps de chacun d'eux, le dieu les a placés, au nombre de sept, dans les sept orbites que décrit la substance de l'Autre [...][7]. »

Le maître d'œuvre des spectacles, Giovanni de' Bardi (1534-1612), poète et musicien, avait été l'animateur, entre 1576 et 1582, de la Camerata Fiorentina, rassemblant des érudits et des artistes florentins, qui entendait promouvoir une réforme du mélodrame antiquisant en le soustrayant aux conventions rigides imposées par les spectacles de cour. Les spectacles de 1589 donnaient l'occasion à Bardi de mettre à l'épreuve ses idées en produisant une image « archéologique » de l'Antiquité qui pût s'accorder aux critères de l'imitation réaliste. Dans son discours « Sopra la musica e il cantar bene », Bardi distingue trois sortes de rythmes : d'une part celui du corps, qui se manifeste au regard ; d'autre part celui de l'harmonie et celui des paroles qui se manifestent à l'oreille – et c'est, selon lui, de la combinaison de ces trois rythmes que doit naître le sens[8]. Tout autant que par les paroles et par le chant, la signification des *Intermezzi* devait donc se transmettre par la danse, les décors, la scénographie, les accessoires, la chorégraphie et les costumes qui occupent dans les spectacles de 1589 une fonction figurative dont Aby Warburg avait déjà reconnu l'importance en peinture, dès 1893, dans une étude consacrée à la représentation des figures en mouvement dans la peinture de Botticelli[9]. À propos des Intermezzi, l'historien de l'art insiste sur la mise entre parenthèses des significations procédant du discours au profit de l'expressivité des corps et de la gestuelle : « Ceux-ci ne relevaient pas essentiellement de l'art dramatique qui se manifeste au moyen de la parole, mais bien plutôt de l'art du cortège mythologique. Celui-ci, muet par nature, demandait, on le comprendra facilement, l'aide des gestes, des accessoires et des ornements ; toutes ces formes *intermédiaires*, aujourd'hui disparues, entre la vie et l'art dramatique, dans lesquelles affleurait la procession mythologique ou allégorique, si fréquente dans les fêtes publiques des XVe, XVIe siècles [...][10]. »

C'est à l'ingénieur Buontalenti qu'il revint d'*animer* les concepts de Bardi en donnant l'illusion de l'espace et du mouvement au moyen des décors, des dispositifs scéniques et des machines. Bernardo Buontalenti (1536-1608) était entré au service des Médicis en 1547, à l'âge de dix ans. Une anecdote rapportée par Filippo Baldinucci fait état de l'intérêt précoce qu'il manifesta pour les mobiles et les figures en mouvement : « À cet âge encore tendre [15 ans], il conçut pour distraire le jeune prince [Francesco, fils de Cosme de Médicis] une crèche que l'on trouva fort singulière et étonnante. Car non seulement on voyait s'ouvrir les cieux, s'abaisser les nuages, voler çà et là une foule d'anges et marcher sur terre d'autres figures, mais ces figurines innombrables qui se dirigeaient vers la crèche, avec des mouvements variés, semblaient vraiment réelles[11]. On lui prête aussi la mise au point d'un jouet, préfiguration des zootropes, qui donnait l'illusion du mouvement et la maîtrise des figures éphémères : « Dans les mêmes circonstances, il inventa un jouet fait de silhouettes découpées et disposées sur un cercle, puis placées à l'intérieur d'un grand cylindre de papier. Tournant sous l'effet de la fumée d'une bougie, elles projetaient leur ombre sur la feuille interposée entre elles et le regard. L'objet fut nommé girandole. Et c'est ainsi qu'on commença à l'appeler l'homme aux girandoles, puis Bernard des girandoles[12]. » Buontalenti supervisa pendant plus d'un demi-siècle les cérémonies du duché, construisant les machines et dessinant costumes et décors pour le théâtre ; il était le « fabricant d'accessoires » (*skeuopoios*) dont l'art, selon Aristote, « pour l'exécution technique du spectacle, [...] est plus décisif que celui des poètes[13]. »

Les machines de Buontalenti apportaient des améliorations importantes à la conception de la scène ; au vieux système des périactes, ou prismes tournants (*scaena versatilis*), qui étaient employés pour les changements de décor à vue et les effets d'apparition, il substitue la scène à coulisses (*scaena ductilis*) où les perspectives ouvrantes, montées sur des glissières, ménagent des effets successifs d'approfondissement de l'espace, système qui allait se généraliser dans le théâtre européen du XVIIe siècle : « Ces effets répondaient mieux à l'idéal baroque de fuite illusoire vers l'infini, de changement continu. Au caractère plastique et constructif de la scène du XVIe siècle dont l'horizon était borné par des architectures succédaient les effets picturaux, la toile de fond devenant l'instrument majeur de l'illusion d'espace. La perspective aérienne l'emportait peu à peu sur la géométrie linéaire. Les périactes, instruments imparfaits d'un décor voué aux métamorphoses rapides dans les intermèdes, allaient céder la place aux coulisses plates latérales, plus légères, issues du même principe que la *forme* ouvrante médiane[14]. »

Pour les « Intermèdes » de 1589, Buontalenti devait concevoir une scénographie qui réponde analogiquement aux exigences nouvelles du *stile rappresentativo* : le spectacle d'une Antiquité féerique donnant le sentiment d'une résurrection de la fable devait naître de la combinaison de l'illusion spatiale et de la reconstitution archéologique, de la vraisemblance et de la rationalité (*verosimiglianza* [...] *congiunta col ragionevole*)[15]. Les « Intermèdes », au nombre de six, représentaient successivement : l'harmonie des sphères célestes, la dispute des Muses et des Piérides, le combat d'Apollon et du serpent Python, le monde des démons, le chant d'Arion, la descente d'Apollon et de Dionysos accompagnés du Rythme et de l'Harmonie. Dans le premier « Intermède », un temple rustique apparaissait au sol et dans le ciel un nuage sur lequel se tenaient quelques figures féminines en train de jouer de la musique et de chanter. On voyait le nuage descendre à l'intérieur du temple, puis le temple à son tour descendre dans le sol : à sa place apparaissait un ciel étoilé d'où tombait une lumière « semblable à celle que par une nuit claire on voit tomber de la lune », dit Bastiano de' Rossi dans le commentaire à chaud qu'il a laissé des intermèdes[16]. C'est alors que, masquant la perspective, passait un défilé de nuages montés par des sirènes. Peu à peu, les nuages bas s'élevaient dans le ciel, la lumière s'intensifiait et ils semblaient éclairés par les rayons du soleil. Au cours du sixième intermède, sans changement de décor, tous les instruments se mettaient à jouer ensemble : orgues, cymbales, harpes, violes, cithares, lyres, guitares espagnoles et napolitaines, luths, théorbes, trombones, flûtes... Le ciel dont procédait cette harmonie s'ouvrait, la scène était envahie de rayons solaires si clairs et si brillants que, sans les vapeurs qui s'élevaient de la terre, l'œil de l'homme, dit Rossi, n'aurait pu soutenir longtemps son éclat[17]. Sept nuages apparaissaient sur lesquels étaient montés Apollon et Dionysos accompagnés de l'Harmonie, du Rythme et du cortège des Grâces et des Muses. Ils posaient le pied sur la scène en chantant, accompagnés de quarante figurants hommes et femmes en costume rustique, et se mettaient à danser ensemble.

Le théâtre maniériste avait utilisé les ressources de la scène perspective construite en profondeur et les changements de décor à vue pour représenter, conformément à la doctrine platonicienne, l'harmonie des sphères. *Mars et Vénus, phases d'opposition* présente la même dimension allégorique : mais au dispositif de la scène construite en profondeur se substitue la forme circulaire du plateau. Animé par le double mouvement excentrique de la caméra et de la danseuse, l'espace se referme sur lui-même, réactivant, en-deçà de la scène perspective, l'espace choral qui était celui de la tragédie antique : « Si le chœur, écrit Nietzsche, est le spectateur idéal (*Zuschauer*), c'est qu'en réalité il est le seul voyant (*Schauer*), le voyant du monde visionnaire de la scène. Tel que nous le connaissons en effet, un public de simples spectateurs était inconnu des Grecs. Dans leurs théâtres qui s'élevaient en gradins concentriques, il était au contraire loisible à chacun de ne pas *voire*, proprement, l'ensemble du monde civilisé qui l'entourait, et, le regard saturé par le spectacle qui lui était offert, de s'imaginer soi-même en choreute[18]. » Cet espace circulaire, où au spectateur est assigné un point de vue impossible, c'est l'espace du film qui échappe, à travers la dialectique de la figure et du plan et la combinaison du mouvement des mobiles et de celui de l'appareil, à la fixité de la scène théâtrale. C'est ainsi que pour construire sa fable astrale, une fiction extatique qui trouve dans la représentation dansée du ciel sa mise en abîme allégorique, Audebert utilise les deux ressorts fondamentaux de la mise-en-cadre tels qu'Eisenstein a pu les décrire, soit l'*obrez*, la rencontre de la figure avec le bord du cadre qui coïncide avec les apparitions et les disparitions de la danseuse évoluant entre le champ et le hors-champ, et le *rakurs*, qui désigne l'angle formé par la caméra dans sa rencontre avec le plan, angle dont l'ouverture vient fugitivement se résoudre dans la stricte perpendiculaire des phases d'opposition[19].

Dans les premières pages d'*Origine du drame baroque*, Walter Benjamin notait que l'effet de connaissance ne peut éviter le moment de la représentation et décrivait la formation du savoir comme un balancement rythmique entre image et concept. Et selon Benjamin : « Les idées, écrit-il, se rapportent aux choses comme les constellations se rapportent aux étoiles[20]. » La représentation de Mars et de Vénus est un topos de la culture maniériste : on trouve au XVIe siècle d'innombrables occurrences dans la littérature comme dans les arts visuels, de leur encontre où s'exprime l'union dissonante des contraires dont procède l'harmonie, *discordia concors* ou *concordia discors*. Au rythme régulier qui scande leur révolution lente, projetant le ciel maniériste dans l'espace du film, Julien Audebert donne à voir en un jeu de coïncidences et d'évitements la transfiguration de l'éros en harmonie dansée, c'est-à-dire en *représentation*, et nous permet de reconnaître, dans la figure de danseuse tournant sur le disque du ciel, l'origine même de la fiction.

1 Erwin Panofsky, *Galilée critique d'art* [*Galileo as a critic of the Arts*, 1954], trad. Nathalie Heinich, Bruxelles, Les Impressions Nouvelles, 2016, p. 62.
2 Alexandre Koyré, « Attitude esthétique et pensée scientifique » [1955], dans *Galilée critique d'art*, op. cit., p. 101.
3 E. Panofsky, *Galilée critique d'art*, op. cit., p. 65.
4 A. Koyré, « Attitude esthétique et pensée scientifique », dans *Galilée critique d'art*, op. cit., p. 105-106.
5 A. Koyré, « Attitude esthétique et pensée scientifique », dans *Galilée critique d'art*, op. cit., p. 103 et E. Panofsky, *Galilée critique d'art*, op. cit., p. 65-67.
6 A. Koyré, « Attitude esthétique et pensée scientifique », dans *Galilée critique d'art*, op. cit., p. 108.
7 Platon, *Timée*, 38, trad. Albert Rivaud, Paris, Les Belles Lettres, 1949, p. 152.
8 Giovanni de' Bardi, in *Trattato della musica scenica*, éd. Giovanni Battista Doni, chap. 4, *Trattati di musica*, Florence 1763, II, p. 233-248. Sauf indication contraire, les adaptations des textes originaux ont été réalisées par le traducteur.
9 Citation originale in Aby Warburg, *Sandro Botticellis Geburt der Venus und Frühling. Eine Untersuchung über die Vorstellungen von der Antike in der italienischen Frührenaissance*, éd. Léopold Voss, Hamburg et Leipzig, 1893. Trad. Sibylle Muller in *Essais florentins*, Paris, Klincksieck, 1990, p. 47-81.
10 Citation originale in Aby Warburg, « I Costumi Teatrali per gli Intermezzi del 1589. I disegni di Bernardo Buontalenti e il Libro di Conti di Emilio de' Cavalieri », dans *La rinascita del paganesimo antico*, éd Gertrud Bing, Florence, La Nuova Italia Editrice, 1991, p. 281.
11 Citation originale in Filippo Baldinucci, « Vita di Bernardo Buontalenti », *Notizie*, II, Florence, 1974, p. 493-494.
12 Ibid.
13 Aristote, *La Poétique*, 6, 50 b 15, éd. et trad. Roselyne Dupont-Roc et Jean Lallot, Paris, Seuil, 1980, p. 57
14 Hélène Leclerc, « La scène d'illusion et l'hégémonie du théâtre à l'italienne », *Histoire des spectacles*, Paris, Gallimard, Bibliothèque de la Pléiade, 1965, p. 598.
15 G. de Bardi, in G. B. Doni, *Trattato della musica scenica*, chap. 4, *Trattati*, II, op. cit., p. 16.
16 Citation originale in Bastiano de' Rossi, *Descrizione dell'Apparato e degli Intermedi Fatti per la Commedia rappresentata in Firenze. Nelle nozze de' Serenissimi don Ferdinando Medici, e Madama Cristina di Lorena Gran Duchi di Toscana*, Florence, Anton Padovani, 1589.
17 Citation originale in B. de' Rossi, *Descrizione dell'Apparato e degli Intermedi*... op. cit.
18 Friedrich Nietzsche, *La Naissance de la tragédie*, § 8, trad. M. Haar, Ph. Lacoue-Labarthe & J.-L. Nancy, Paris, Gallimard, 1977, p. 72.
19 Citation originale in Sergueï Eisenstein, « Montage 1937 », in *Towards a Theory of Montage*, éds. Michael Glenny et Richard Taylor, Londres, BFI, 1991, p. 15.
20 Walter Benjamin, *Origine du drame baroque allemand*, trad. Sibylle Muller, Paris, Flammarion, coll. Essais, 2000.

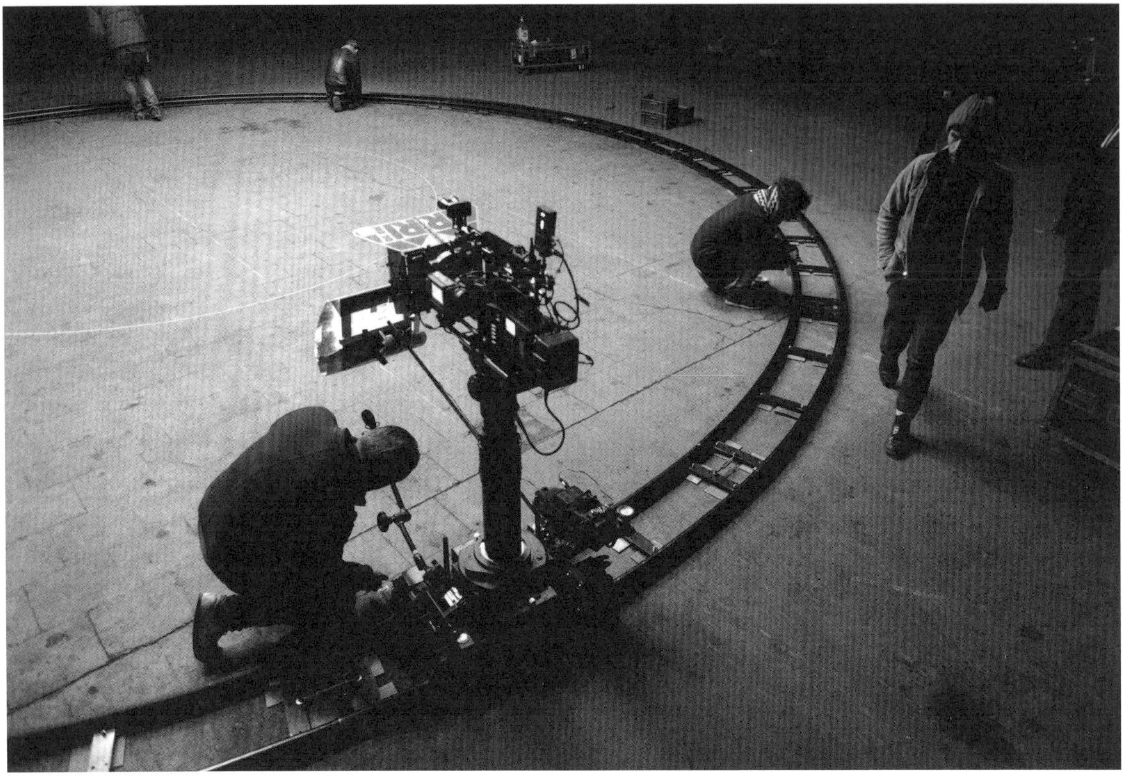

Photographie de plateau de / Set photography of *Mars et Vénus, phases d'opposition*

In a vast warehouse, intensely lit in its center and otherwise plunged into darkness, a dancer moves to the sound of a metronome on a circular line, periodically performing twirls without deviating from its axis. On the outer edge, on a larger circle, a camera mounted on a dolly and remotely controlled follows the movement of the dancer who sometimes leaves the frame before entering it again. The circle on which the camera evolves is slightly off-center compared to the axis on which the dancer evolves, so that the curve drawn by the double revolution of the two mobiles doesn't form a circle, but rather an ellipse. The dancer and the camera do not move at the same speed and if the movement of the camera is uniform, that of the dancer is marked by accelerations and delays. They regularly meet, fleetingly, at the moment when the two mobiles are strictly aligned.

Mysterium Cosmographicum
Philippe-Alain Michaud

Apart from the figure of the dancer, the only element appearing at irregular intervals in the image is the track of the dolly rails which outlines the ground of the performance space and marks the division between shadow and light. Thanks to a panoramic shot, the camera loses itself in the darkness of the warehouse three times, away from light, beyond the frame created by the circular tracking shot. The double trajectory that regulates the dance of the camera along-side the ballerina represents both that of Mars and Venus, inspired by an illustration of *Astronomia Nova* by Johannes Kepler, published in Prague in 1609, representing Mars epicycles system, calculated with the help of astronomers in the Paris Observatory. Audebert asked Alice Renavand, a star of the Paris Opera, to dance this diagram: the contraction in about ten minutes of a phenomenon that takes place over several months and observed from an impossible point of view. It is therefore fiction. But then what is *Mars et Vénus, phases d'opposition* the fiction of?

In a famous study of 1954, *Galileo as a Critic of the Arts*, where he undertakes to show the rigorous matching point in Galileo's aesthetic and scientific attitudes, Erwin Panofsky dwells on the mathematician astronomer's ties with Johannes Kepler. According to the art historian, Galileo completely ignored Kepler's fundamental astronomical discovery that the orbits of the planets are not circles, but ellipses: a discovery that provided answers to questions left unanswered by the heliocentric theory of Copernic which did not account for the apparent retrogradation of the planets nor the variation in their shining intensity. However, according to Panofsky, it was not for lack of information but deliberately that Galileo ignored the Keplerian elliptical hypothesis, and "one must ask oneself why."[1]

In the opening lines of the *Dialogue Concerning the Two Chief World Systems, Ptolemaic and Copernican* (1632), Galileo exposes the perfection of the circular movement, "which always starts from a natural term and moves towards a natural term; in which revulsion and inclination are always of equal force which, therefore, is neither retarded nor accelerated, but uniform and, therefore, capable of perpetual renewal, which wouldn't be possible in rectilinear motion continually delayed or accelerated."[2] How Aristotle trusts the material world to be set in rectilinear motion is one of the most fundamental theses of his physics. If for him circular motion is natural in the skies, it is precisely because the spheres and the stars are not material, or at least because their nature is different from that of the sublunar world.

The rectilinear motion therefore encompasses the finitude and the relative imperfection of the world as it was created. Thus adopting the ellipse simplifies the understanding of the planetary movements system; an elliptical trajectory is more attuned to a dynamic conception of these movements than a trajectory relying on circular movements. Such a trajectory, in its imperfection, is more suited to the mobile, temporal, and changing world than the supreme perfection of the sphere. But it was impossible for Galileo to visualize the solar system as a combination of ellipses because he could not help seeing the ellipse as a distorted circle, a shape in which he felt the perfect order was disturbed by the intrusion of rectilinearity; a form which, it may be added, "was as strenuously rejected in the Golden Age of High Renaissance art as it was cherished by Mannerism."[3]

Therefore, in Galileo's eyes, Keplerian astronomy was mannerist. For Kepler as for Galileo, the universe has always kept the shape of a finite and well-centered sphere. Also, to force the planets to describe ellipses in the sky, he was forced to endow their own motors and vector rays with libration so as to help them do this movement. Under the influence of the action of the sun, the planets would thus draw circles: the action of their own motors diverting them from their path.[4] Galileo sees the essence of animal and human movement in the rotation of their limbs around their "concave or convex" points of attachment and thus reduces it to a system of circles and epicycles, while Kepler states, on the contrary, that all the muscles operate on the principle of rectilinear motion, thus mapping the motion of the planets on that of the human body.[5]

Kepler identified terrestrial physics with celestial physics. This identification relies on Copernicus ending the division of the world into sublunar and astral. But it trusts just as much in its fidelity to the Aristotelian conception of movement, a process in which any continuous movement yields the equally continuous action of a motor. Where Galileo's progressive empiricism prevented him from distinguishing between the ideal form of the circle and mechanical action and thereby helped to ascertain his theory of motion under the aegis of circularity, Kepler's conservative idealism allowed to make this distinction. Envisioning elliptical trajectories allowed Kepler to maintain the material identity of the world, that is to say the assimilation of the earth to the planets and therefore of the planets to the earth. But uniting terrestrial physics and celestial physics was based on an astral animism, an animism which was to appear to Galileo as a return to magical conceptions, yet henceforth free, in the words of Alexandre Koyré, from "the dreaded circularity."[6]

According to the Ancient doctrine of the laws of motion, renaissance artists and thinkers thought that the cosmos was ruled eurhythmically around a central point. This is how Bernardo Buontalenti represented complex shows combining dance, music, and theater in a series of "Intermezzi," presented in Florence at Palazzo Pitti in 1589 for the wedding of Ferdinando de' Medici and Christine de Lorraine. He then staged the harmony of the spheres of the universe following Plato's *Timaeus* words to the letter: "The Sun, the Moon, and the five other stars, the 'wandering stars' as we tend to call them, were born to define the numbers of time and ensure their safeguard. Having fashioned the body of each of them, the god placed them, seven in number, in the seven orbits outlined by the substance of the Other [. . .]."[7]

Giovanni de' Bardi (1534–1612), poet and musician, masterminded the performances. He had been the animator, between 1576 and 1582, of the Camerata Fiorentina, gathering Florentine scholars and artists, which intended to promote a reform of antiquist melodrama by shielding it from the rigid conventions imposed by performances for the Court. The performances of 1589 gave Bardi the opportunity to test his ideas. He designed an "archeological" image of antiquity that could meet the criteria of realistic imitation. In his speech "Sopra la musica e il cantar bene," Bardi distinguishes three kinds of rhythms: on the one hand that of the body, which manifests itself to the gaze; on the other hand, that of harmony and that of the words that manifest themselves to the ear and it is, according to him, the combination of these three rhythms that makes sense.[8] As much as thanks to words and song, the meaning of the Intermezzi was therefore to be shared through dance, sets, scenography, accessories, choreography, and costumes which are given a figurative dimension in the shows of 1589. Aby Warburg had already recognized the importance of this figuration in painting, as early as 1893, in a study devoted to the moving figures in Sandro Botticelli's painting representations.[9] Regarding the Intermezzi, the art historian wishes the discourse and its meaning be set aside so that the bodies and the gestures could be appreciated: "[Their true origins] did not lie in the spoken drama so much as in the mythological peagant; and this, being an essentially mute and gestural art, naturally relies on accessories and adornments. All those now extinct transitional forms between real life and dramatic art, which the fifteenth, sixteenth and seventeenth centuries produced in such abundance [. . .] afforded a unique opportunity for members of the public to see the revered figures of Antiquity standing before them in flesh and blood."[10]

It was up to engineer Buontalenti to *animate* Bardi's concepts by giving the illusion of space and movement through sets, stage devices, and machines. Bernardo Buontalenti (1536–1608) had been offered a position at the service of the Medici family in 1547, at the age of ten. An anecdote reported by Filippo Baldinucci mentions his early interest in mobiles and moving figures: "At this tender age [15], he designed a nativity scene which was found to be very singular and astonishing only to distract the young prince [Francesco, son of Cosmo de' Medici]. For not only were the heavens opened, the clouds lowered, a multitude of angels flying here and there, and other figures walking on the ground, but these innumerable figurines heading for the manger, with various movements, seemed really real."[11] He is also credited with the development of a toy, a prefiguration of zoetropes, which gave the illusion of movement and mastered ephemeral figures: "Under the same circumstances, he invented a toy made of cut-out silhouettes arranged on a circle, then placed inside a large paper cylinder. Turning under the effect of the smoke of a candle, they projected their shadow on the leaf between them and under our eyes. The object was named a *girandola*. And so people began to call him the man with the girandola, then Bernard of the girandola."[12] For more than half a century, Buontalenti supervised the ceremonies of the duchy, building the machines and designing costumes and sets for the theater; he was the "maker of accessories" (*skeuopoios*), according to Aristotle, "the beauty of which depends more on the art of the mechanic, than on that of the poet."[13]

Buontalenti's machines significantly improved stage design; instead of the old system of periacts, or rotating prisms (*scaena versatilis*), which were used for scenery on-sight changes and appearance effects, he envisioned a sliding backstage stage (*scaena ductilis*) where the opening perspectives, mounted on slides, provide successive effects in order to deepen the scene. A system which would soon be widely used in the European theater venues of the seventeenth century: "These effects adorned the Baroque ideal of illusion of our elevation towards infinity and of continuous change. The pictorial effects had overthrown the plastic and constructive sixteenth century stage, whose horizon was framed within limited architectures, the backdrop would become the major instrument of the illusion of space. Aerial perspective gradually prevailed over linear geometry. The periacts, imperfect instruments of a setting designed to accommodate for rapid metamorphoses in the interludes, were to give way to flat and lighter lateral slides, which resulted from the same principle as the median opening 'form'."[14]

For the "Interludes" of 1589, Buontalenti had to conceive a scenography which would meet the analogical criteria of the *stile rappresentativo*: staging the magic of Antiquity giving the feeling that the fable was resurrected, had to be created from combining spatial illusion and archeological reconstruction, verisimilitude and rationality (*verosimiglianza . . . congiunta col ragionevole*).[15] The six "Interludes," successively represented: the harmony of the celestial spheres; the dispute between the Muses and the Pierides; the fight between Apollo and the serpent Python; the world of demons; the song of Arion, the descent of Apollo and Dionysos alongside Rhythm and Harmony. In the first "Interlude," a rustic temple would appear on the ground and in the sky a cloud on which stood a few female figures playing music and singing. We could see the cloud descending inside the temple, then the temple in its turn descending into the ground: in its stead a starry sky from which fell a light "similar to that which on a clear night we see falling from the moon," Bastiano de' Rossi says off the cuff in the commentary of the interludes.[16] Then a procession of clouds ridden by sirens would mask the perspective as it passed. The low clouds gradually rising in the sky seemed to be illuminated by the rays of the sun as the light intensified. During the sixth interlude, without any change of scenery, all the instruments would begin to play together: organs, cymbals, harps, viols, zithers, lyres, Spanish and Neapolitan guitars, lutes, theorbos, trombones, flutes. . . The sky from which this harmony opened, the scene invaded by solar rays so clear and so bright that, without the steam which rose from the earth, the eye of man, says Rossi, could not have long sustained its brightness.[17] Seven clouds would then appear which Apollo and Dionysus had climbed alongside Harmony, Rhythm, and the procession of the Graces and the Muses. They would set foot on stage singing, accompanied by forty male and female extras in rustic costumes, and begin to dance together.

The mannerist theater had used the resources of the perspective stage built in depth and the changes of scenery for the viewers to see in order to represent, in accordance with the Platonic doctrine, the harmony of the spheres. *Mars et Vénus, phases d'opposition* presents the same allegorical dimension: but the device of the scene built in depth is replaced by the stage's circular shape. Animated by the eccentric double movement of the camera and the dancer, the space closes in on itself, reactivating, below the perspective scene, the choral space that was that of ancient tragedy: "If the chorus, writes Nietzsche, is the ideal spectator (*Zuschauer*) in so far as it is the only beholder, the beholder of the visionary world of the scene. A public of spectators, as known to us, was unknown to the Greeks. In their theatres the terraced structure of the spectators' space rising in concentric arcs enabled every one, in the strictest sense, to overlook the entire world of culture around him, and in surfeited contemplation to imagine himself a chorist."[18] This circular space assigns the viewer an impossible view point. This viewpoint escapes the fixity of the theatrical stage, through the dialectic of the figure and the shot, as well as through the combination of the movement of the mobiles and that of the apparatus.

This is how his astral fable is built, as an ecstatic fiction which meets its allegorical mise-en-abîme in the dancing performance of the sky, Audebert uses the two fundamentals of framing as Eisenstein was able to describe them, either the *obrez*, the meeting of the figure with the edge of the frame which coincides with the appearances and disappearances of the dancer evolving between the frame and the off-screen, and the *rakurs*, which designates the angle formed by the camera in its encounter with the set, an angle whose fleetingly opening is resolved in the strict perpendicular of the phases of opposition.[19]

In the opening pages of *The Origin of German Tragic Drama*, Walter Benjamin noted that the knowledge effect cannot give the moment of representation a miss and described the formation of knowledge as a rhythmic swing between image and concept. Also according to Benjamin, "Ideas relate to things as constellations relate to stars."[20] The representation of Mars and Venus is a topos of Mannerist culture: in the sixteenth century there are innumerable occurrences of their encounter where from the dissonant union of opposites rises harmony in literature as well as in the visual arts, *discordia concors or concordia discors*. To the regular rhythm that punctuates their slow revolution, projecting the Mannerist sky into the space of the film, Audebert shows how eros is transfigured in danced harmony, in a game of coincidences and mishaps that is to say in representation, and allows us to recognize, in the figure of the dancer revolving on the ring of the sky, the very origin of fiction.

1 Erwin Panofsky, *Galileo as a Critic of the Arts* (La Haye: Martinus Nijhoiff, 1954).
2 Alexandre Koyré, "Aesthetic attitude and Scientific Thought," [1955] in Erwin Panofsky, *Galileo as a Critic of the Arts*, p. 101.
3 Panofsky, *Galileo as a Critic of the Arts*, 65.
4 Koyré, "Aesthetic attitude and Scientific Thought," in Panofsky, *Galileo as a Critic of the Arts*, 105–106.
5 Panofsky, *Galileo as a Critic of the Arts*, 65–67.
6 Koyré, "Aesthetic attitude and Scientific Thought," in Panofsky, *Galileo as a Critic of the Arts*, 108.
7 Plato, *Timaeus*, 38, trans. Donald J. Zeyl, in Plato, *Complete Works* (Indianapolis: Hackett, 1997), 1242.
8 Original quote in Giovanni de' Bardi, *Trattato della musica scenica*, Giovanni Battista Doni, ed, chap. 4, Trattati di musica, Florence, 1763, II, 233–248. Unless otherwise noted, original texts in this essay are rendered in English by the translator.
9 Aby Warburg, "Sandro Botticelli's Birth of Venus an Spring," in *The Renewal of Pagan Antiquity*, trans. David Britt (Los Angeles: Getty Research Institute, 1999).
10 Aby Warburg, "The Theatrical Costumes for the Intermedi of 1589," in *The Renewal of Pagan Antiquity*, 369.
11 Original quote in Filippo Baldinucci, "Vita di Bernardo Buontalenti," *Notizie*, II (Florence, 1974), 493–494.
12 Original quote in Baldinucci, "Vita di Bernardo Buontalenti," 493–494.
13 Aristotle, *Poetics*, 6, 1450 b. 20., ed. Jonathan Barnes (Princeton: Princeton University Press, 1984), vol. 2.
14 Original quote in Hélène Leclerc, "La scène d'illusion et l'hégémonie du théâtre à l'italienne," in *Histoire des spectacles* (Paris: Gallimard, Bibliothèque de la Pléiade, 1965), 598.
15 de Bardi, in Doni, *Trattato della musica scenica*, chap. 4, Trattati, II, 16.
16 Original quote in Bastiano de' Rossi, *Descrizione del' Apparato e degli Intermedi Fatti per la Commedia rappresentata in Firenze. Nelle nozze de' Serenissimi don Ferdinando Medici, e Madama Cristina di Lorena Gran Duchi di Toscana* (Florence: Anton Padovani, 1589).
17 de' Rossi, *Descrizione del'Apparato e degli Intermedi.*
18 Friedrich Nietzsche, *The Birth of Tragedy or Hellenism and Pessimism*, trans. William August Haussmann (London/New York: George Allen/ The Macmillan Company, 2016).
19 Sergei Eisenstein, "Montage 1937," in *Towards a Theory of Montage*, Michael Glenny and Richard Taylor, eds. (London: BFI, 1991), 15.
20 Walter Benjamin, *The Origin of German Tragic Drama* [1928], trans. John Osborne, intro George Steiner, (London/New York: Verso, 1998).

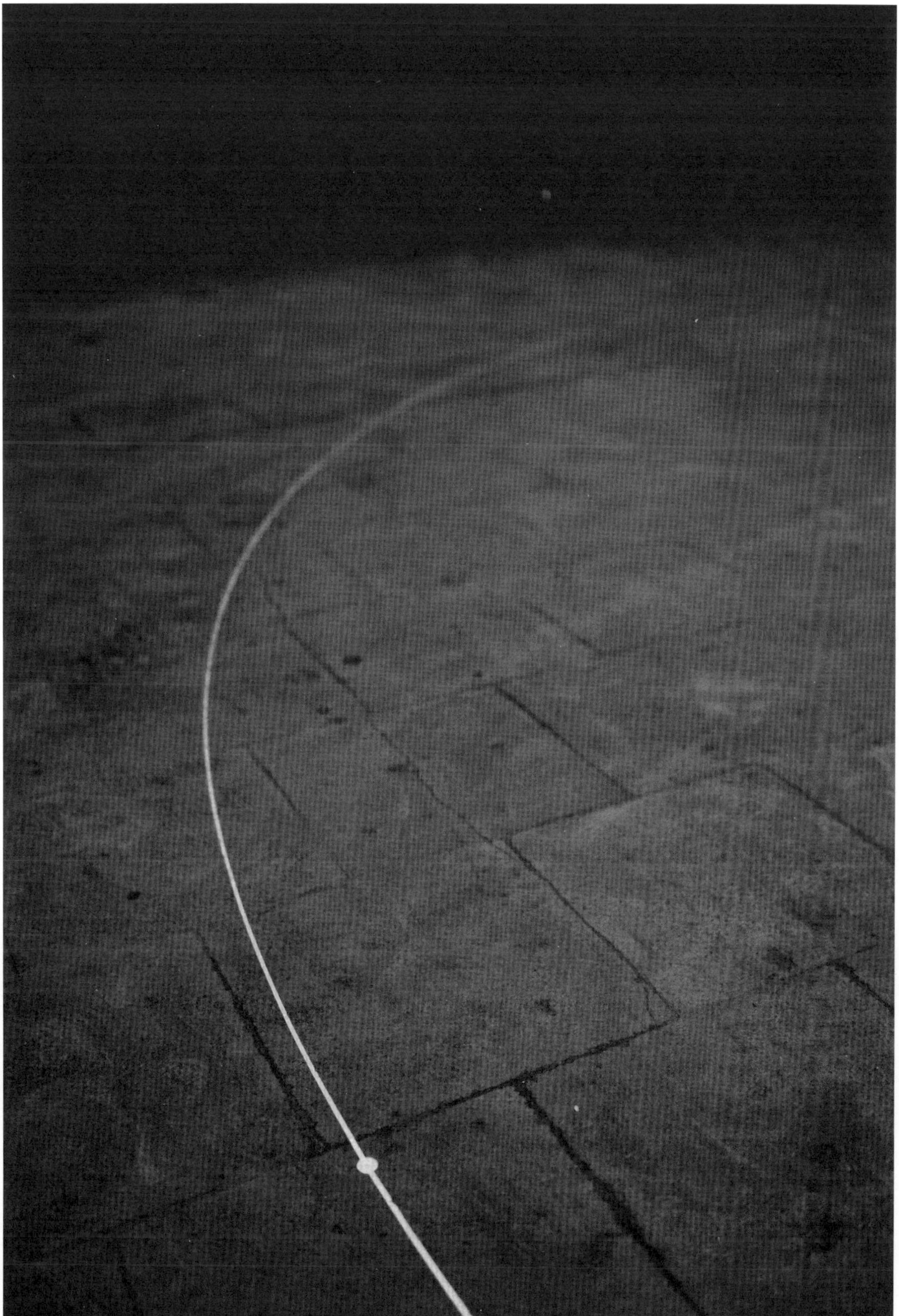

Marquage au sol de la trajectoire de Vénus / Floor marking of Venus's trajectory

Mars et Vénus, phases d'opposition, 2016
Film numérique 35 mm, couleur, son / 35 mm digital film, color, sound, 10:30 min.

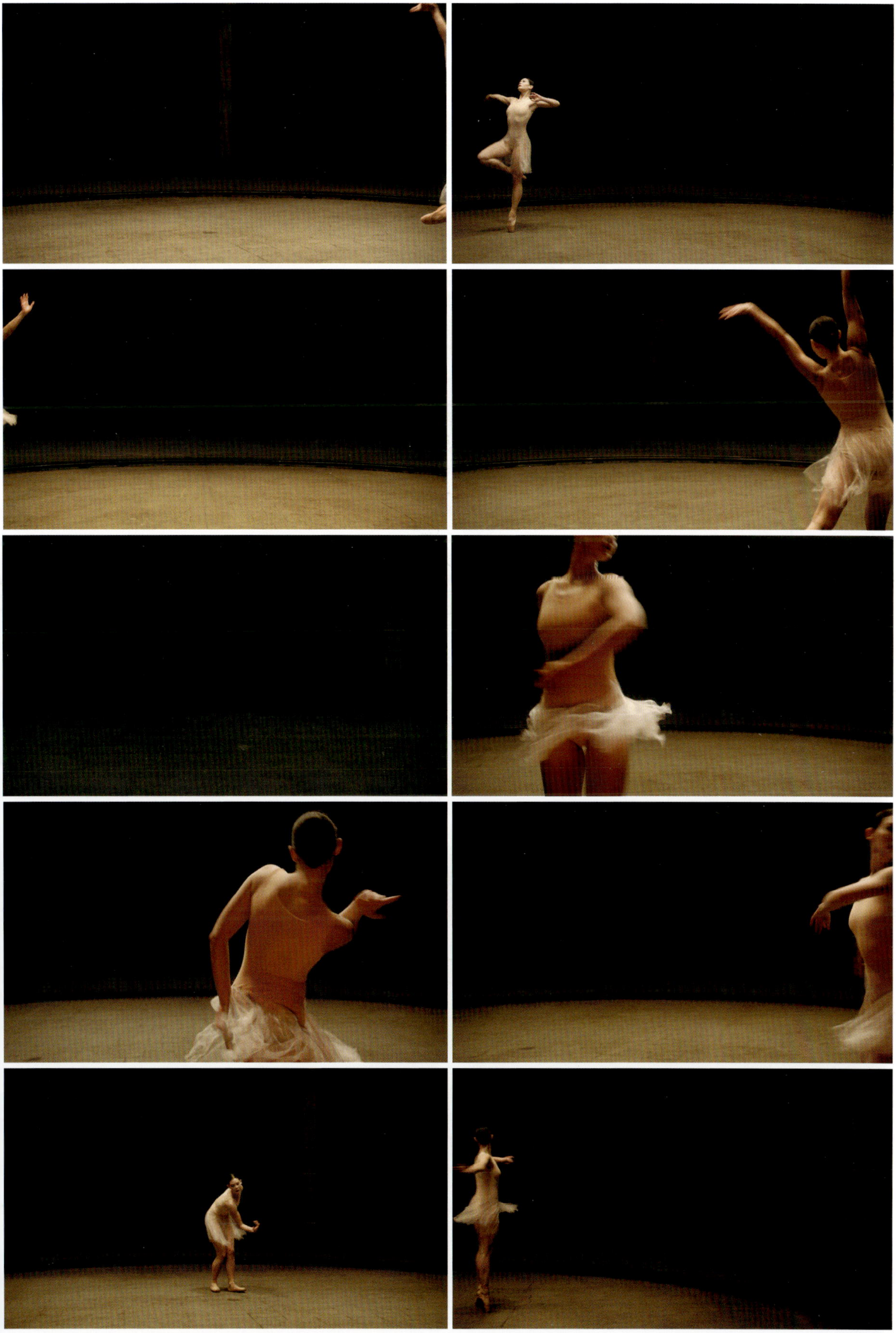

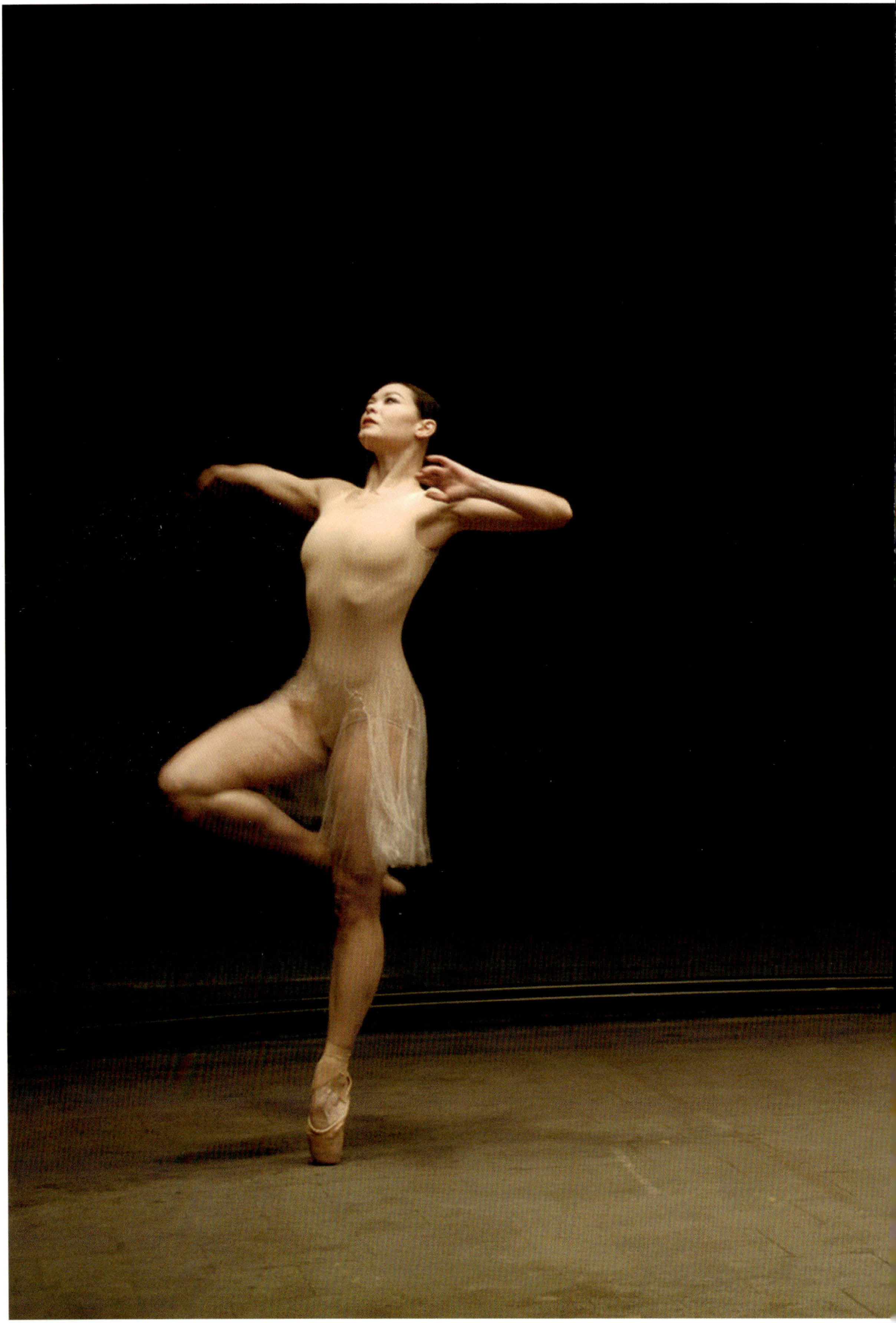

132 *Chant 23*, 2011
Film 15/70 mm (chant 23 de l'*Iliade* d'Homère), disque en marbre de Thassos, socle en bois / 70 mm film (Chant 23 of Homer's *Iliad*), marble slab, and wood pedestal, socle / plinth: 132 × 67 cm

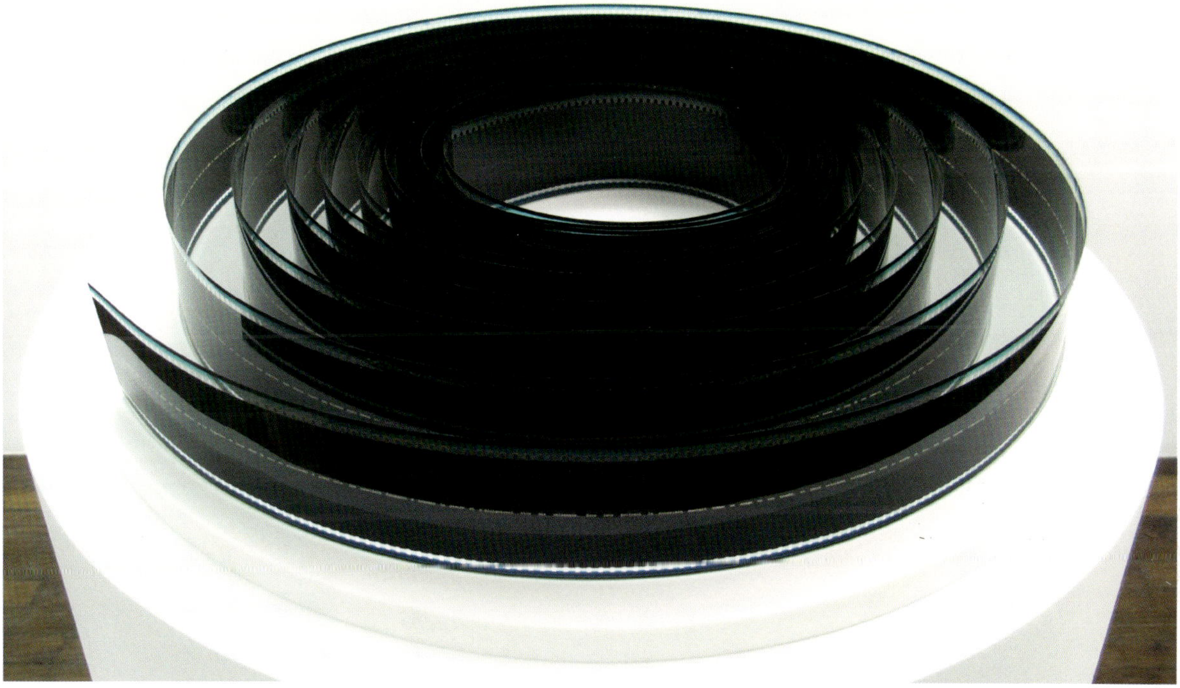

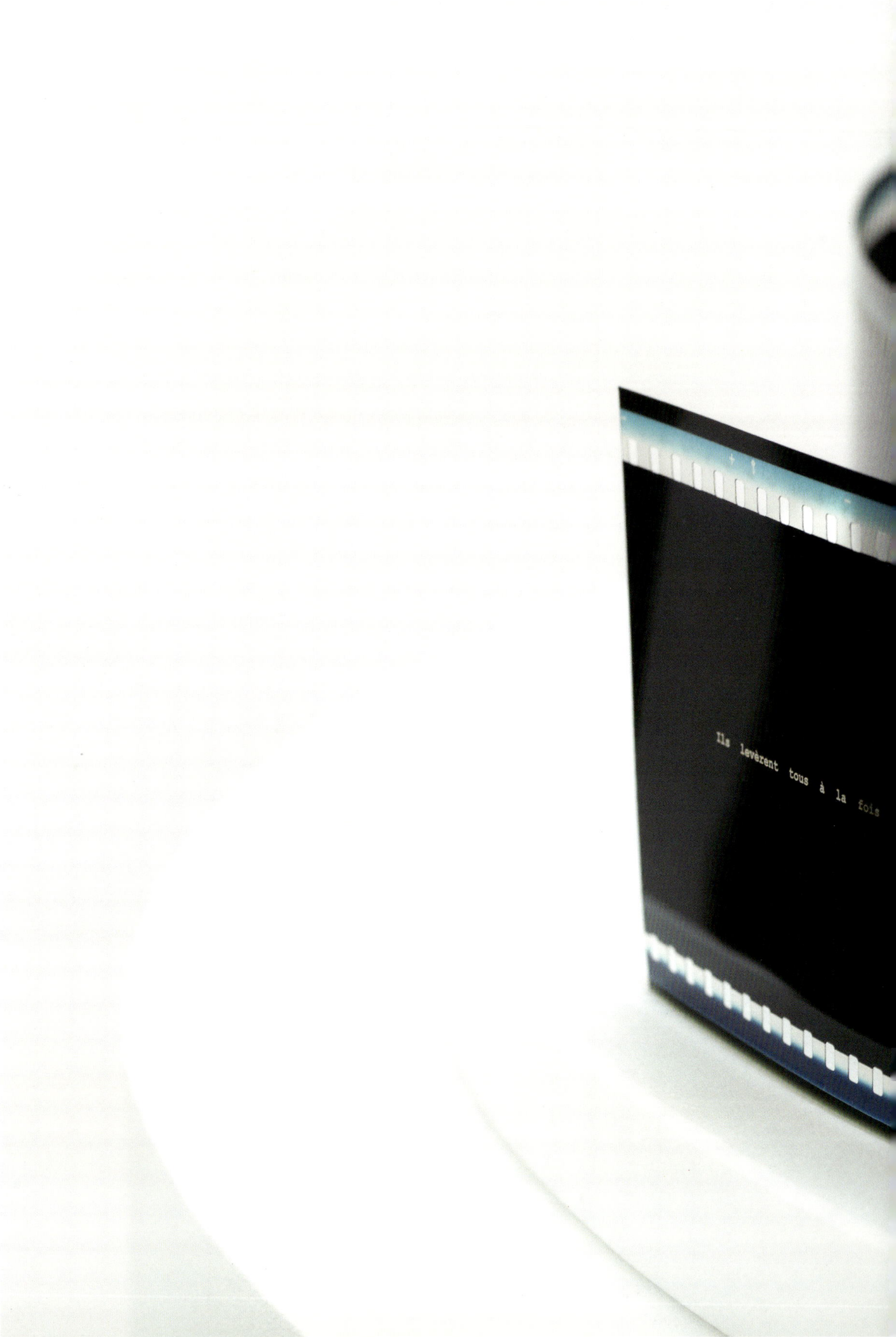
Ils levèrent tous à la fois

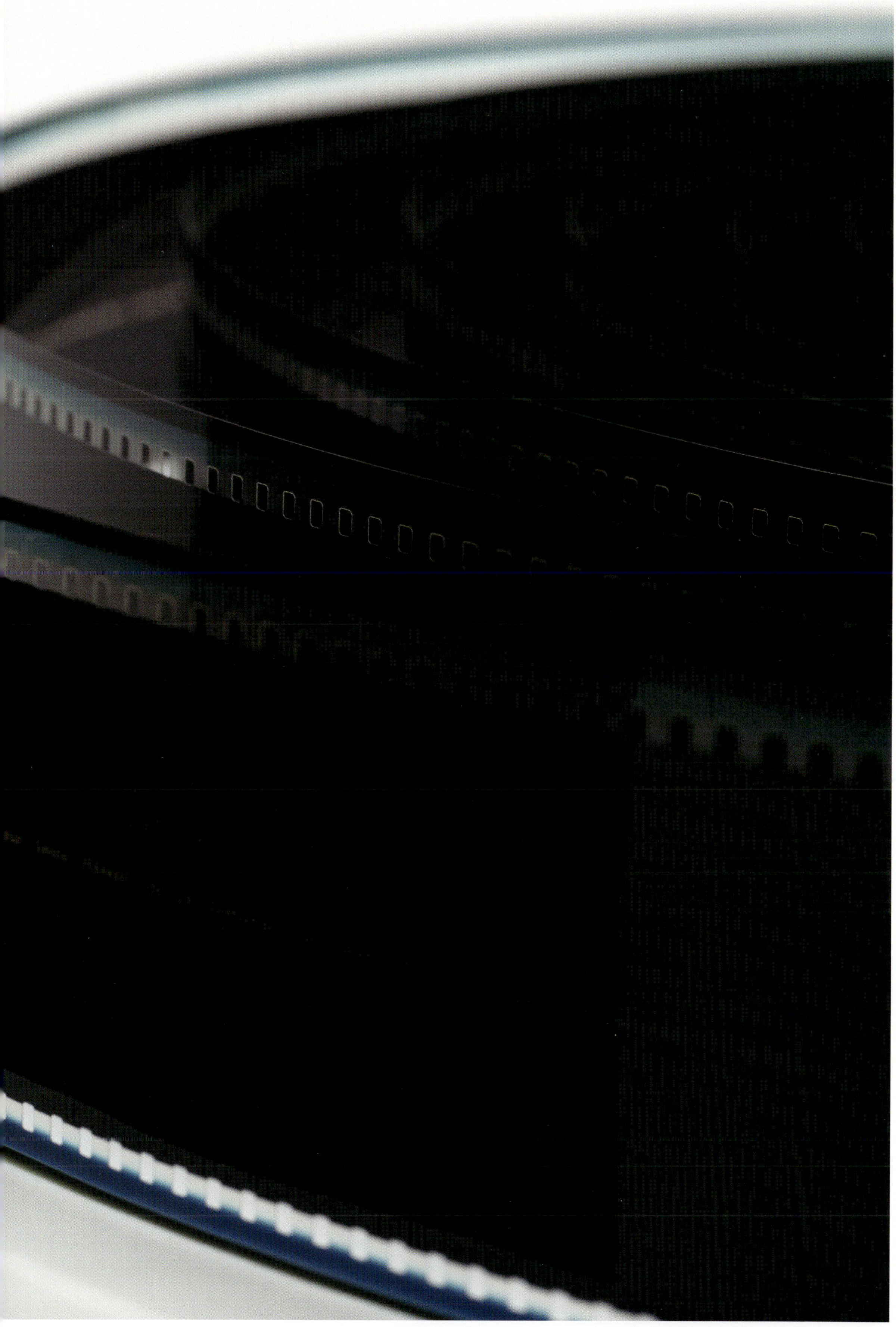

1925-1964, 2008
Tirage Lambda / Lambda print, 123 × 143 cm

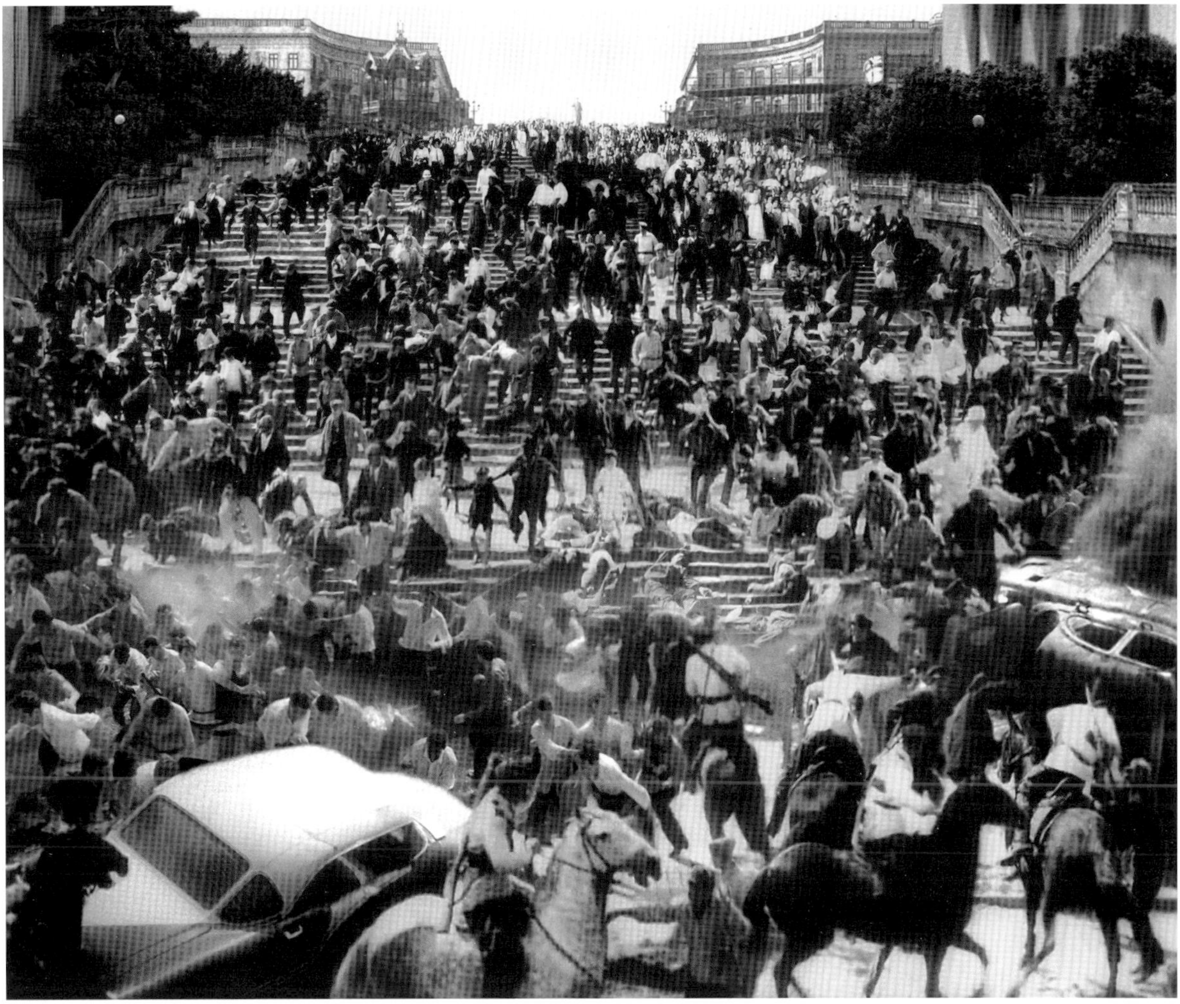

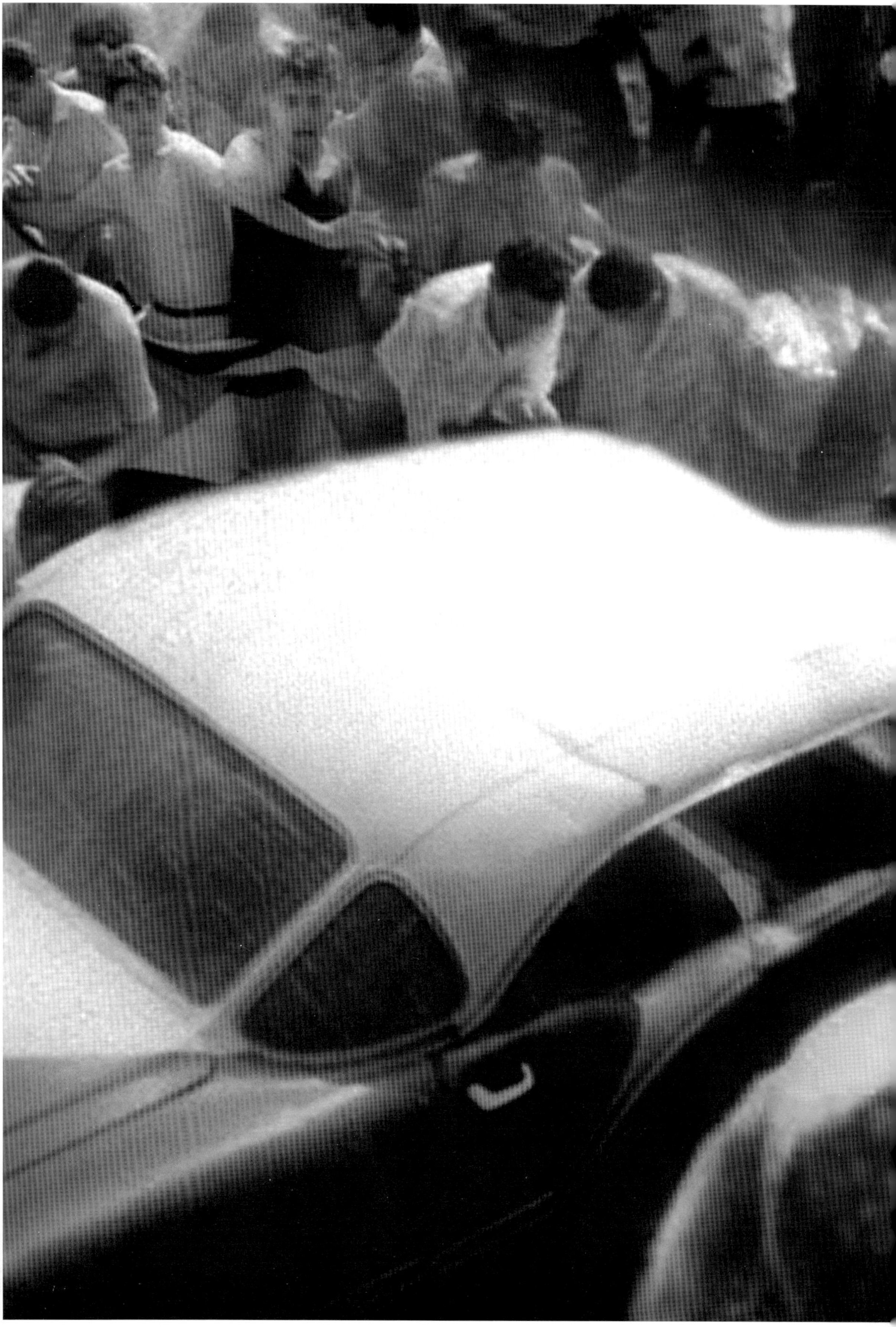

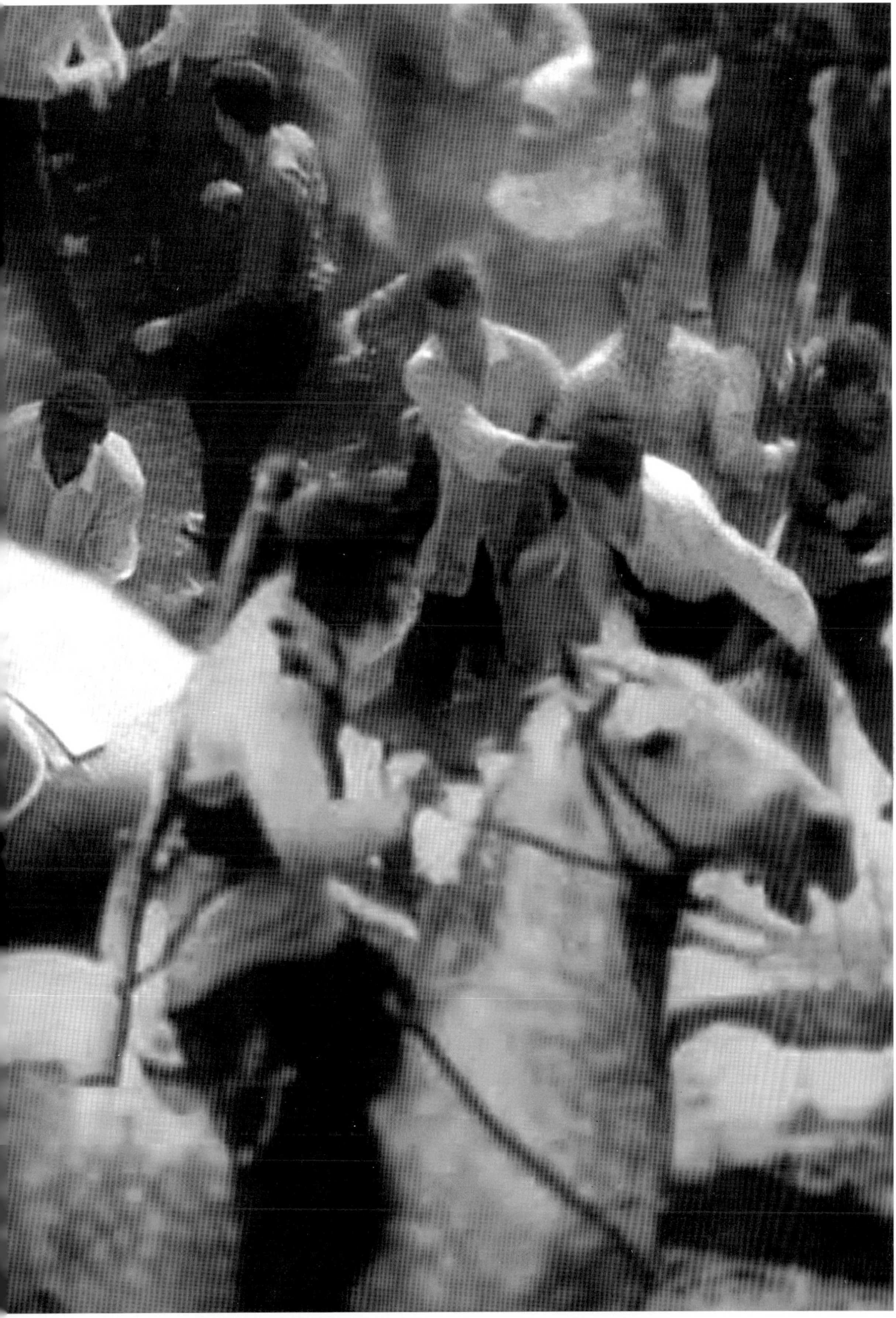

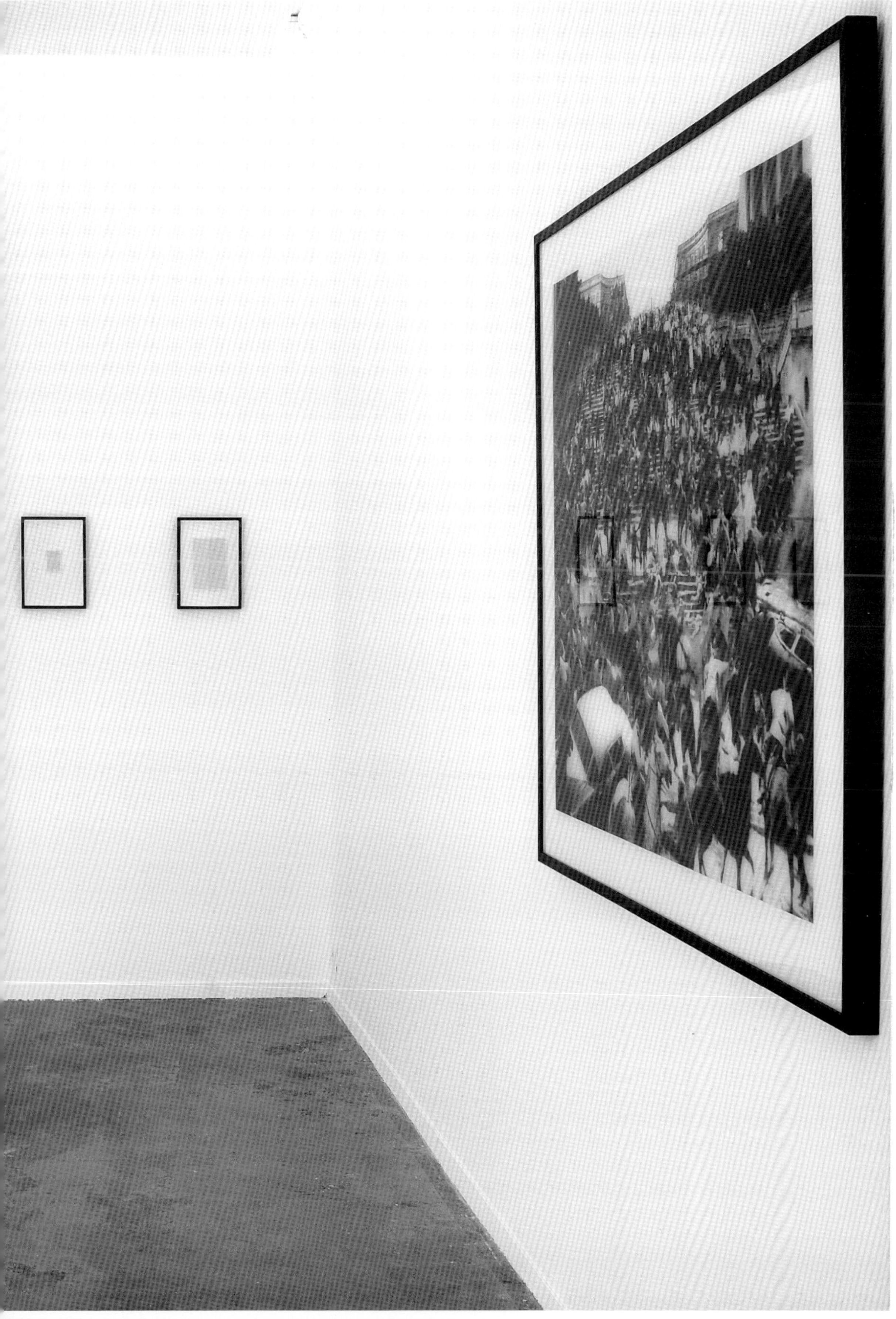

L'œuvre d'art à l'époque de sa reproduction mécanisée (pour W. Benjamin), 2003
Tirage photographique par contact sur bromure d'argent / Contact print on silver bromide, 21 × 29.7 cm

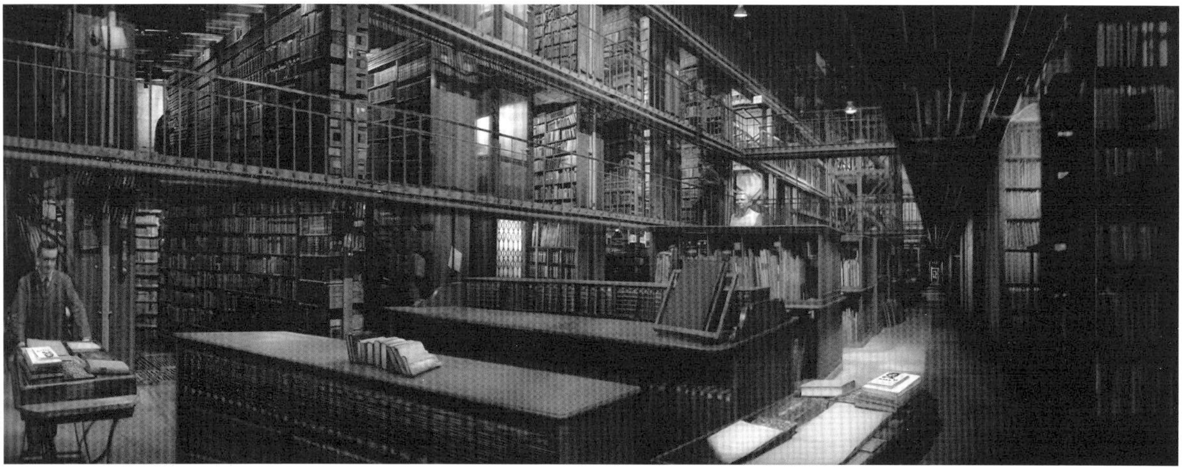

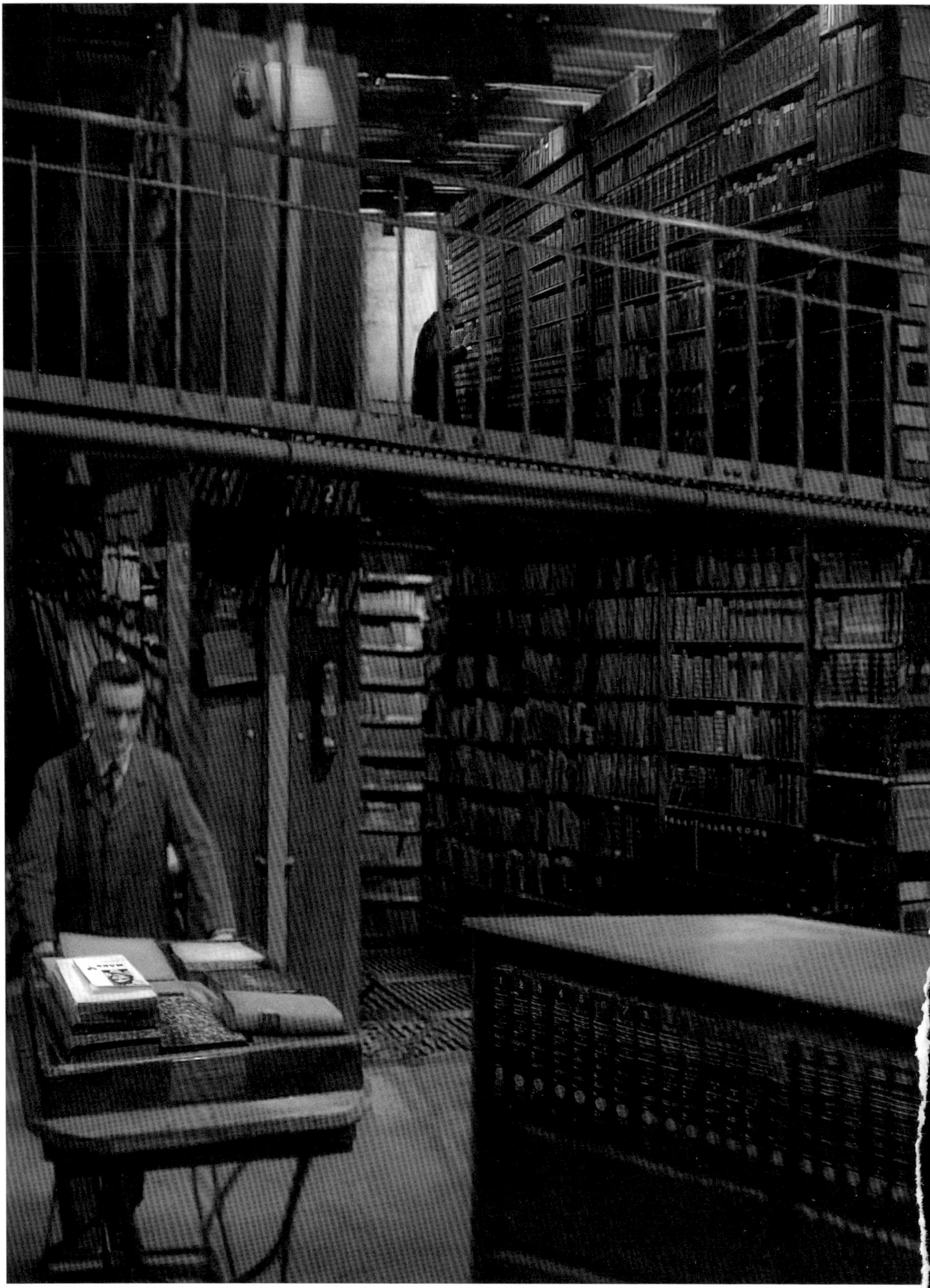

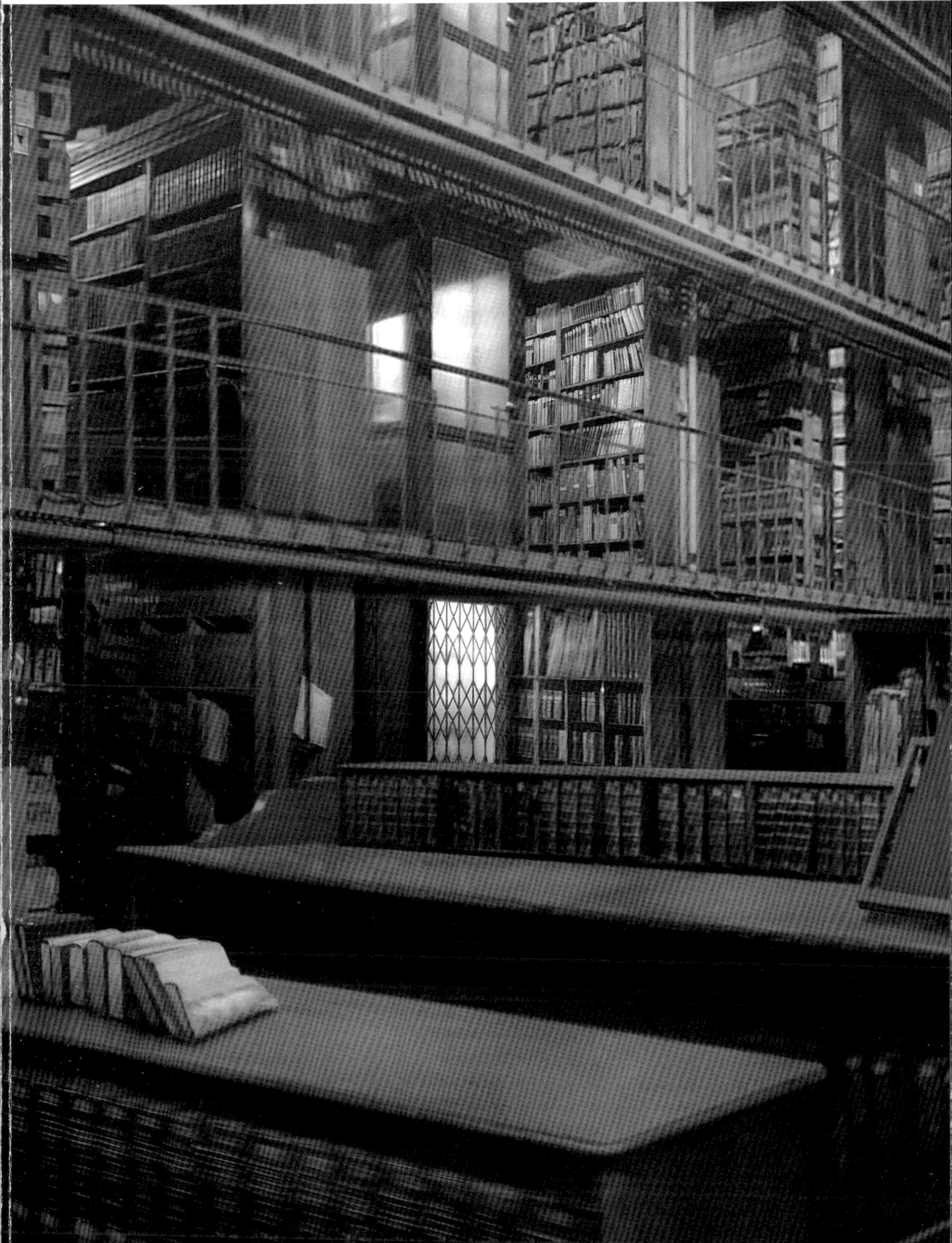

Le Chariot de Mars, 2018
Tirage pigmentaire noir et blanc / Black and white pigment print, 150 × 354 cm

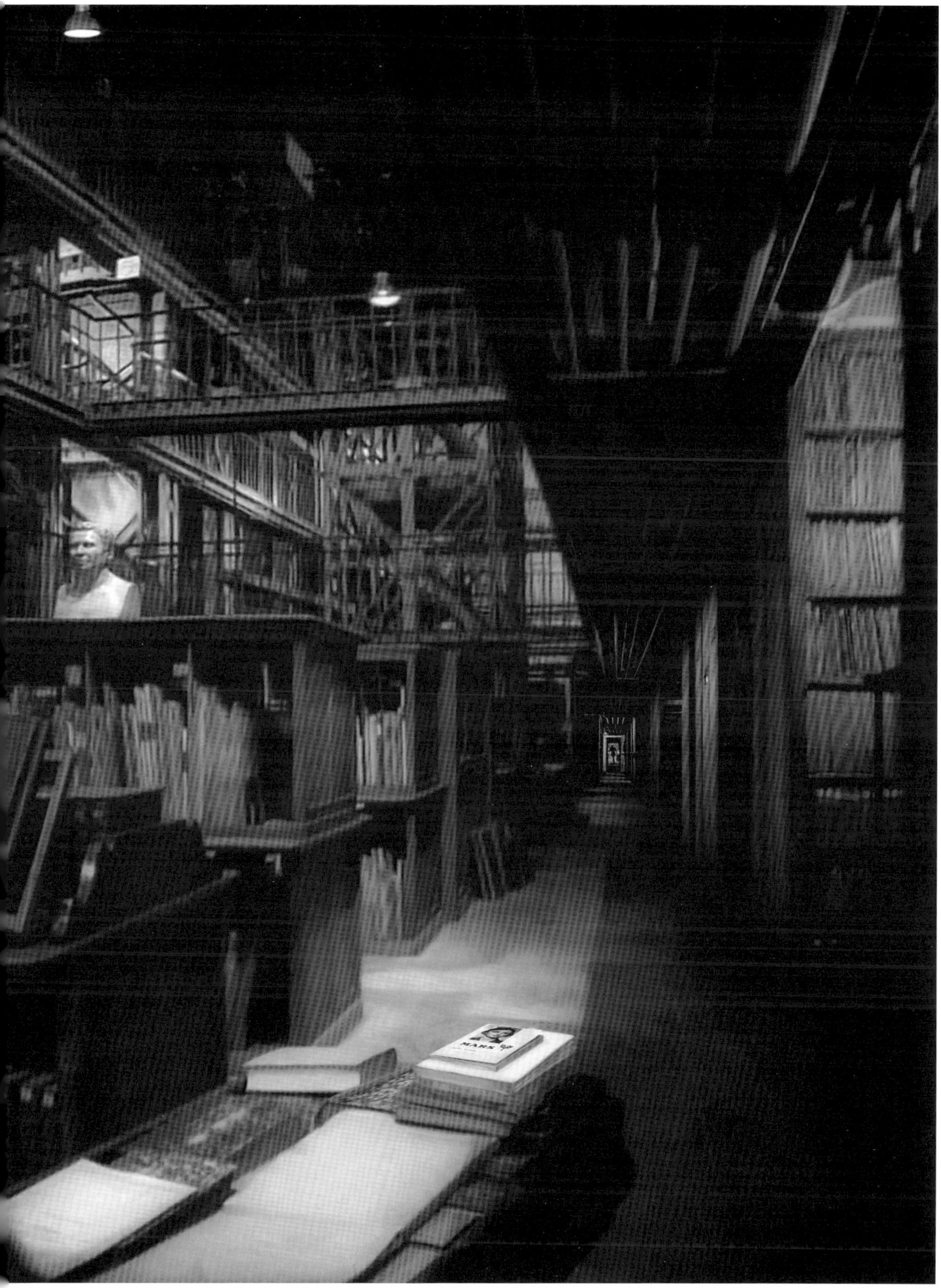
MARS

L'Éternité par les astres, 2006
Tirage photographique par contact sur bromure d'argent / Contact print on silver bromide on aluminum, 23 × 29.7 cm

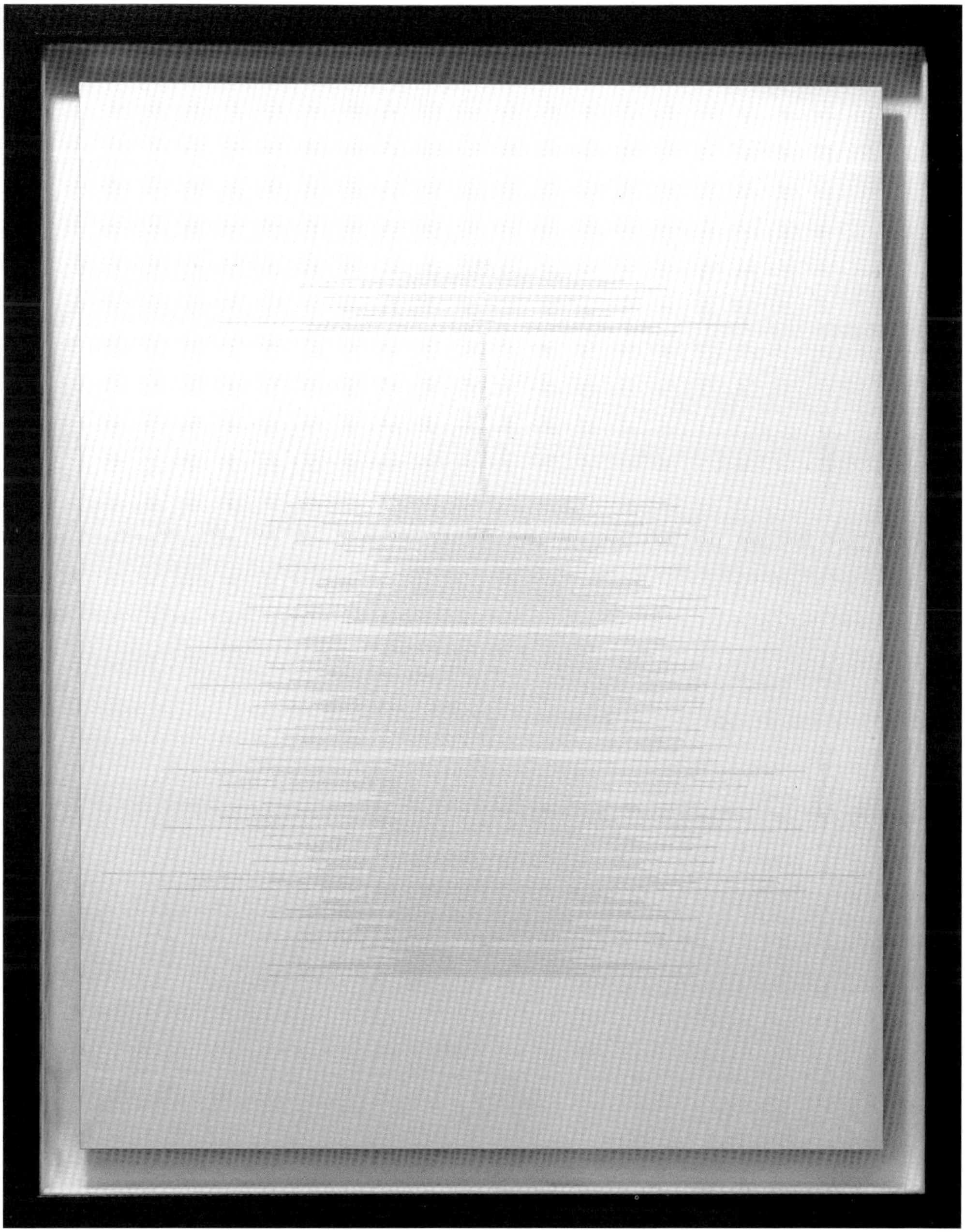

151-153
Landschaft

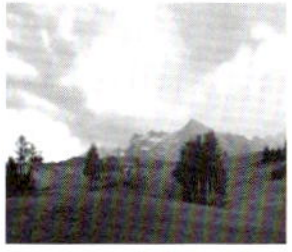

155-157
nwsfrmnwhr

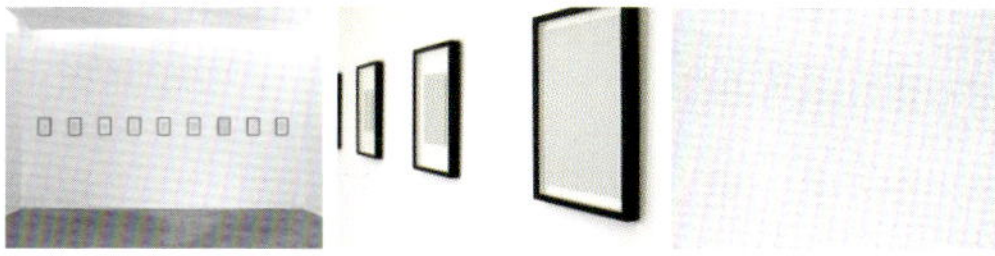

159-161
Tutto sta in un pugno

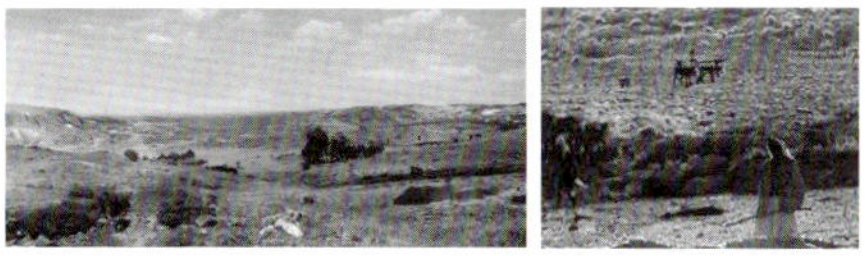

163
L'Élan pour l'Amérique

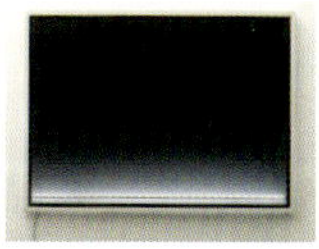

165-167
Diagram of the sea

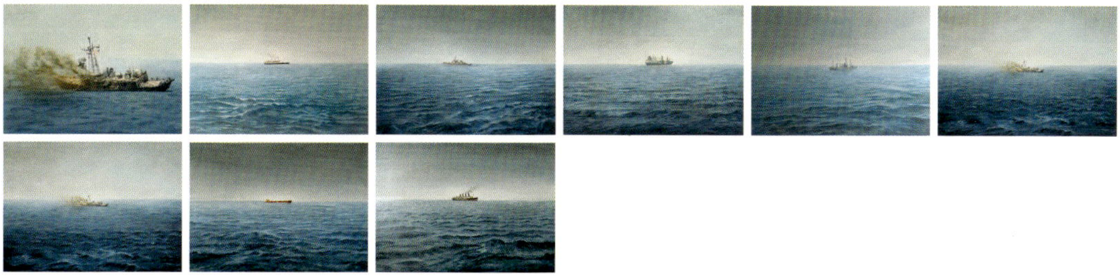

168
Searchers

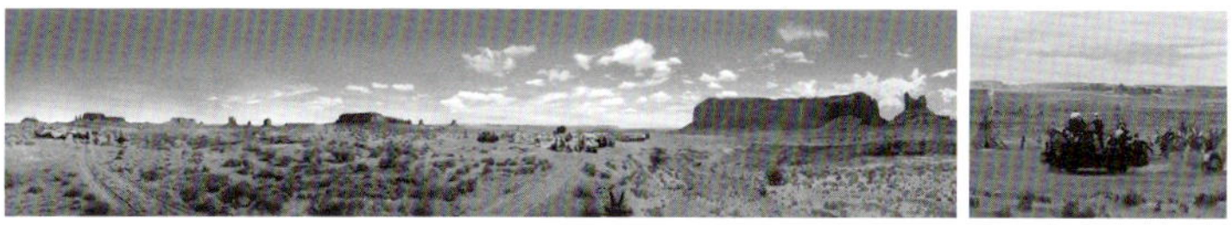

L'Atelier fermé

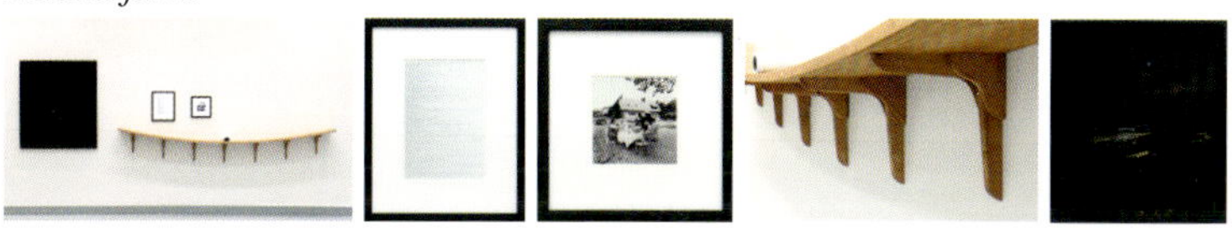

Landschaft, 2005
Tirage Lambda sur papier baryté / Lambda print on baryta paper, 120 × 144 cm

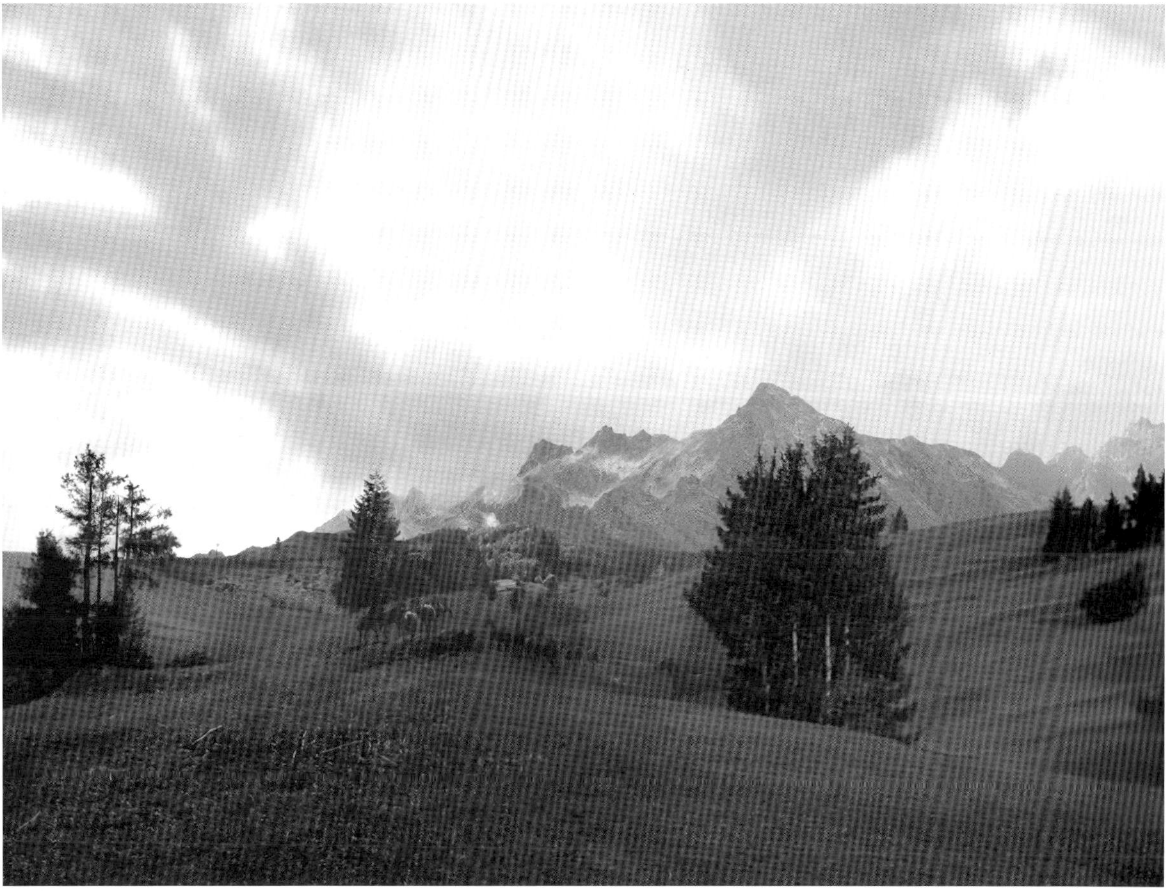

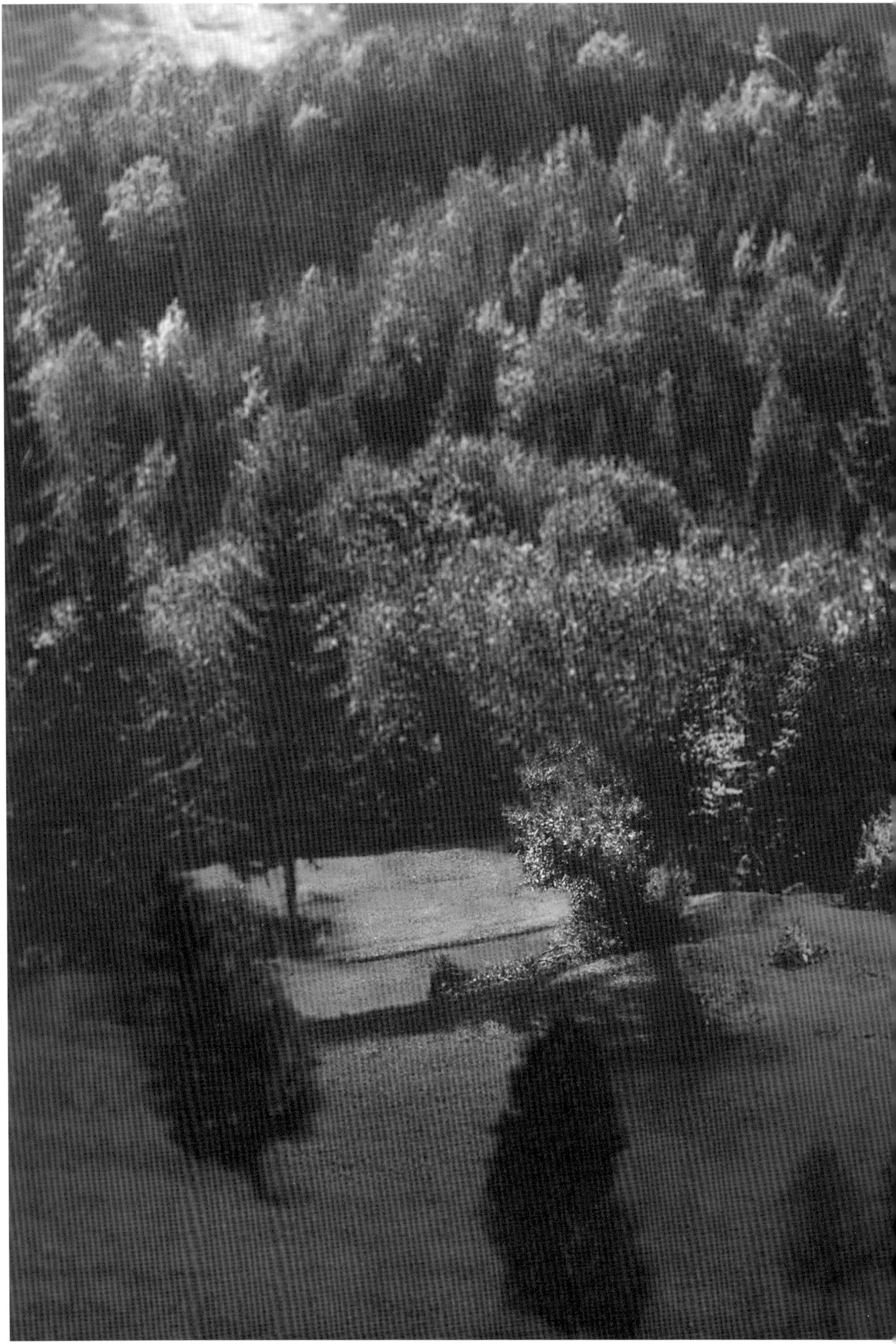

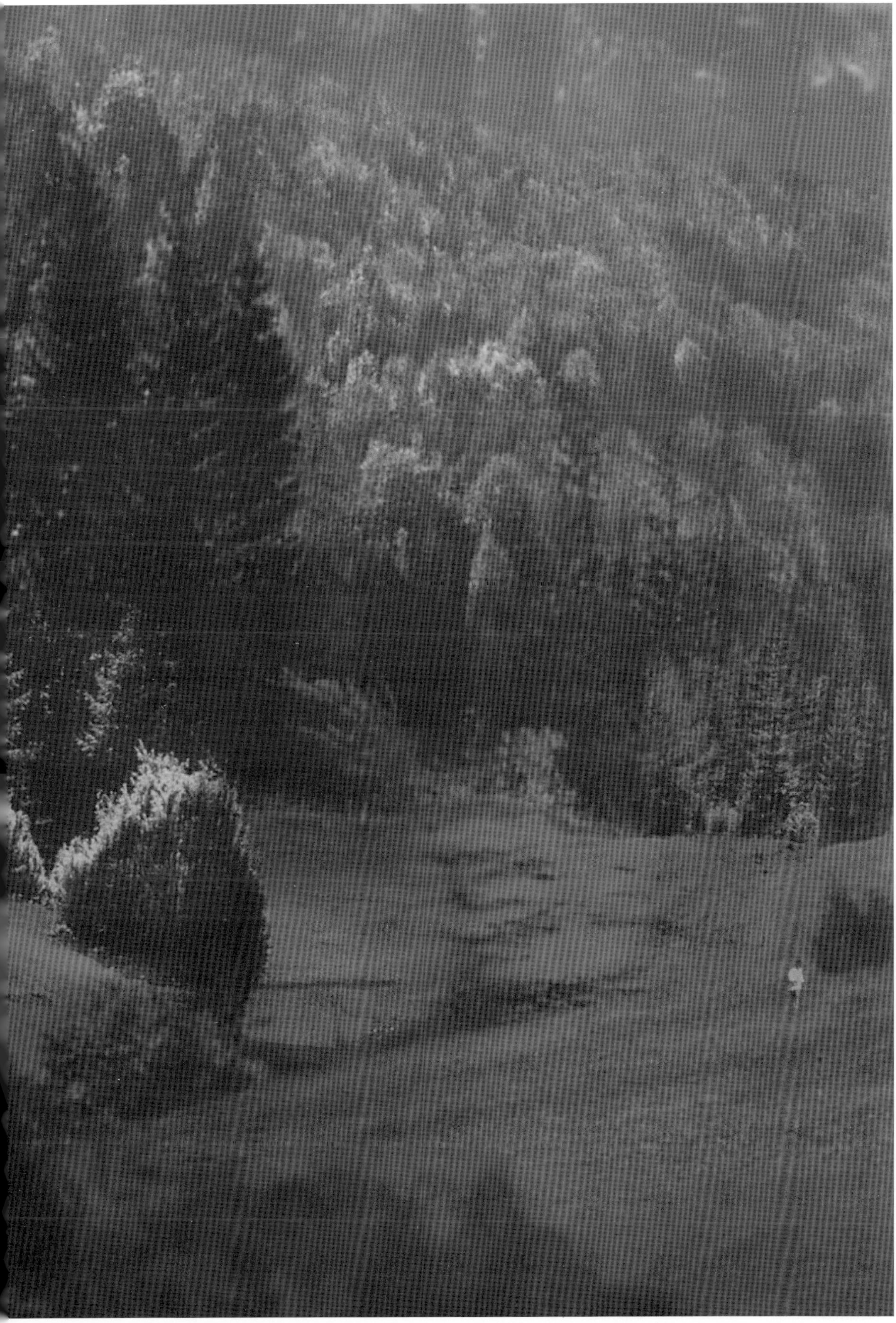

nwsfrmnwbr, 2009
Polyptyque de 9, tirages photographiques par contact sur bromure d'argent / Polyptych of 9, contact print on silver bromide, chaque / each: 23 × 31.5 cm encadrées / framed

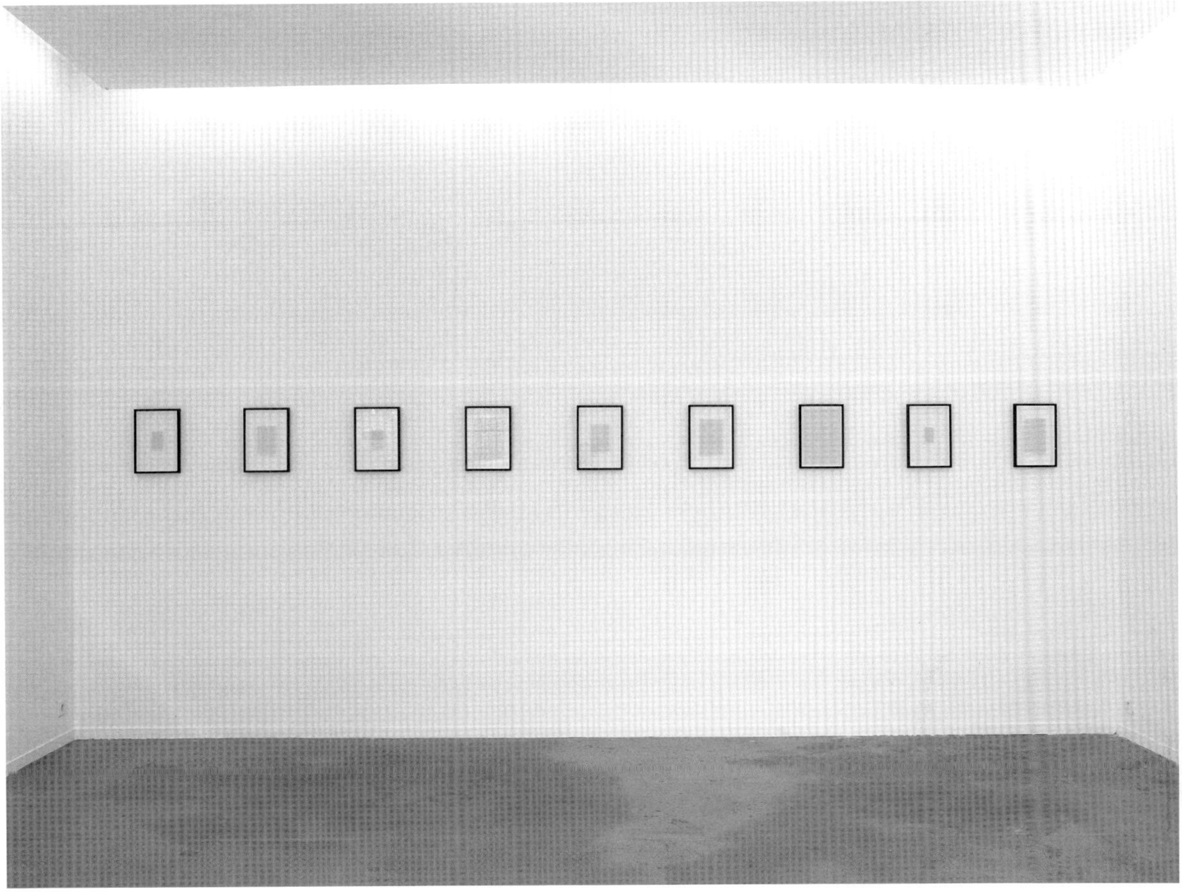

ut sit quam minime malum nam ut omnia bene sint fieri non potest nisi omnes boni sint quod ad aliquot abhinc annos adhuc non expecto hac inquit arte nihil fieret aliud quam ne dum aliorum furori mederi studeo ipse cum illis insaniam nam nam essent ut certe sunt meliora tamen aliena uideri possint quod hic singulorum priuatae sunt possessiones illic omnia sunt communia mea uero oratio—nisi quod ad eos qui statuissent secum ruere diuersa uia praecipites iucundus esse ari usqueadeo uetuit ut ea quoque quae ipse in aures insusurrasset suis palam in tectis iussent praedicari quorum maxima pars ab istis moribus longe est alienior quam mea fuit oratio nisi quod concionatores homines callidi tuum illud consilium sentiam quod perinde fuerit ac si nihil sentiam aut eadem et ipsorum adiutor sim ut inquit Micio Terentianus insaniae nam obliquus ille ductus tuus non uideo quid sibi uelit quo censes adnitendum si non possint omnia reddi bona tamen ut tra n eos delatus collegas qui uel optimum uirum facilius corruperint quam ipsi corrigantur quorum peruersa consuetudine uel deprauaberis uel ipse integer atque innocens alienae malitiae stultitiaeque praetexeris tantum abest ut aliquid possit in n tur semet intra tecta continent habentes satis quando alienae stultitiae non possunt mederi si ipsi saltem sint in tuto quamquam profecto mi More—ut ea uere dicam quae meus animus fert—mihi uidetur ubicumque priuatae sunt possessiones ru rudentissima atque sanctissima instituta Utopiensium apud quos tam paucis legibus tam commode res administrantur ut et uirtuti pretium sit et tamen aequatis rebus omnia abundent omnibus tum ubi his eorum moribus ex aduerso comparo tot n infinita illa tam assidue nascentia quam nummum finienda litigia haec inquam dum apud me considero aequior Platoni fio minusque demiror dedignatum illis leges ferre ullas qui recusabant eas quibus ex aequo omnes omnia partirentur com liquis relinquunt inopiam fereque accidit ut alteri sint alterorum sorte dignissimi cum illi sint rapaces improbi atque inutiles contra hi modesti uiri ac simplices et cotidiana industria in publicum quam in semet benigniores adeo mihi certe persuad non posse nempe si statuatur ne quis supra certum agri modum possideat et uti sit legitimus cuique census pecuniae si fuerit legibus quibusdam cautum ut neque sit princeps nimium potens neque populus nimis insolens tum magistratus ne ar oque mala leniri queant ac mitigari ut sanentur uero atque in bonum redeant habitum nulla omnino spes est dum sua cuique sunt propria quin dum unius partis curae studes aliarum uulnus exasperaueris ita mutuo nascitur ex alterius medela al entur inopia neque quod quisquam fuerit nactus id pro suo tueri ulla possit lege an non necesse est perpetua caede ac seditione laboretur sublata praesertim authoritate ac reuerentia magistratuum cui quis esse locus possit apud homines tales em tum plane faterere populum recte institutum nusquam alibi te uidisse quam illic atqui profecto inquit Petrus Aegidius aegre persuadeas mihi melius institutum populum in nouo illo quam in hoc noto nobis orbe reperiri ut in quo neque deteric quibus si fides haberi debet prius apud eos erant urbes quam homines apud nos iam uero quicquid hactenus uel ingenium inuenit uel casus repperit hoc utrobique potuit extitisse ceterum ego certe puto ut illis praestemus ingenio studio tam Romani quidam atque Aegyptii qui postea numquam inde discessere hanc unam occasionem uide quam commodam illis sua fecit industria nihil artis erat intra Romanum imperium unde possit aliquis esse usus quod non illi aut ab expositis hosp est fecerunt suum sic diu futurum puto priusquam nos accipiamus quicquam quod apud illos melius quam nobis est institutum quod unum maxime esse reor in causa cur cum neque ingenio neque opibus inferiores simus eis ipsorum tamen res libentius nam haec in promptu habeo sed res otium poscit eamus ergo inquam intro pransum mox tempus nostro arbitratu sumemus fiat inquit ita ingressi prandemus pransi in eundem reuersi locum in eodem sedili consedimus ac iussis n nam Morum ciuem et uicecomitem Londinensem [Raphaelis sermo pomeridianus] [de Utopiensium insula] Utopiensium insula in media sui parte—nam hac latissima est—milia passuum ducenta porrigitur magnumque per insulae spatium non magis quam saeuiens omnem prope eius terrae aluum pro portu facit magnoque hominum usu naues quaqua uersus transmittit fauces hinc uadis inde saxis formidolosae in medio ferme interstitio una rupes eminet eoque innoxia cui inaedificat n traherent ab altera parte non infrequentes portus at ubique descensus in terram ita natura munitus aut arte ut ingentes copiae paucis inde queant propugnatoribus arceri ceterum uti fertur utique ipsa loci facies prae se fert ea tellus olim non ar ac mare circum terram duxit cumque ad id operis non incolas modo coegisset—ne contumeliae loco laborem ducerent—sed suos praeterea milites omnes adiungeret in tantam hominum multitudinem opere distributo incredibili celeritate res perf ac uiginti separant nulla rursus est tam deserta e qua non ad aliam urbem pedibus queat unius itinere diei perueniri ciues quaque ex urbe terni senes ac rerum periti tractatum de rebus insulae communibus quotannis conueniunt nam Amaurotu do promouendorum finium quippe quos habent agricolas magis eorum se quam dominos putant habent ruri per omnes agros commode dispositas domos rusticis instrumentis instructas hae habitantur ciuibus per uices eo commigrantibus nulla ut ab his qui annum ibi fuere atque ideo rusticarum peritiores rerum instituantur alios anno sequente docturi ne si pariter omnes ibi noui agricolationisque rudes essent aliquid in annona per imperitiam peccaretur is innouandorum agricolarun eque enim incubant oua gallinae sed magnum eorum numerum calore quodam aequabili fouentes animant educantque hi simul atque e testa prodiere homines uice matrum comitantur et agnoscunt equos alunt perquam paucos nec nisi ferocier solum panem utuntur nam aut uuarum uinum bibunt aut pomorum pirorumue aut denique aquam nonnumquam meram saepe etiam qua mel aut glycyrizam incoxerint cuius haud exiguam habent copiam cum exploratum habeant—habent eni stratibus urbanis nullo negotio consequuntur nam illo singulo quoque mense plerique ad festum diem conueniunt cum frumentandi dies instat magistratibus urbanis agricolarum phylarchi denunciant quantum ciuium numerum ad se mitti conu sed quam potius quam Amaurotum qua nec ulla dignior est quippe cui senatus gratia reliquae deferunt nec ulla mihi notior ut in qua annos quinque perpetuos uixerim situm est igitur Amaurotum in leni deiectu montis figura fere quadrata nar c amplior sexaginta milia prolapsus excipitur oceano hoc toto spacio quod urbem ac mare interiacet ac supra urbem quoque aliquot milia sex horas perpetuas influens aestus ac refluus alternat celeri flumine cum sese pelagus infert triginta lapideo egregie arcuato ponte commissa est ab ea parte quae longissime distat a mari quo naues totum id latus urbis possint inoffensae praeteruehi habent alium praeterea fluuium haud magnum quidem illum sed perquam placidum ac iucur riores urbis partes aqua diriuatur id sicubi locus fieri uetat cisternis capacibus collecta pluuia tantumdem usus adfert murus altus ac latus oppidum cingit turribus ac propugnaculis frequens arida fossa sed alta lataque ac ueprium sepibus im quanta est uici longitudo hortus adiacet latus et uicorum tergis undique circumseptus nulla domus est quae non ut hostium in plateam ita posticum in hortum habeat quin bifores quoque facili tractu manus apertiles ac dein sua sponte coeuntes i cultu certamen accendit et certe non aliud quicquam temere urbe tota reperias siue ad usum ciuium siue ad uoluptatem commodius eoque nullius rei quam huiusmodi hortorum maiorem habuisse curam uidetur is qui condidit nam totam hanc ur uant aedes initio humiles ac ueluti casas et tuguria fuisse e quolibet ligno temere factas parietes luto obductos culmina in aciem fastigiata stramentis operuerant at nunc omnis domus uisenda forma tabulatorum trium parietum facies aut silice a d perlucido oleo aut succino perlinunt gemino nimirum commodo siquidem ad eum modum fit ut et plus lucis transmittat et uentorum minus admittat [de magistratibus] triginta quaeque familiae magistratum sibi quotannis eligunt quem sua pris a quaque urbis quarta parte selectus unus commendatur senatui principis magistratus perpetuus est in omnem illius uitam nisi tyrannidis affectatae suspicio impediat Traniboros quotannis eligunt ceterum haud temere commutant reliqui magistr cam pertineat de quo non tribus in senatu diebus ante agitatum quam decretum sit extra senatum aut comitia publica de rebus communibus inire consilia capitale habetur haec eo ferunt instituta ne procliue esset coniuratione principis ac Tranib die primum proponitur eodem disputetur sed in sequentem senatum differatur ne quis ubi quod in buccam primum uenerit temere effutierit ea potius excogitet postea quibus decreta tueatur sua quam quae ex reipublicae usu sint malitque salutis itis praeceptis partim in agros uiciniores urbi quasi per ludum educti non intuentes modo sed per exercitandi corporis occasionem tractantes etiam praeter agriculturam—quae est omnibus ut dixi communis—quilibet unam quampiam tamquam omne aeuum perpetua nec ad oculum indecora et ad corporis motum habilis tum ad frigoris aestusque rationem apposita eas inquam quaeque sibi familia conficit sed ex aliis illis artibus unusquisque aliquam discit nec uiri modo sed muliere modo eius sed magistratibus etiam praestita ut graui atque honesto patrifamilias mancipetur quin si quis unam perdoctus artem aliam praeterea cupiuerit eodem modo permittitur utramque nactus utram uelit exercet nisi alterutra ciuitas magis s Utopiensibus qui cum in horas uiginti quattuor aequales diem connumerata nocte diuidant sex dumtaxat operi deputant tres ante meridiem a quibus prandium ineunt atque a prandio duas pomeridianas horas cum interquieuerint tres deinde r ollocet has intercapedines plerique impendunt litteris solemne est enim publicas cotidie lectiones haberi antelucanis horis quibus ut intersint ii dumtaxat adiguntur qui ad litteras nominatim selecti sunt ceterum ex omni ordine mares simul ac fem tate in hortis hieme in aulis illis communibus in quibus comedunt ibi aut musicen exercent aut se sermone recreant aleam atque id genus ineptos ac perniciosos ludos ne cognoscunt quidem ceterum duos habent in usu ludos latrunculorum lud quo adoriantur quo praesidio uirtutes uitiorum uires infringant quibus artibus eorum conatus eludant quibus denique modis alterutra pars uictoriae compos fiat sed hoc loco ne quid erretis quiddam pressius intuendum est etenim quod sex dumta s quam magna populi pars iners degit primum mulieres fere omnes totius summae dimidium aut sicubi mulieres negotiosae sunt ibi ut plurimum earum uice uiri stertunt ad haec sacerdotum ac religiosorum quos uocant quanta quamque otiosa constant haec omnia quibus mortales utuntur expende nunc tecum ex his ipsis quam pauci in necessariis opificiis uersantur siquidem ubi omnia pecuniis metimur multas artes necesse est exerceri inanes prorsus ac superfluas luxus tantum ac lib o ac desidia languescens turba quorum unus quiuis earum rerum quae aliorum laboribus suppeditantur quantum duo earundem operatores consumit in opera uniuersi atque eadem utilia collocarentur facile animaduertis quantulum temporis ad ufficit uacatio permittitur in iis syphogranti—quamquam leges eos labore soluerunt—ipsi tamen sese non eximunt quo facilius exemplo suo reliquos ad labores inuitent eadem immunitate gaudent hi quos commendatione sacerdotum persuasus classem prouehatur ex hoc litteratorum ordine legati sacerdotes Tranibori ac ipse denique deligitur princeps quem illi prisca ipsorum lingua Barzanem recentiore Ademum appellant reliqua fere multitudo omnis cum neque otiosa sit nec inutilib quae pater aedificauit haeres parum frugi paulatim dilabi sinit ita quod minimo tueri potuit successor eius de integro impendio magno cogitur instaurare quin frequenter etiam quae domus alii ingenti sumptu stetit hanc alius delicato animo contemr durent aedificia et id genus opifices uix habeant interdum quod agant nisi quod materiam dolare domi et lapides interim quadrare atque aptare iubentur quo—si quod opus incidat—maturius possit exurgere iam in uestibus uide quam paucis oper multo minoris impendii est at lini minor est labor eoque usus crebrior sed in lineo solus candor in laneo sola mundicies conspicitur nullum tenuioris fili pretium est itaque fit ut cum alibi nusquam uni homini quattuor aut quinque togae laneae diue um etiam opera pauciora sufficiant fit nimirum ut abundante rerum omnium copia interdum in reficiendas—si quae detritae sunt—uias publicas immensam multitudinem educant persaepe etiam cum nec talis cuiuspiam operis usus occurrat paucio e felicitatem putant [de commerciis mutuis] sed iam quo pacto sese mutuo ciues utantur quae populi inter se commercia quaeque sit distribuendarum rerum forma uidetur explicandum cum igitur ex familiis constet ciuitas familias ut plurimum cauetur ne ulla familia quarum milia sex quaeque ciuitas excepto conuentu complectitur pauciores quam decem pluresue quam sexdecim puberes habeat impuberum enim nullus praefiniri numerus potest hic modus facile seruatur transcripti gibus propagant ascitis una terrae indigenis si conuiuere secum uelint cum uolentibus coniuncti in idem uitae institutum eosdemque mores facile coalescunt idque utriusque populi bono efficiunt enim suis institutis ut ea terra utrisque abunda s debeant usum ac possessionem interdicat si quando ullas ex suis urbibus aliquis casus eousque imminuerit ut ex aliis insulae partibus seruato suo cuiusque urbis modo resarciri non possint—quod bis dumtaxat ab omni aeuo pestis grassante tes diuiditur in medio cuiusque partis forum est omnium rerum eo in certas domos opera cuiusque familiae conuehuntur atque in horrea singulae seorsum species distributae sunt ab iis quilibet paterfamilias quibus ipse suique opus habent petit it in omni animantum genere aut in homine sola reddit superbia quae gloriae sibi ducit superflua rerum ostentatione ceteros antecellere quod uitii genus in Utopiensium institutis nullum omnino locum habet adiuncta sunt foris—quae commerc nimalium cuius usu clementiam humanissimum naturae nostrae affectum paulatim deperire putant neque sordidum quicquam atque immundum cuius putredine corruptus aer morbum posset inuehere—perferri in urbem sinunt habet praeterea qui d prima ratio aegrotorum habetur qui in publicis hospitiis curantur nam quattuor habent in ambitu ciuitatis hospitia paulo extra muros tam capacia ut totidem oppidulis aequari possint tum ut neque aegrotorum numerus quamlibet magnus anguste nemo mittatur inuitus nemo tamen fere in tota urbe sit qui aduersa ualetudine laborans non ibi decumbere quam domi suae praeferat cum aegrotorum obsonator cibos ex medicorum praescripto receperit deinceps optima quaeque inter aulas langore commonefacta nisi qui aut in hospitiis aut domi decumbunt quamquam nemo prohibetur postquam aulis est satis factum e foro domum cibum petere sciunt enim neminem id temere facere nam et si domi prandere nulli uetitum sit nemo fa e mulieres exercent cuiusque uidelicet familiae per uices tribus pluribusue mensis pro numero conuiuarum discumbitur uiri ad parietem feminae exterius collocantur ut si quid his subiti oboriatur mali quod uterum gerentibus interdum solet accid aut mors aut morbus impediat id cum accidit uxores Syphograntorum propere nutricem quaerunt nec id difficile est nam quae id praestare possunt nulli officio sese offerunt libentius quoniam et omnes eam misericordiam laude prosequuntur et entibus porrigitur eo uescuntur nec aliud discretum prandendi tempus habent in medio primae mensae qui summus locus est et cui—nam ea mensa suprema in parte cenaculi transuersa est—totus conuentus conspicitur Syphograntus cum ux immiscentur quod ideo ferunt institutum ut senum grauitas ac reuerentia—cum nihil ita in mensa fieri dicique potest ut eos ab omni parte uicinos effugiat—iuniores ab improba uerborum gestuumque licentia cohibeat ciborum fercula non a primo lo nmodi tantumdem tamen ad omneis peruenit omne prandium cenamque ab aliqua lectione auspicantur quae ad mores faciat sed breui tamen ne fastidio sit ab hac seniores honestos sermones sed neque tristes nec infacetos ingerunt at nec lo cem putant nulla cena sine musica transigitur nec ullis caret secunda mensa bellariis odores incendunt et unguenta spargunt nihilque non faciunt quod exhilarare conuiuas possit sunt enim hanc in partem aliquanto procliuiores ut nullum uolu commorantium aut ipsius etiam uidendi loci desiderium coeperit a Syphograntis ac Traniboris suis ueniam facile impetrant nisi si quis usus impediat mittitur ergo simul numerus aliquis cum epistola principis quae et datam peregrinandi copiam tes isdem opificiis humanissime tractantur si semet authore quisquam extra suos fines uagetur deprehensus sine principis diplomate contumeliose habitus pro fugitiuo reducitur castigatus acriter idem ausus denuo seruitute plectitur quod si quem iset iam uidetis quam nulla sit usquam otiandi licentia nullus inertiae praetextus nulla taberna uinaria nulla ceruisiaria nusquam lupanar nulla corruptelae occasio nullae latebrae conciliabulum nullum sed omnium praesentes oculi necessitate s quoque loco abundet rursum cuius alicubi malignior prouentus fuerit alterius inopiam alterius protinus ubertas explet atque id gratuito faciunt nihil uicissim ab his recipientes quibus donant sed quae de suis rebus unicuipiam urbi dederint nihil cerae seui corii ad haec animalium quoque in alias regiones exportant quarum rerum omnium septimam partem inopibus eius regionis dono dant reliquam pretio mediocri uendítant quo ex commercio non eas modo merces quibus domi egent ciendis non priuatorum umquam sed confectis ex more instrumentis publicam urbis fidem sequuntur ciuitas ubi solutionis dies aduenerit a priuatis debitoribus exigit creditum atque in aerarium redigit eiusque pecuniae quoad ab Utopiensibus rep domi seruant uti aut extremis in periculis aut in subitis praesidio sit potissimum quo milites externos—quos libentius quam suos ciues obiiciunt discrimini—immodico stipendio conducant gnari multitudine pecuniae hostes ipsos plerumque mercabi se perduci ut alteri idem recensenti crederem necesse est enim fere quam quicque est ab eorum qui audiunt moribus alienum tam idem procul illis abesse a fide quamquam prudens rerum aestimator minus fortasse mirabitur cum reliqua eorum meruit quam rerum ipsarum natura meretur qua quis non uidet quam longe infra ferrum sunt ut sine quo non hercule magis quam absque igni atque aqua uiuere mortales queant cum interim auro argentoque nullum usum quo non facile careamus uulgi stulta solertia—ne deluso per technam populo ipsi aliquo inde commodo fruerentur porro si phyalas inde aliaque id genus opera fabre excusa conficerent si quando incidisset occasio ut conflanda sint rursus atque in militum eroganda stipend ue elegantissimis quidem illis sed uilibus tamen edant bibantque ex auro atque argento non in communibus aulis modo sed in priuatis etiam domibus matellas passim ac sordidissima quaeque uasa conficiunt ad haec catenas et crassas compedi

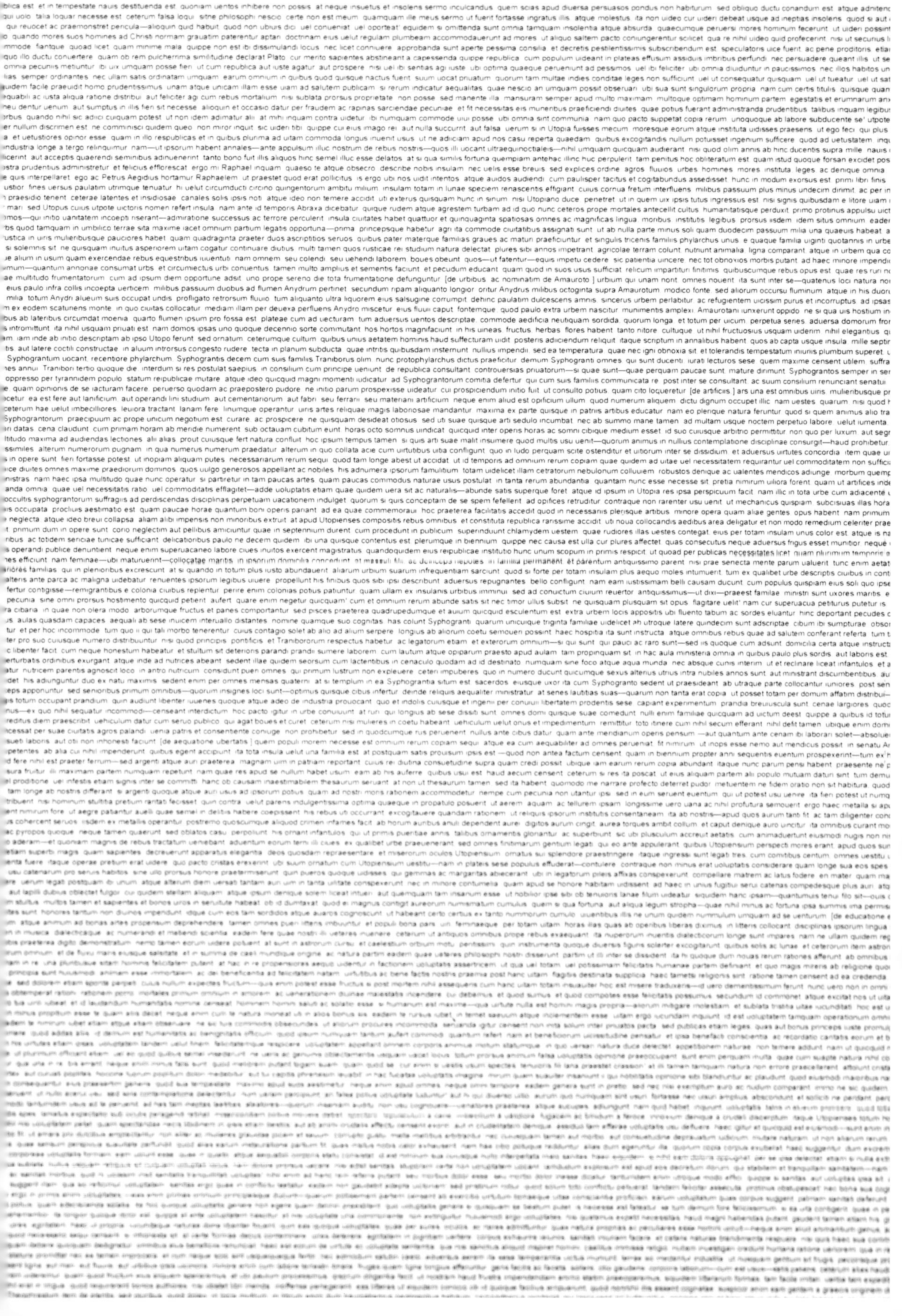

blica est et in tempestate nauis destituenda est quoniam uentos inhibere non possis at neque insuetus et insolens sermo inculcandus quem scias apud diuersa persuasos pondus non habiturum sed obliquo ductu conandum est atque adnitenc
qui uolo talia loquar necesse est ceterum falsa loqui sitne philosophi nescio certe non est meum quamquam ille meus sermo ut fuerit fortasse ingratus illis atque molestus ita non uideo cur uideri debeat usque ad ineptias insolens quod si aut
qui reuocet ac praemonstret pericula—alioquin quid habuit quod non ubiuis dici uel conueniat uel oporteat equidem si omittenda sunt omnia tamquam insolentia atque absurda quaecumque peruersi mores hominum fecerunt ut uideri possint
o quando mores suos homines ad Christi normam grauatim paterentur aptari doctrinam eius uelut regulam plumbeam accommodauerunt ad mores ut aliquo saltem pacto coniungerentur scilicet qua re nihil uideo quid profecerint nisi ut securius li
mmode fiantque quoad licet quam minime mala quippe non est ibi dissimulandi locus nec licet conniuere approbanda sunt aperte pessima consilia et decretis pestilentissimis subscribendum est speculatoris uice fuerit ac pene proditoris etiai
quo illo ductu conuertere quam ob rem pulcherrima similitudine declarat Plato cur merito sapientes abstineant a capessenda quippe republica cum populum uideant in plateas effusum assiduis imbribus perfundi nec persuadere queant illis ut se
omnia pecuniis metiuntur ibi uix umquam posse fieri ut cum republica aut iuste agatur aut prospere nisi uel ibi sentias agi iuste ubi optima quaeque perueniunt ad pessimos uel ibi feliciter ubi omnia diuiduntur in paucissimos nec illos habitos un
lias semper ordinantes nec ullam satis ordinatam umquam earum omnium in quibus quod quisque nactus fuerit suum uocat priuatum quorum tam multae indies conditae leges non sufficiunt uel ut consequatur quisquam uel ut tueatur uel ut sat
uidem facile praeuidit homo prudentissimus unam atque unicam illam esse uiam ad salutem publicam si rerum indicatur aequalitas quae nescio an umquam possit observari ubi sua sunt singulorum propria nam cum certis titulis quisque quan
equabili ac iusta aliqua ratione distribui aut feliciter agi cum rebus mortalium nisi sublata prorsus proprietate non posse sed manente illa mansuram semper apud multo maximam multoque optimam hominum partem egestatis et erumnarum an
neu dentur uenum aut sumptus in illis fieri sit necesse alioquin et occasio datur per fraudem ac rapinas sarciendae pecuniae et fit necessitas eis muneribus praeficiendi diuites quae potius fuerant administranda prudentibus talibus inquam legibu
rbus quando nihil sic adiici cuiquam potest ut non idem adimatur alii at mihi inquam contra uidetur ibi numquam commode uiui posse ubi omnia sint communia nam quo pacto suppetat copia rerum unoquoque ab labore subducente se utpote
er nullum discrimen est ne comminisci quidem queo non miror inquit sic uideri tibi quippe cui eius imago rei aut nulla succurrit aut falsa uerum si in Utopia fuisses mecum moresque eorum atque instituta uidisses praesens ut ego feci qui plus
et uetustiores opinor esse quam in illo respublicas et in quibus plurima ad uitam commoda longus inuenit usus ut ne adiiciam apud nos casu reperta quaedam quibus excogitandis nullum potuisset ingenium sufficere quod ad uetustatem inqu
industria longe a tergo relinquimur nam—ut ipsorum habent annales—ante appulsum illuc nostrum de rebus nostris—quos illi uocant ultraequinoctiales—nihil umquam quicquam audierant nisi quod olim annis ab hinc ducentis supra mille nauis
icerint aut acceptis quaerendi seminibus adinuenerint tanto bono fuit illis aliquos hinc semel illuc esse delatos at si qua similis fortuna quempiam antehac illinc huc perpulerit tam penitus hoc obliteratum est quam istud quoque forsan excidet pos
stra prudentius administretur et felicius efflorescat ergo mi Raphael inquam quaeso te atque obsecro describe nobis insulam nec uelis esse breuis sed explices ordine agros fluuios urbes homines mores instituta leges ac denique omnia
e quis interpellaret ego ac Petrus Aegidius hortamur Raphaelem ut praestet quod erat pollicitus is ergo ubi nos uidit intentos atque auidos audiendi cum paulisper tacitus et cogitabundus assedisset hunc in modum exorsus est primi libri finis
ustior fines uersus paulatim utrimque tenuatur hi uelut circumducti circino quingentorum ambitu milium insulam totam in lunae speciem renascentis effigiant cuius cornua fretum interfluens milibus passuum plus minus undecim dirimit ac per in
praesidio tenent ceterae latentes et insidiosae canales solis ipsis noti atque ideo non temere accidit uti exterus quisquam hunc in sinum nisi Utopiano duce penetret ut in quem uix ipsis tutus ingressus est nisi signis quibusdam e litore uiam
mari sed Utopus cuius utpote uictoris nomen refert insula nam ante id temporis Abraxa dicebatur quique rudem atque agrestem turbam ad id quo nunc ceteros prope mortales antecellit cultus humanitatisque perduxit primo protinus appulsu uict
mos—qui initio uanitatem inceepti riserant—admiratione successus ac terrore perculerit insula ciuitates habet quattuor et quinquaginta spatiosas omnes ac magnificas lingua moribus institutis legibus prorsus iisdem idem situs omnium eader
bs quod tamquam in umbilico terrae sita maxime iacet omnium partium legatis opportuna—prima princepsque habetur agri ita commode ciuitatibus assignati sunt ut ab nulla parte minus soli quam duodecim passuum milia una quaeuis habeat a
ustica in uiris mulieribusque pauciores habet quam quadraginta praeter duos ascriptitios seruos quibus pater materque familias graues ac maturi praeficiuntur et singulis tricenis familiis phylarchus unus e quaque familia uiginti quotannis in urbe
si solemnis sit ne quisquam inuitus asperiorem uitam cogatur continuare diutius multi tamen quos rusticae rei studium natura delectat plures sibi annos impetrant agricolae terram colunt nutriunt animalia ligna comparant atque in urbem qua co
e alium in usum quam exercendae rebus equestribus iuuentuti nam omnem seu colendi seu uehendi laborem boues obeunt quos—ut fatentur—equis impetu cedere sic patientia uincere nec tot obnoxios morbis putant ad haec minore impendi
mum—quantum annonae consumat urbs et circumiectus urbi conuentus tamen multo amplius et sementis faciunt et pecudum educant quam quod in suos usus sufficiat relicum impartituri finitimis quibuscumque rebus opus est quae res ruri nc
ae multitudo frumentatorum cum ad ipsum diem opportune adsit uno prope sereno die tota frumentatione defunguntur [de urbibus ac nominatim de Amauroto] urbium qui unam norit omnes nouerit ita sunt inter se—quatenus loci natura non
eius paulo infra collis incoepta uerticem milibus passuum duobus ad flumen Anydrum pertinet secundum ripam aliquanto longior oritur Anydrus milibus octoginta supra Amaurotum modico fonte sed aliorum occursu fluminum atque in his duor
milia totum Anydri alueum suis occupat undis profligato retrorsum fluuio tum aliquanto ultra liquorem eius salsugine corrumpit dehinc paulatim dulcescens amnis sincerus urbem perlabitur ac refugientem uicissim purus et incorruptus ad ipsas
m ex eodem scatunens monte in quo ciuitas collocatur mediam illam per deuexa perfluens Anydro miscetur eius fluuii caput fontemque quod paulo extra urbem nascitur muniments amplexi Amaurotani iunxerunt oppido ne si qua uis hostium in
bus ab lateribus circumdat moenia quarto flumen ipsum pro fossa est plateae cum ad uecturam tum aduersus uentos descriptae commode aedificia neutiquam sordida quorum longa et totum per uicum perpetua series aduersa domorum fror
s intromittunt ita nihil usquam priuati est nam domos ipsas uno quoque decennio sorte commutant hos hortos magnifaciunt in his uineas fructus herbas flores habent tanto nitore cultuque ut nihil fructuosius usquam uiderim nihil elegantius qu
am iam inde ab initio descriptam ab ipso Utopo ferunt sed ornatum ceterumque cultum quibus unius aetatem hominis haud suffecturam uidit posteris adiiciendum reliquit itaque scriptum in annalibus habent quos ab capta usque insula mille septir
is aut latere coctili constructae in aluum introrsus congesto rudere tecta in planum subducta quae intritis quibusdam insternunt nullius impendii sed ea temperatura quae nec igni obnoxia sit et tolerandis tempestatum iniuriis plumbum superet
Syphograntum uocant recentiore phylarchum Syphograntis decem cum suis familiis Traniborus olim nunc protophylarchus dictus praeficitur demum Syphogranti omnes qui sunt ducenti iurati lecturos sese quem maxime censent utilem suffra
es annui Tranibori tertio quoque die interdum si res postulat saepius in consilium cum principe ueniunt de republica consultant controuersias priuatorum—si quae sunt—quae perquam paucae sunt mature dirimunt Syphograntos semper in ser
oppresso per tyrannidem populo statum reipublicae mutare atque ideo quicquid magni momenti iudicatur ad Syphograntorum comitia defertur qui cum suis familiis communicata re post inter se consultant ac suum consilium renunciant senatui
quam opinionis de se iacturam facere peruerso quodam ac praepostero pudore ne initio parum prospexisse uideatur cui prospiciendum initio fuit ut consulto potius quam cito loqueretur [de artificiis] ars una est omnibus uiris mulieribusque pr
cetur ea est fere aut lanificium aut operandi lini studium aut cementariorum aut fabri seu ferrarii seu materiarii artificium neque enim aliud est opificium ullum quod numerum aliquem dictu dignum occupet illic nam uestes quarum nisi quod h
ceterum hae uelut imbecilliores leuiora tractant lanam fere linumque operantur uiris artes reliquae magis laboriosae mandantur maxima ex parte quisque in patriis artibus educatur nam eo plerique natura feruntur quod si quem animus alio tra
Syphograntorum praecipuum ac prope unicum negotium est curare ac prospicere ne quisquam desideat otiosus sed uti suae quisque arti sedulo incumbat nec ab summo mane tamen ad multam usque noctem perpetuo labore uelut iumenta
ri datas cena claudunt cum primam horam ab meridie numerent sub octauam cubitum eunt horas octo somnus uindicat quicquid inter operis horas ac somni cibique medium esset id suo cuiusque arbitrio permittitur non quo per luxum aut segr
ltitudo maxima ad audiendas lectiones alii alias prout cuiusque fert natura confluit hoc ipsum tempus tamen si quis arti suae malit insumere quod multis usu uenit—quorum animus in nullius contemplatione disciplinae consurgit—haud prohibetur
ssimiles alterum numerorum pugnam in qua numerus numerum praedatur alterum in quo collata acie cum uirtutibus uitia confligunt quo in ludo perquam scite ostenditur et uitiorum inter se dissidium et aduersus uirtutes concordia item quae ui
in opere sunt fieri fortasse potest ut inopiam aliquam putes necessariarum rerum sequi quod tam longe abest ut accidat ut id temporis ad omnium rerum copiam quae quidem ad uitae uel necessitatem requirantur uel commoditatem non suffici
ice diuites omnes maxime praediorum dominos quos uulgo generosos appellant ac nobiles his adnumera ipsorum famulitium totam uidelicet illam cetratorum nebulonum colluuiem robustos denique ac ualentes mendicos adiunge morbum quemp
nistras nam haec ipsa multitudo quae nunc operatur si partiretur in tam paucas artes quam paucas commodus naturae usus postulat in tanta rerum abundantia quantam nunc esse necesse sit pretia nimirum uiliora forent quam ut artifices inde
anda omnia quae uel necessitatis ratio uel commoditatis efflagitet—adde uoluptatis etiam quae quidem uera sit ac naturalis—abunde satis superque foret atque id ipsum in Utopia res ipsa perspicuum facit nam illic in tota urbe cum adiacente
occultis syphograntorum suffragiis ad perdiscendas disciplinas perpetuam uacationem indulget quorum si quis conceptam de se spem fefellerit ad opifices retruditur contraque non raro usu uenit ut mechanicus quispiam subcisiuas illas hora
is occupata procliuis aestimatio est quam paucae horae quantum boni operis pariant ad ea quae commemoraui hoc praeterea facilitatis accedit quod in necessariis plerisque artibus minore opera quam aliae gentes opus habent nam primum
neglecta atque ideo breui collapsa aliam alibi impensis non minoribus exstruit at apud Utopienses compositis rebus omnibus et constituta republica rarissime accidit uti noua collocandis aedibus area deligatur et non modo remedium celeriter prae
primum dum in opere sunt corio neglectim aut pellibus amiciuntur quae in septennium durent cum procedunt in publicum superinduunt chlamydem uestem quae rudiores illas uestes contegat eius per totam insulam unus color est atque is na
nibus ac totidem sericae tunicae sufficiant delicatioribus paulo ne decem quidem ibi una quisque contentus est plerumque in biennium quippe nec causa est ulla cur plures affectet quas consecutus neque aduersus frigus esset munitior neque
s operandi publice denuntient neque enim superuacaneo labore ciues inuitos exercent magistratus quandoquidem eius reipublicae institutio hunc unum scopum in primis respicit ut quoad per publicas necessitates licet quam plurimum temporis
es efficiunt nam feminae—ubi maturuerint—collocatae maritis in ipsorum domicilia concedunt at masculi filii ac deinceps nepotes in familia permanent et parentum antiquissimo parent nisi prae senecta mente parum ualuerit tunc enim aetat
riores familias qui in plenioribus excrescunt at si quando in totum plus iusto abundauerit aliarum urbium suarum infrequentiam sarciunt quod si forte per totam insulam plus aequo moles intumuerit tum ex qualibet urbe descriptis ciuibus in conti
alteris ante parca ac maligna uidebatur renuentes ipsorum legibus uiuere propellunt his finibus quos sibi ipsi describunt aduersus repugnantes bello confligunt nam eam iustissimam belli causam ducunt cum populus quispiam eius soli quo ipse
fertur contigisse—remigrantibus e colonia ciuibus repientur perire enim colonias potius patiuntur quam ullam ex insulanis urbibus imminui sed ad coniuctum ciuium reuertor antiquissimus—ut dixi—praeest familiae ministri sunt uxores maritis e
pecunia sine omni prorsus hostimento quicquid petient aufert quare enim negetur quicquam cum et omnium rerum abunde satis sit nec timor ullus subsit ne quisquam plusquam sit opus flagitare uelit nam cur superuacua petiturus putetur is
ra cibaria in quae non olera modo arborumque fructus et panes comportantur sed pisces praeterea quadrupedumque et auium quicquid esculentum est extra urbem locis appositis ubi fluento tabum ac sordes eluantur hinc deportant pecudes c
s aulas quasdam capaces aequali ab sese inuicem interuallo distantes nomine quamque suo cognitas has colunt Syphogranti quarum unicuique triginta familiae uidelicet ab utroque latere quindecim sunt adscriptae cibum ibi sumpturae obsor
tur et per hoc incommode tum quo ii qui tali morbo tenerentur cuius contagio solet ab alio ad alium serpere longius ab aliorum coetu semoueri possint haec hospitia ita sunt instructa atque omnibus rebus quae ad salutem conferant referta tum t
ter pro suo cuiusque numero distribuuntur nisi quod principis pontificis et Traniborum respectus habetur ac legatorum etiam et exterorum omnium—si qui sunt qui pauci ac raro sunt—sed iis quoque cum adsunt domicilia certa atque instructa
c libenter facit cum neque honestum habeatur et stultum sit deterioris parandi prandii sumere laborem cum lautum atque opiparum praesto apud aulam tam propinquam sit in hac aula ministeria omnia in quibus paulo plus sordis aut laboris est
erturbatis ordinibus exurgant atque inde ad nutrices abeant sedent illae quidem seorsum cum lactentibus in cenaculo quodam ad id destinato numquam sine foco atque aqua munda nec absque cunis interim ut et reclinare liceat infantulos et a
atur nutricem parentis agnoscit loco in antro nutricum considunt pueri omnes qui primum lustrum non expleuere ceteri impuberes quo in numero ducunt quicumque sexus alterius utrius intra nubiles annos sunt aut ministrant discumbentibus au
det his adiunguntur duo ex natu maximis sedent enim per omnes mensas quaterni at si templum in ea Syphograntia situm est sacerdos eiusque uxor ita cum Syphogranto sedent ut praesideant ab utraque parte collocantur iuniores post sen
eps apponuntur sed senioribus primum omnibus—quorum insignes loci sunt—optimus quisque cibus infertur deinde reliquis aequaliter ministratur at senes lautitias suas—quarum non tanta erat copia ut posset totam per domum affatim distribui
s totum occupant prandium quin audiunt libenter iuuenes quoque atque adeo de industria prouocant quo et indolis cuiusque et ingenii per conuiuii libertatem prodentis sese capiant experimentum prandia breuiuscula sunt cenae largiores quoc
nus—ex quo nihil sequatur incommodi—censeant interdictum hoc pacto igitur in urbe conuiuunt at rur qui longius ab sese dissiti sunt omnes domi quisque suae comedunt nulli enim familiae quicquam ad uictum deest quippe a quibus id totu
reditus diem praescribit uehiculum datur cum seruo publico qui agat boues et curet ceterum nisi mulieres in coetu habeant uehiculum uelut onus et impedimentum remittitur toto itinere cum nihil secum efferant nihil defit tamen ubique enim dom
cessat per suae ciuitatis agros palandi uenia patris et consentiente coniuge non prohibetur sed in quodcumque rus peruenerit nullus ante cibus datur quam ante meridianum operis pensum—aut quantum ante cenam ibi laborari solet—absolue
sueti laboris aut otii non inhonesti faciunt [de aequatione ubertatis] quem populi morem necesse est omnium rerum copiam sequi atque ea cum aequabiliter ad omnes perueniat fit nimirum ut inops esse nemo aut mendicus possit in senatu A
petentes ab alia cui nihil impenderunt quibus egent accipiunt ita tota insula uelut una familia est at postquam satis prouisum ipsis est—quod non antea factum censent quam in biennium propter anni sequentis euentum prospexerint—tum ex
d fere nihil est praeter ferrum—sed argenti atque auri praeterea magnam uim in patriam reportant cuius rei diutina consuetudine supra quam credi possit ubique iam earum rerum copia abundant itaque nunc parum pensi habent praesente ne
sura fruitur illi maximam partem numquam repetunt nam quae res apud se nullum habet usum eam ab his auferre quibus usui est haud aequum censent ceterum si res ita poscat ut eius aliquam partem alii populo mutuam daturi sint tum demu
proditione uel infestis etiam signis inter se committi hanc ob causam inaestimabilem thesaurum seruant at non ut thesaurum tamen sed ita habent quomodo me narrare profecto deterret pudor metuentem ne fidem oratio non sit habitura quod
tam longe ab nostris differant si argenti quoque atque auri usus ad ipsorum potius quam ad nostri moris rationem accommodetur nempe cum pecunia non utantur ipsi sed in eum seruent euentum qui ut potest usu uenire ita fieri potest ut num
tribuent nisi hominum stultitia pretium raritati fecisset quin contra uelut parens indulgentissima optima quaeque in propatulo posuerit ut aerem aquam ac tellurem ipsam longissime uero uana ac nihil profutura semouerit ergo haec metalla si apu

Tutto sta in un pugno, 2014
Impression digigraphie sur papier baryté / Digigraphic print on baryta paper, 62 × 115 cm

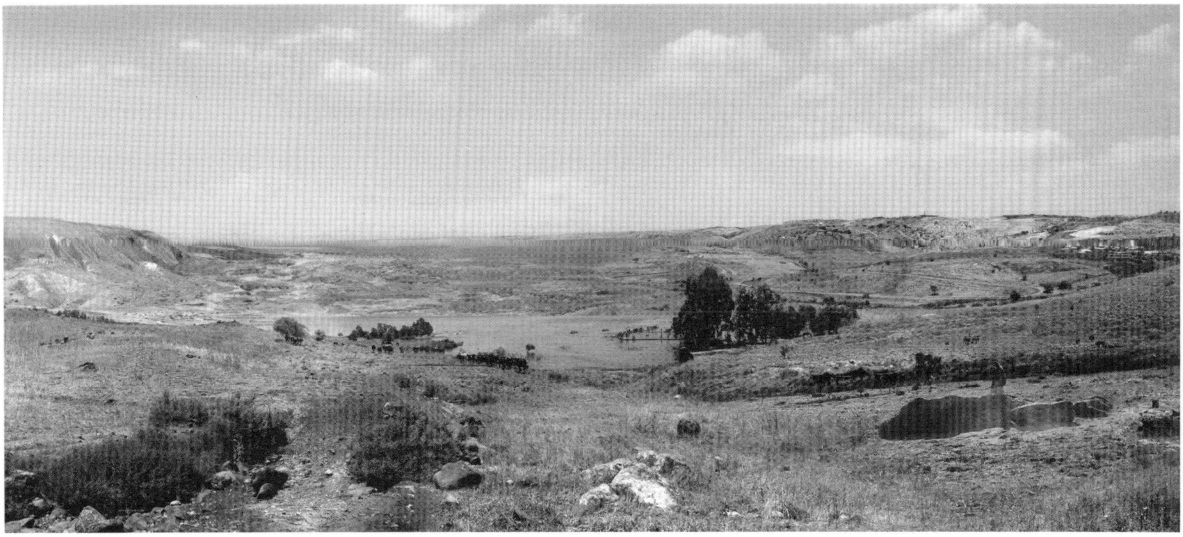

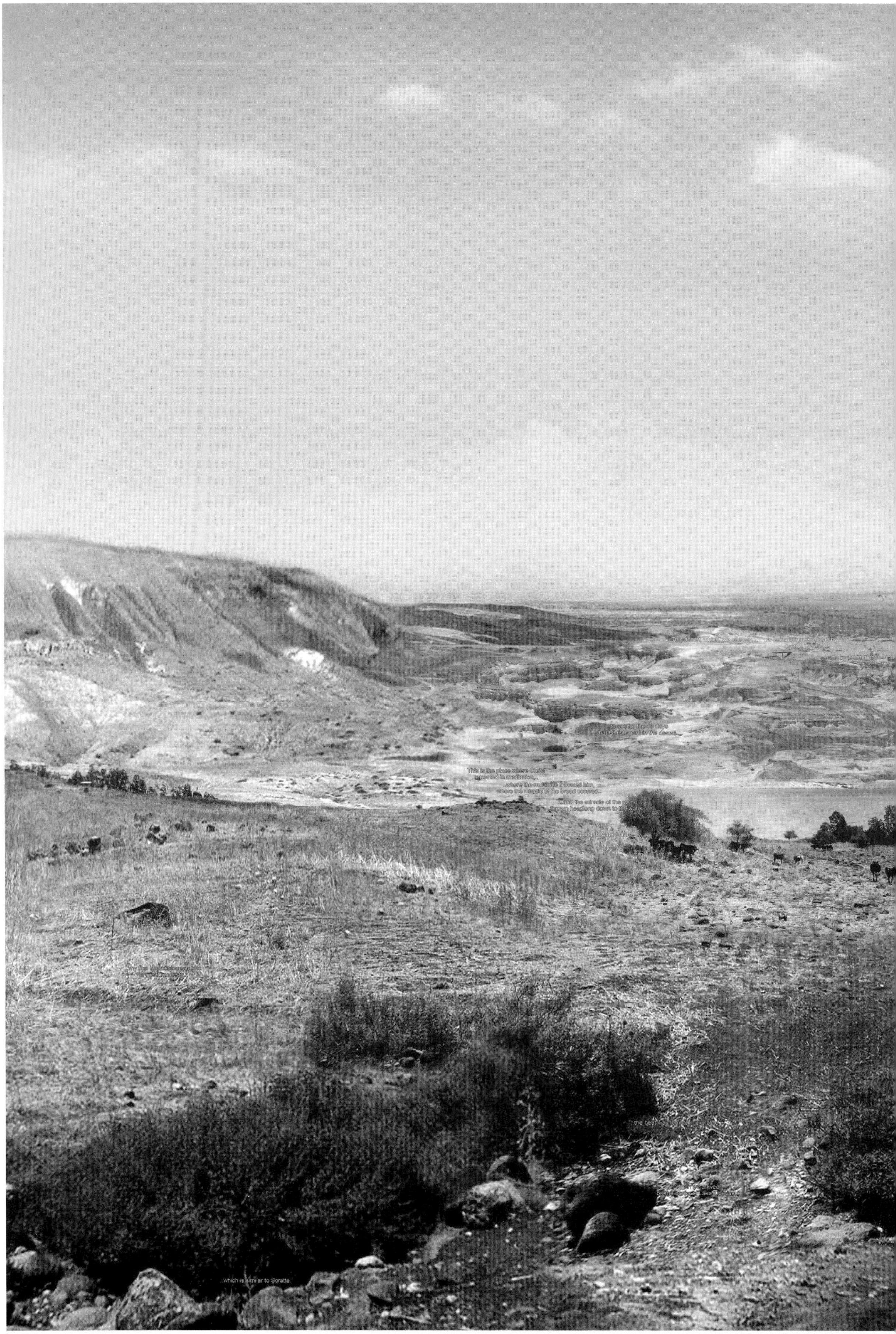
This is the place where Christ
...which is similar to Soratte.

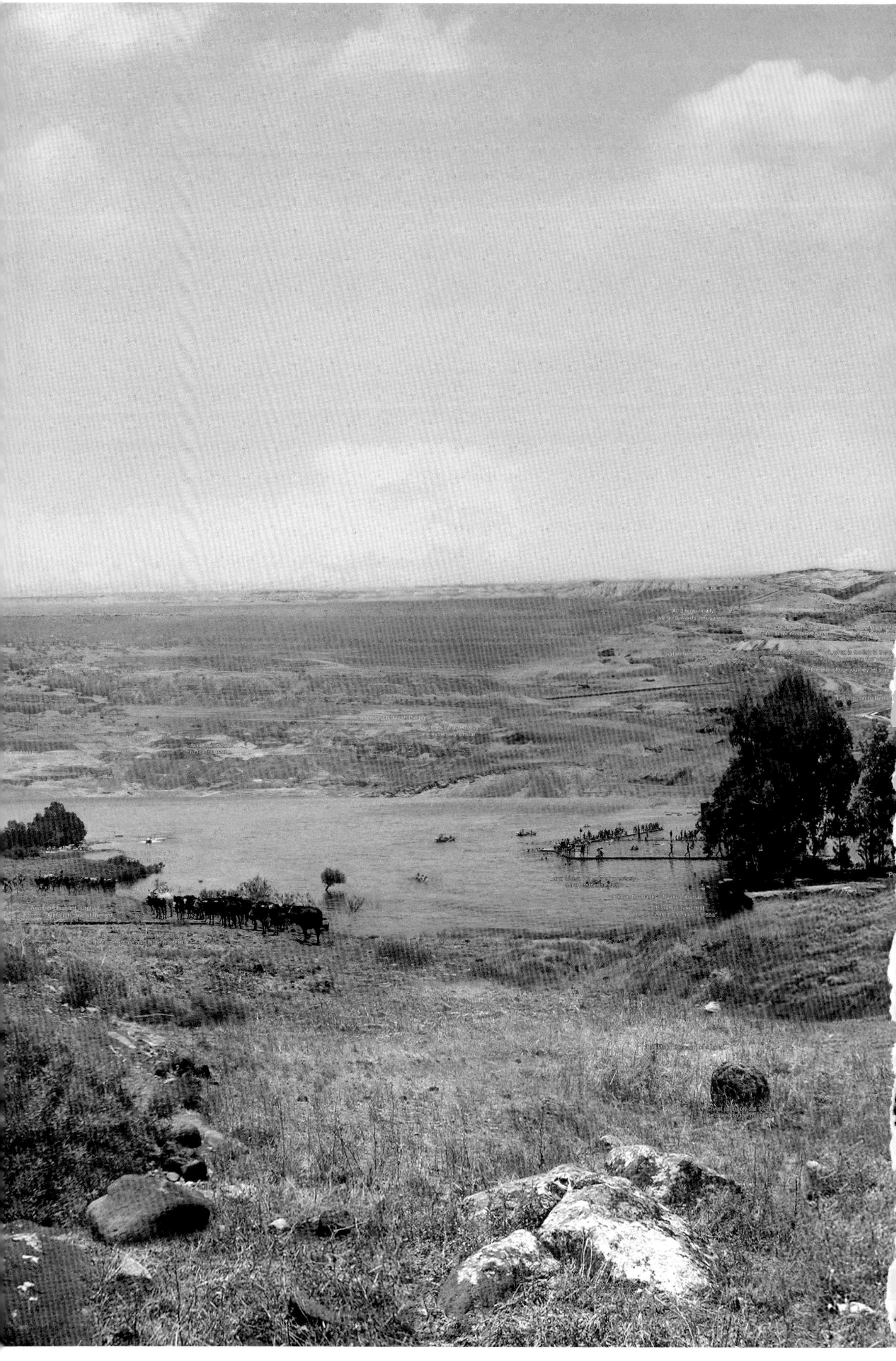

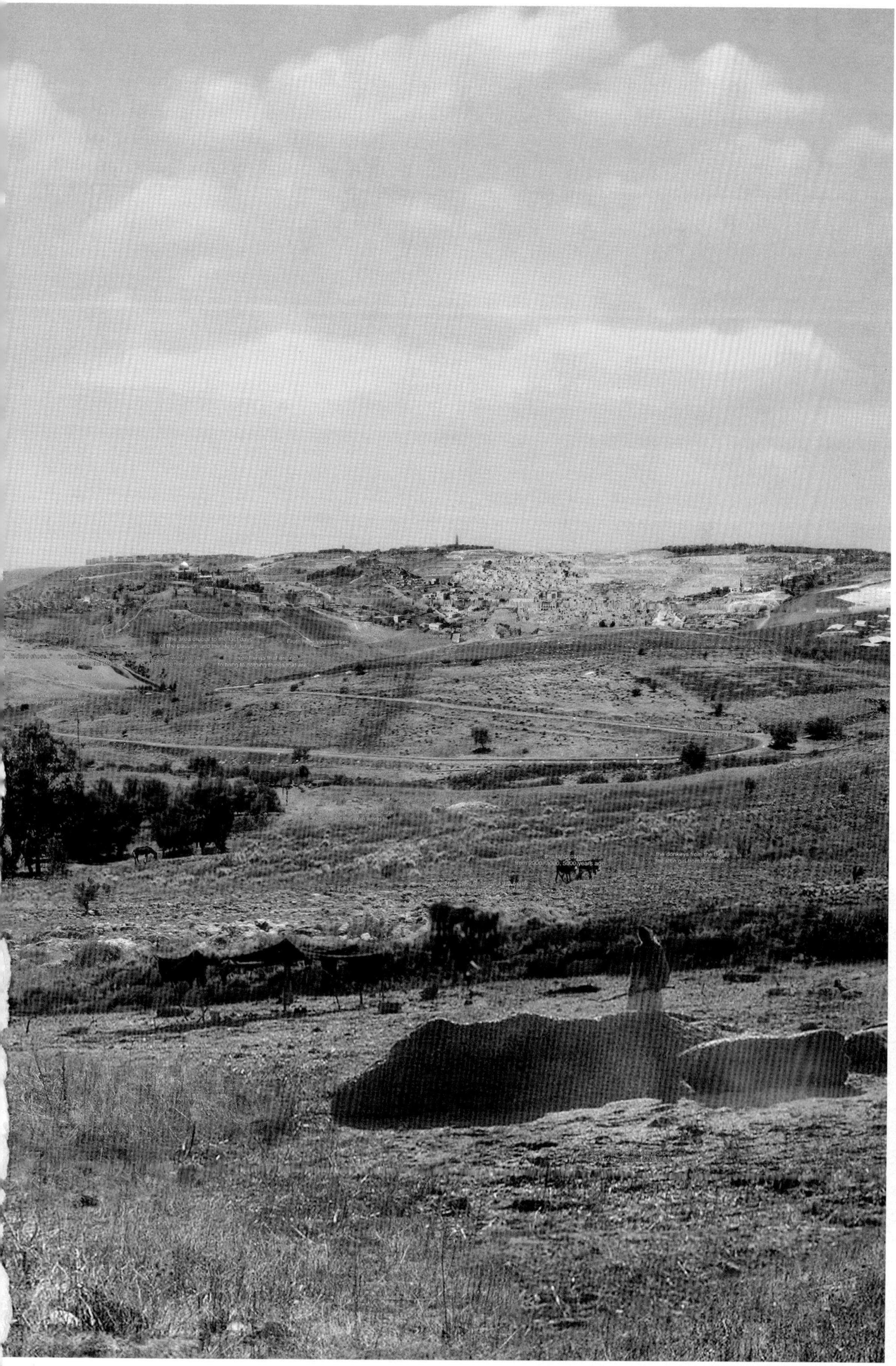
It's a world within a world
the area crucial to the last days
of the passion and the life of Jesus
From here you can see
even things that are not
to bring to nothing things that are
this landscape
from 2000, 3000, 5000 years ago
the donkeys from the Bible
the little girl from the Bible

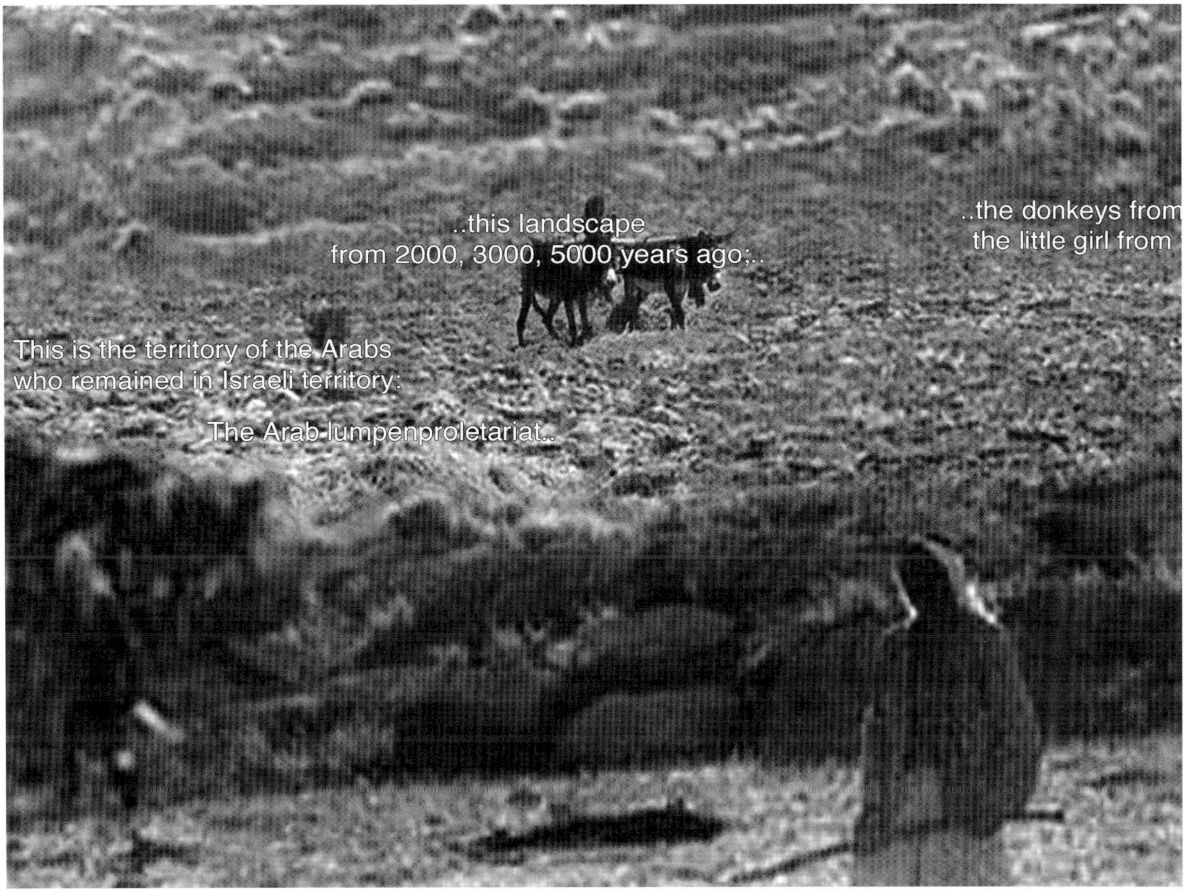
..this landscape
from 2000, 3000, 5000 years ago;..
..the donkeys from
the little girl from
This is the territory of the Arabs
who remained in Israeli territory:
The Arab lumpenproletariat..

162 *L'Élan pour l'Amérique*, 2010
Film négatif (*Histoire de France* de Jules Michelet), néon / Negative film (*Histoire de France* by Jules Michelet), neon light, 81.5 × 113.5 cm

Diagram of the sea, 2015–16
Huile sur toile / Oil on canvas, chaque / each: 38 × 55 cm

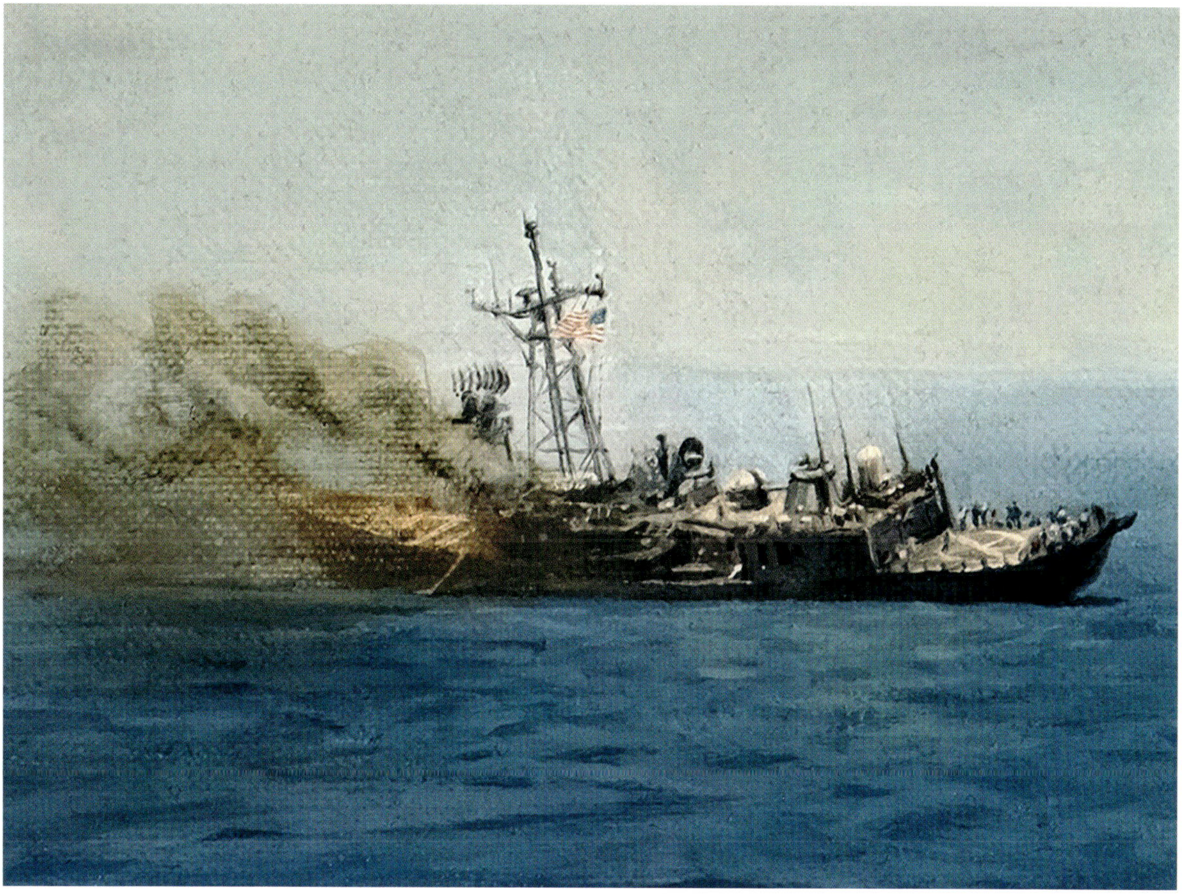

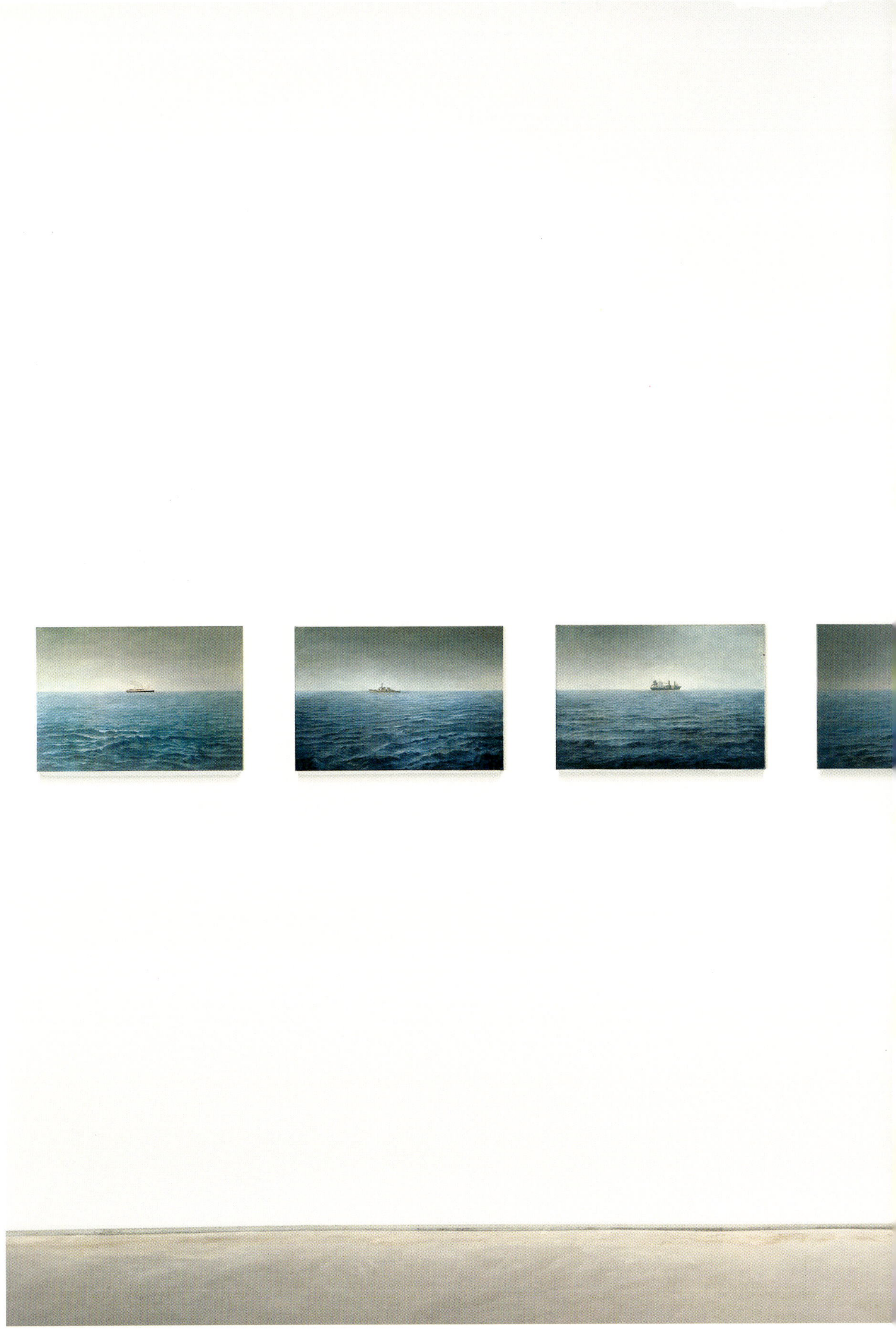

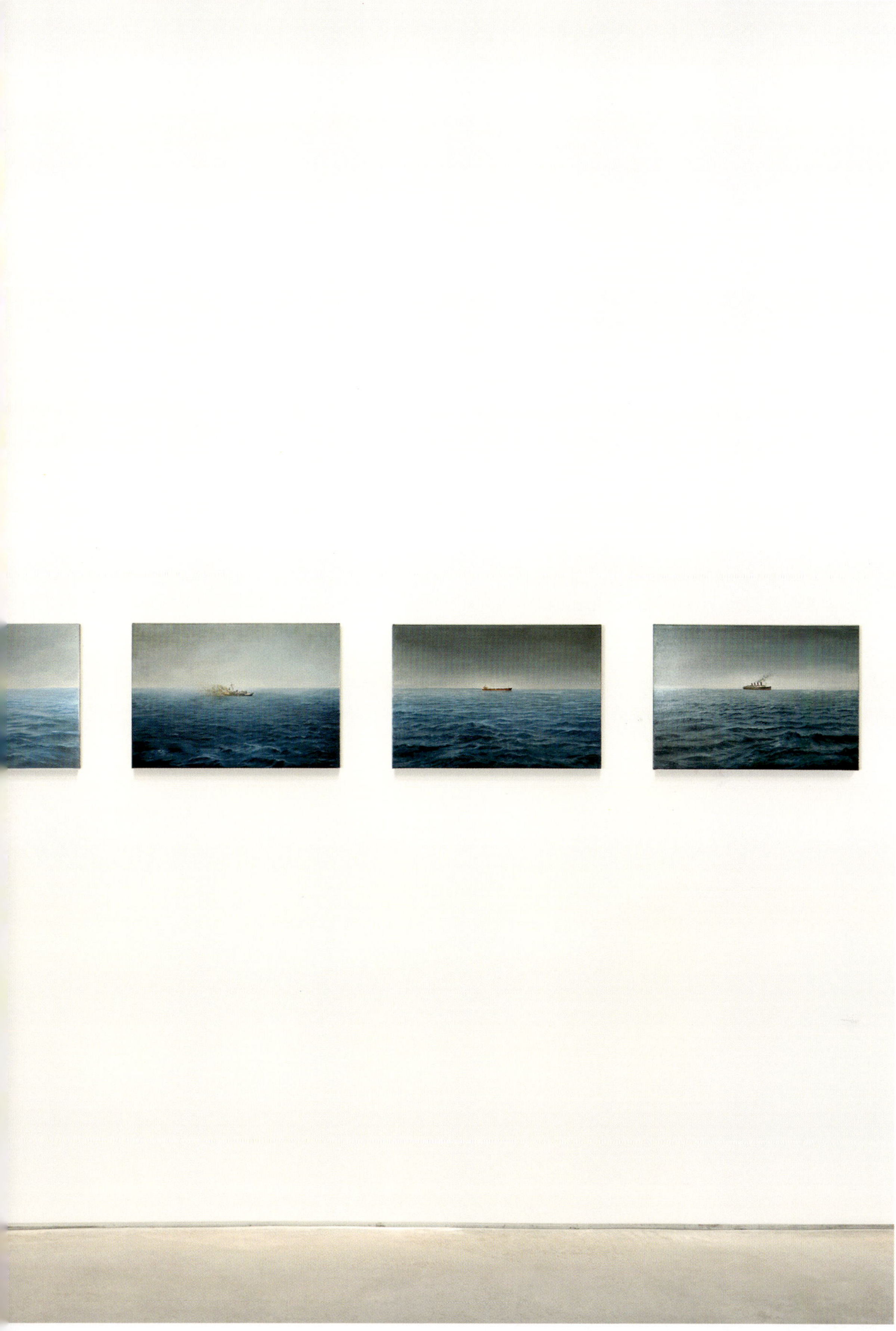

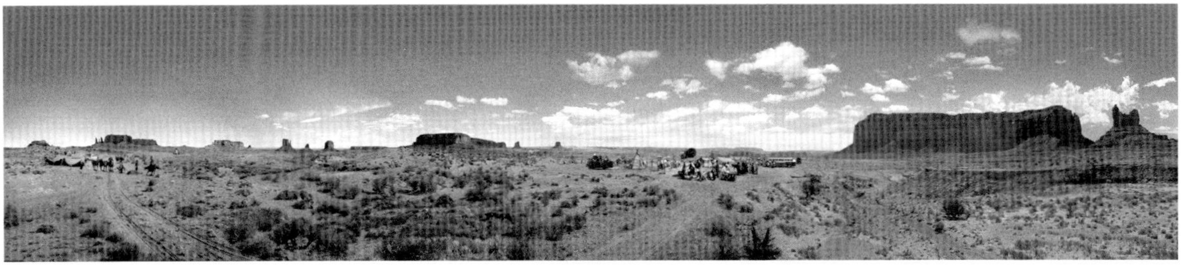

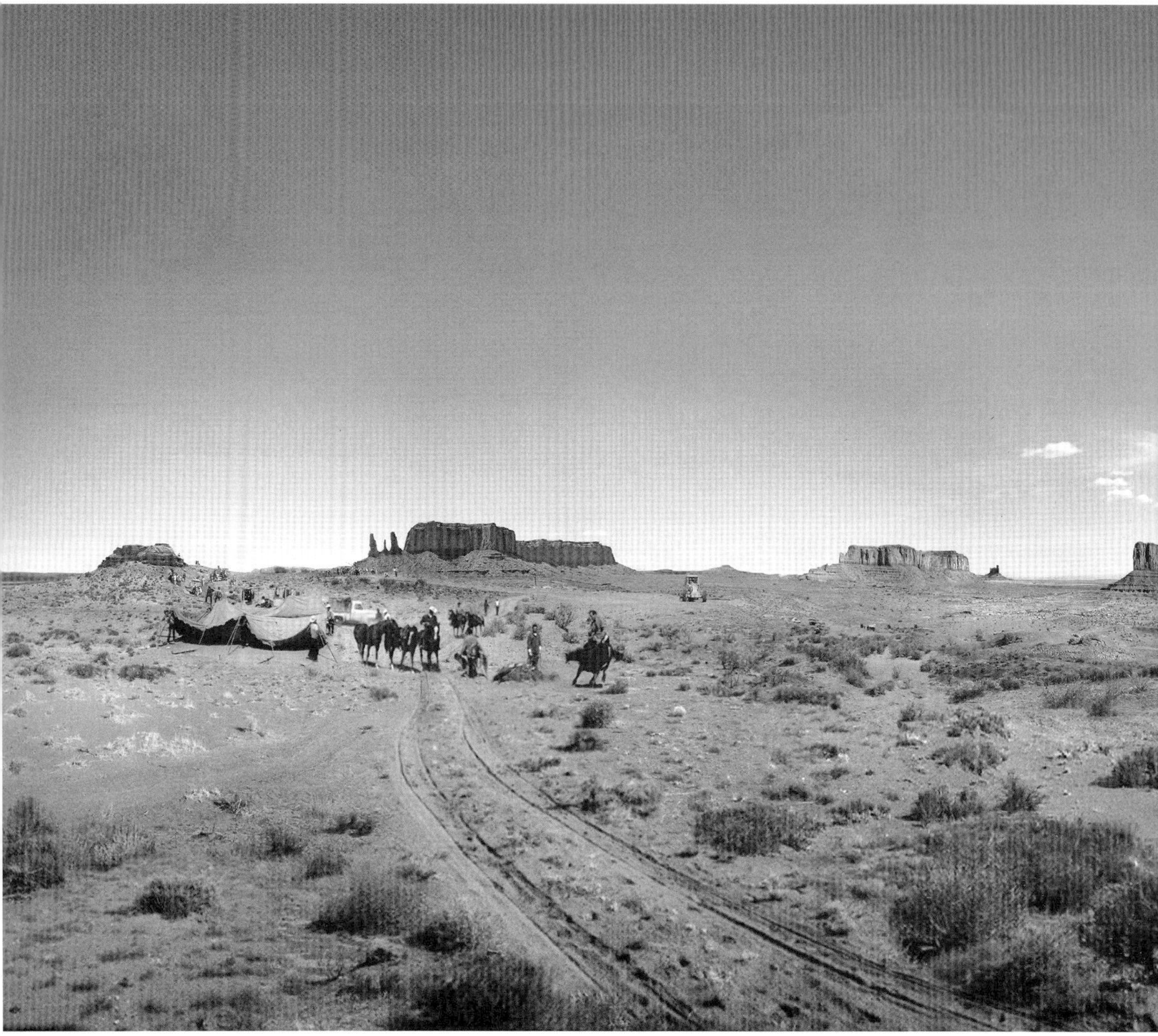

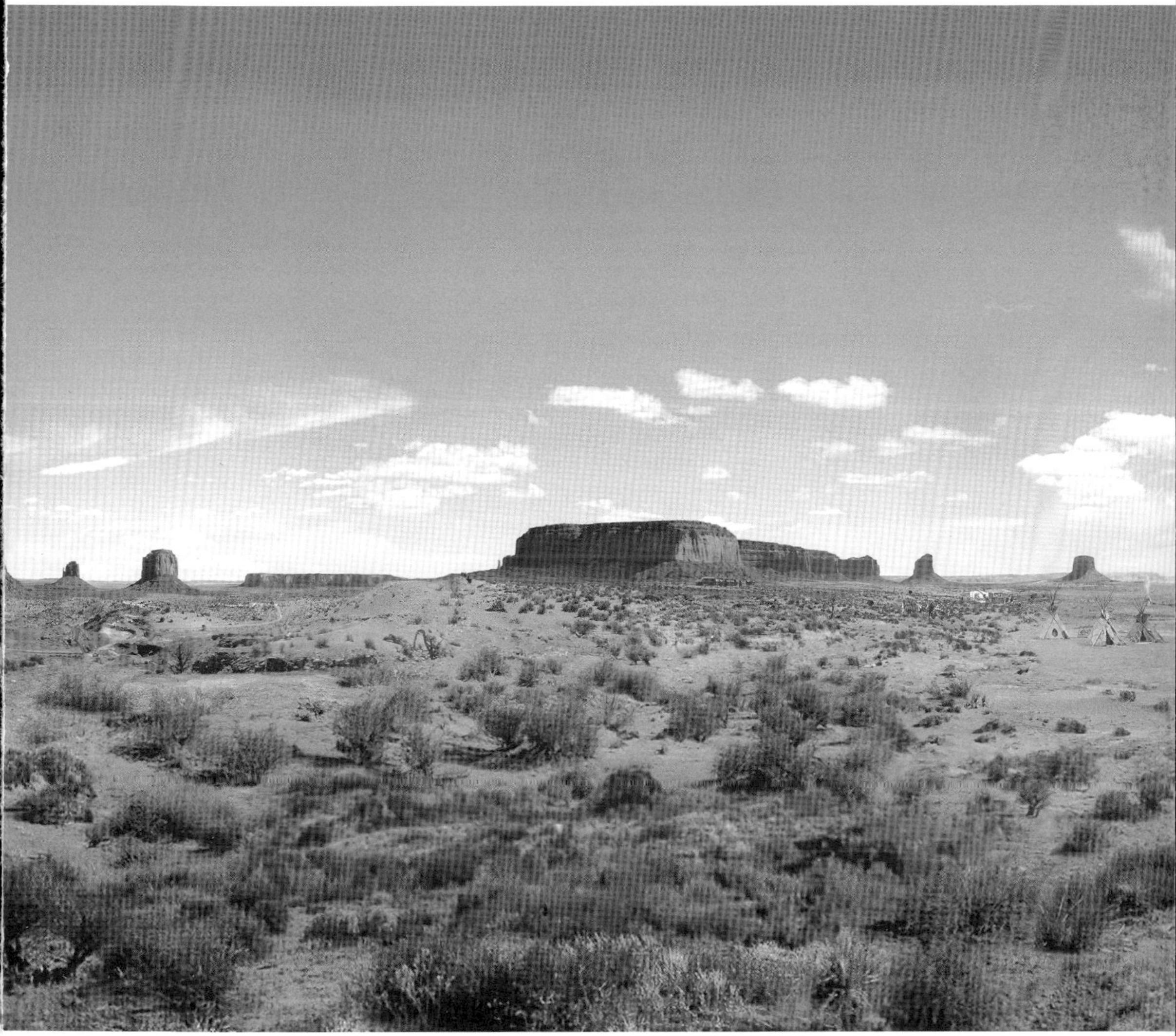

Searchers, 2009–10
Impression digigraphie sur papier photo / Digigraphic print on photo paper, 86 × 304 cm

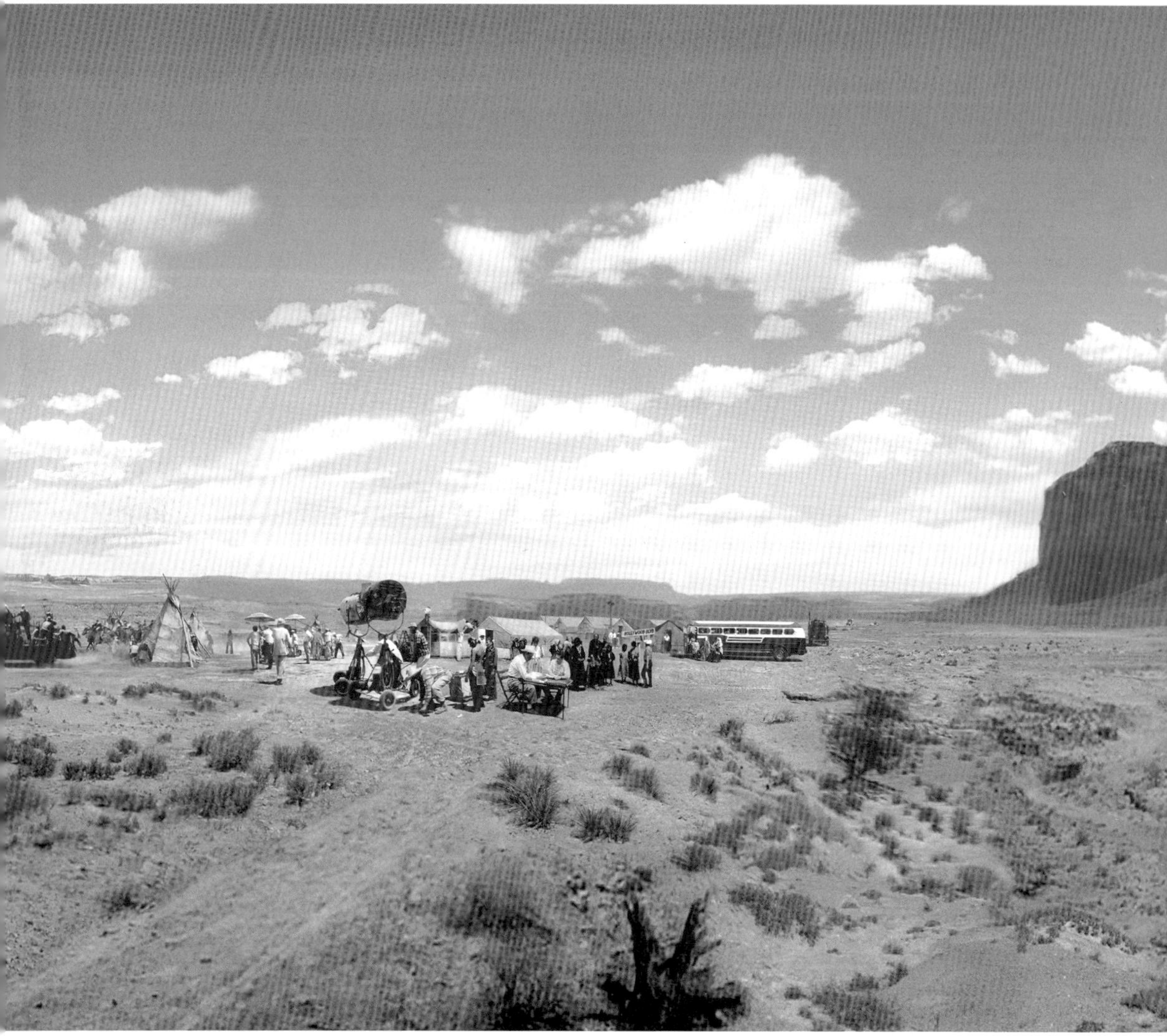

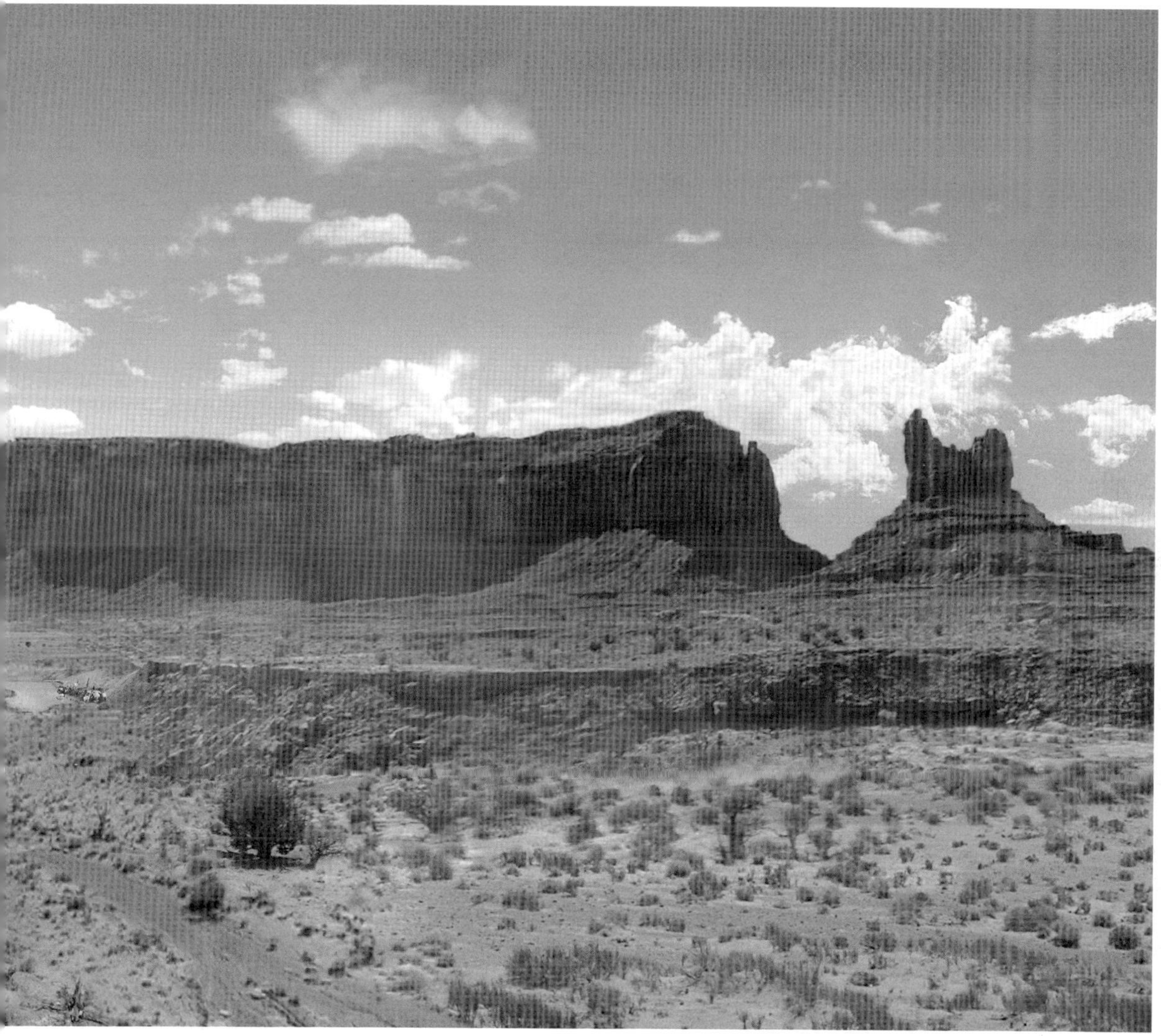

171
60 œuvres irréalisées

173
Red sunset over a lake

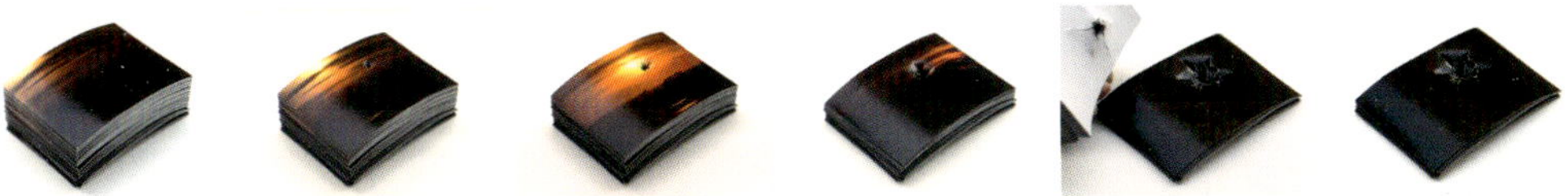

175
Julius Magneticus

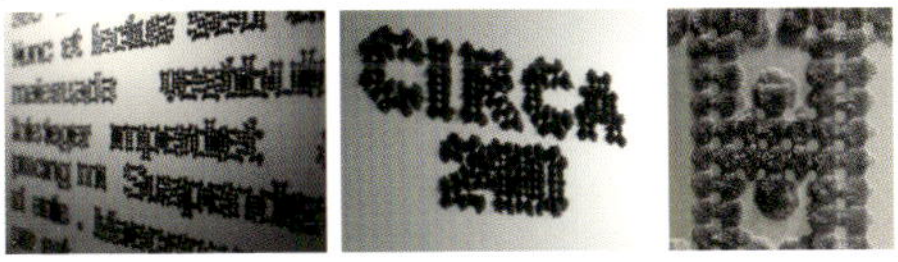

177-179
Premier feu

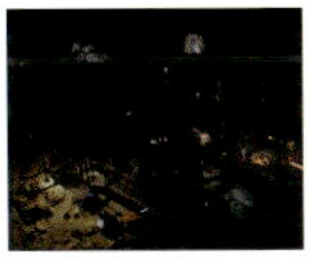

181-187
Eden

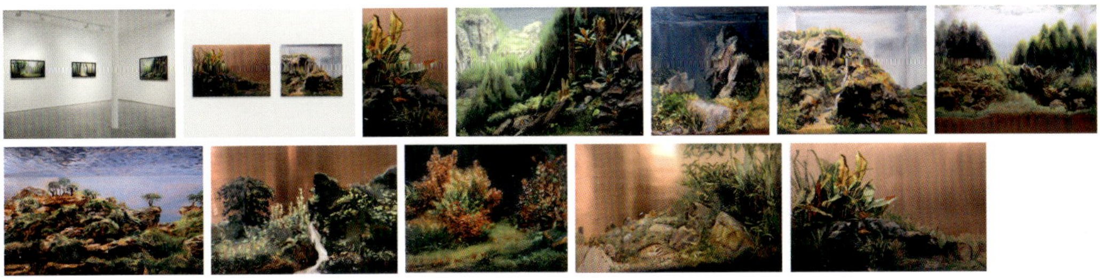

189-191
Livres

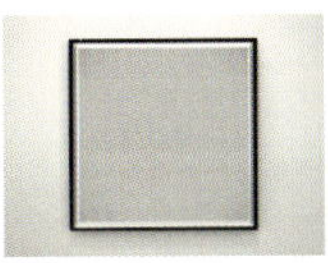

Livres

Parasites

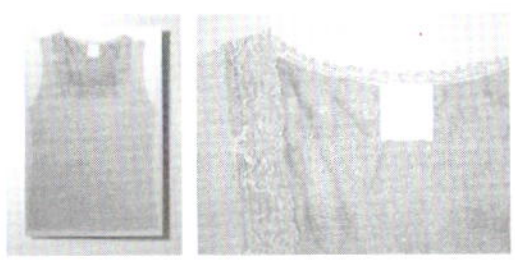

60 œuvres irréalisées, 2002–5
Tirage photographique par contact sur bromure d'argent / Contact print on silver bromide, 29.7 × 21 cm

Red sunset over a lake, 2011
211 cartes postales, tir à la carabine / 211 postcards, carbine shooting

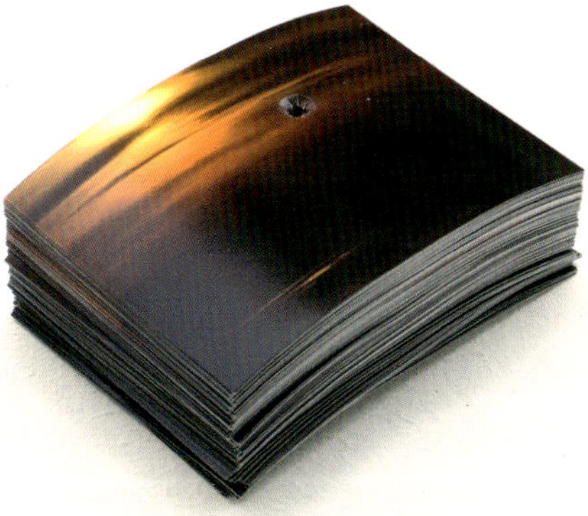

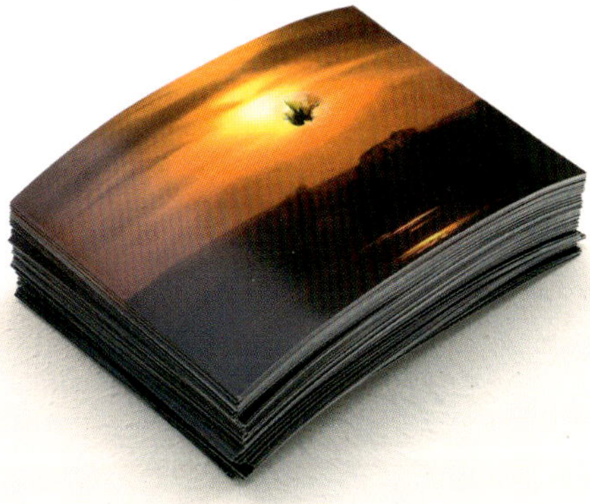

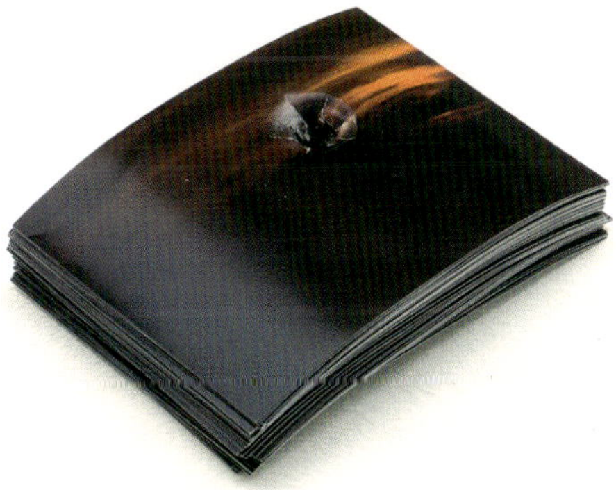

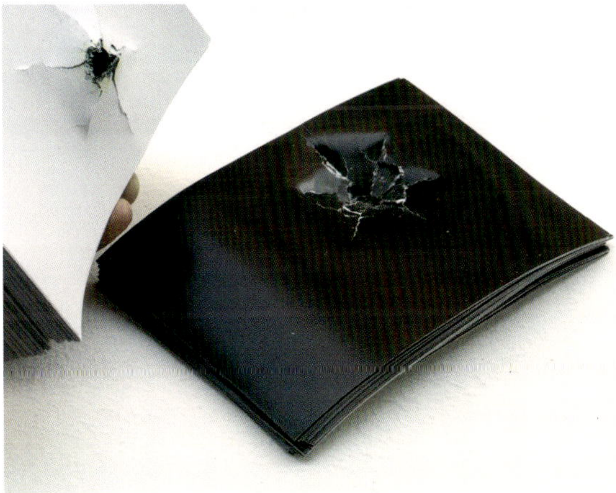

Julius Magneticus (H), 2008
Poussière de fer, aimants et aluminium anodisé / Iron dust, magnets, and anodized aluminum, 91 × 69 × 4 cm

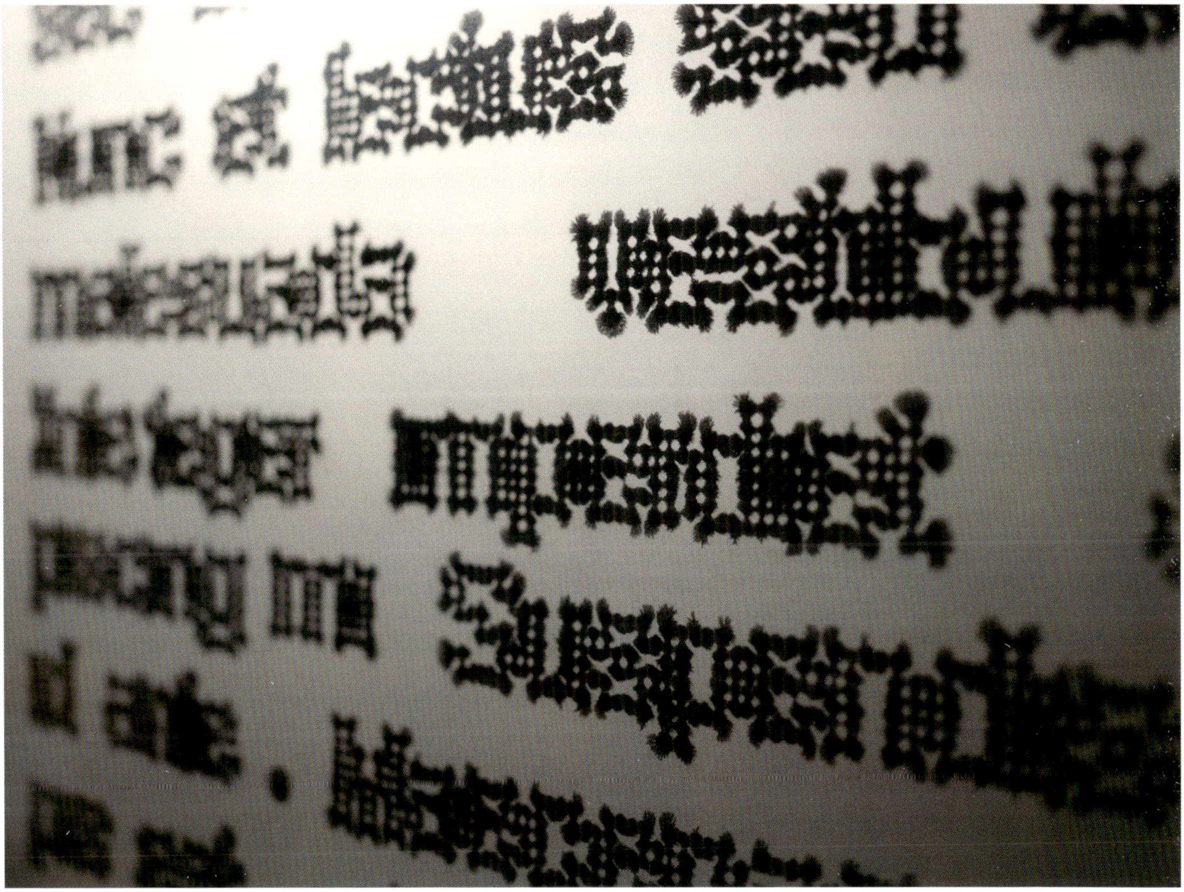

176 *Premier feu*, 2008
Photographie numérique transférée sur plan-film ektachrome / Digital photograph transferred to Ektachrome sheet film, 10 × 12 cm

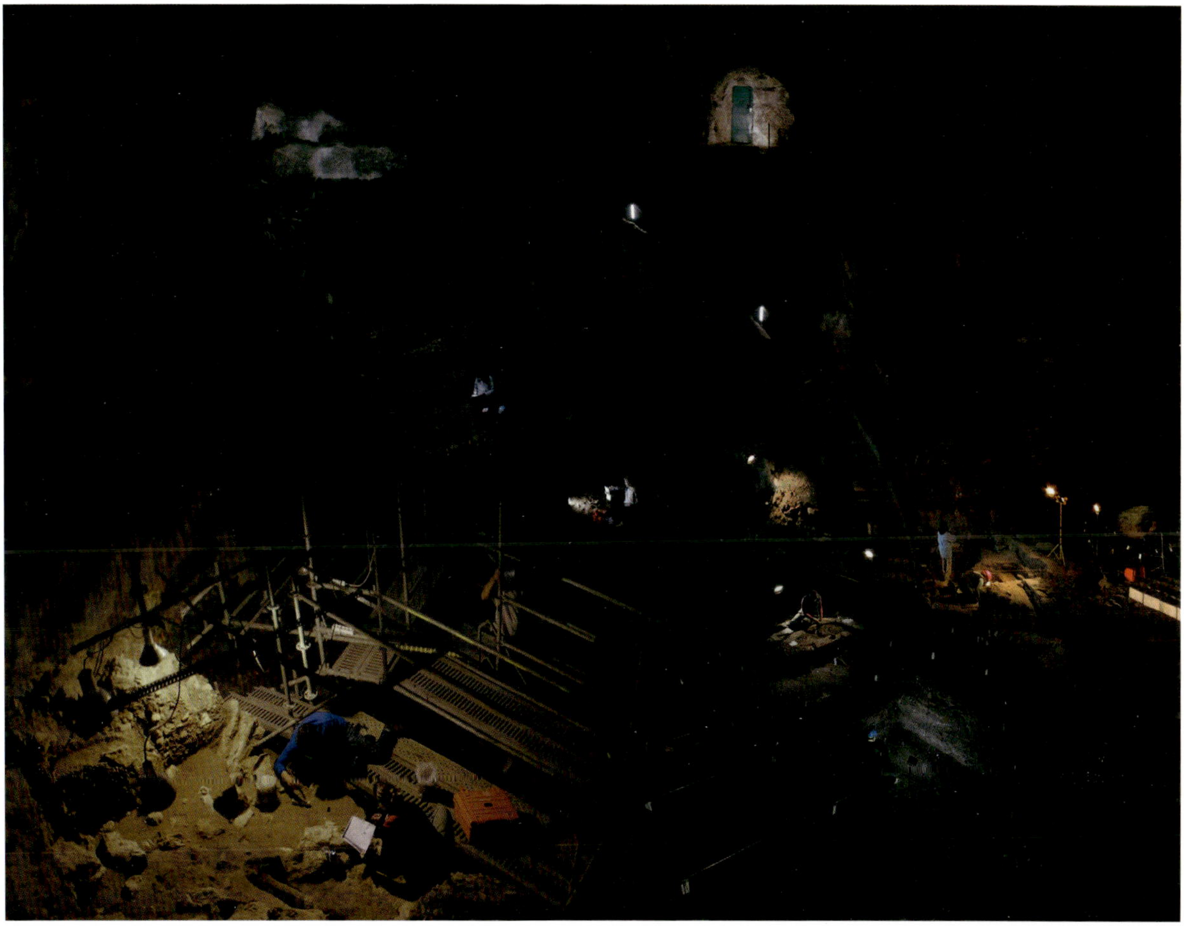

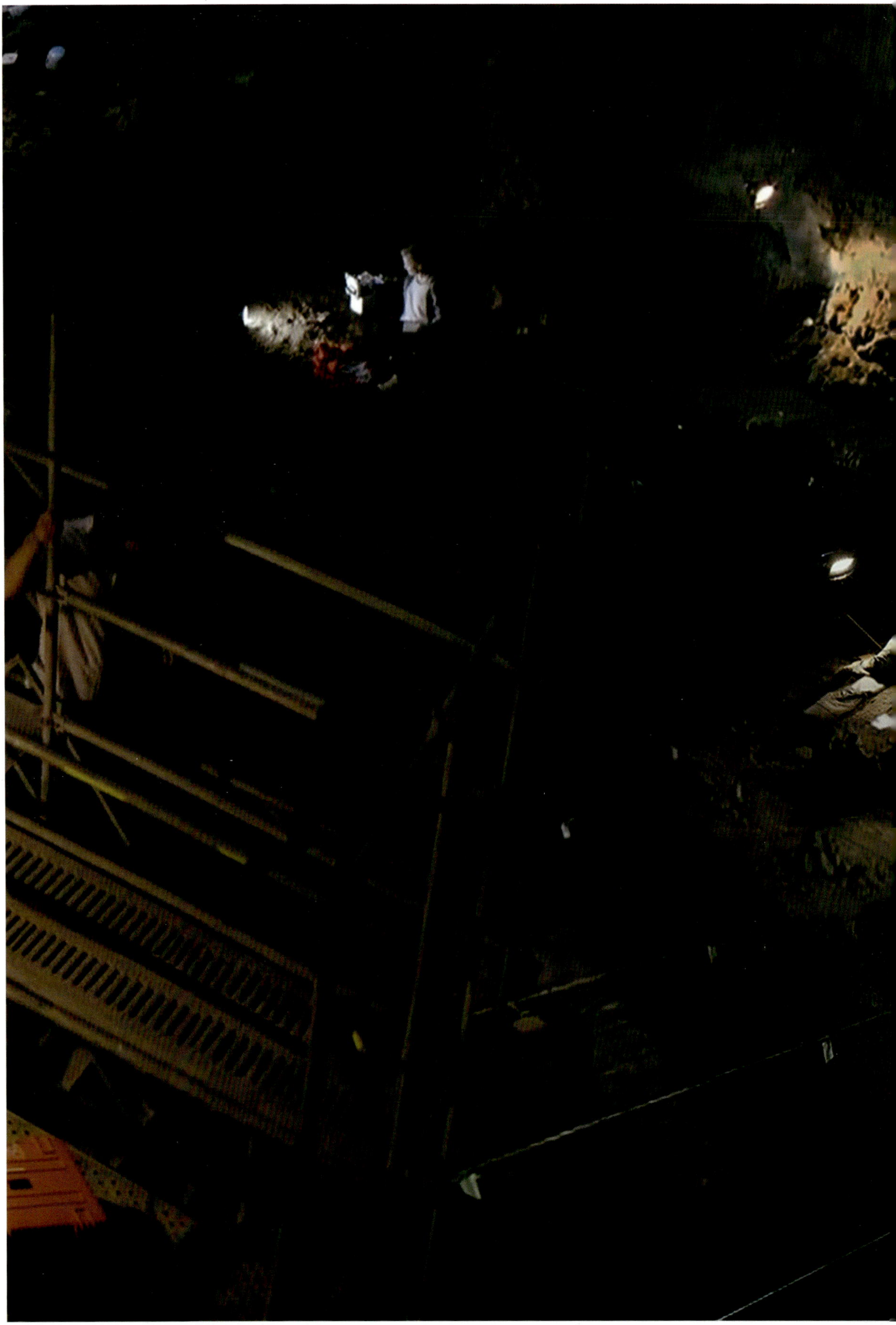

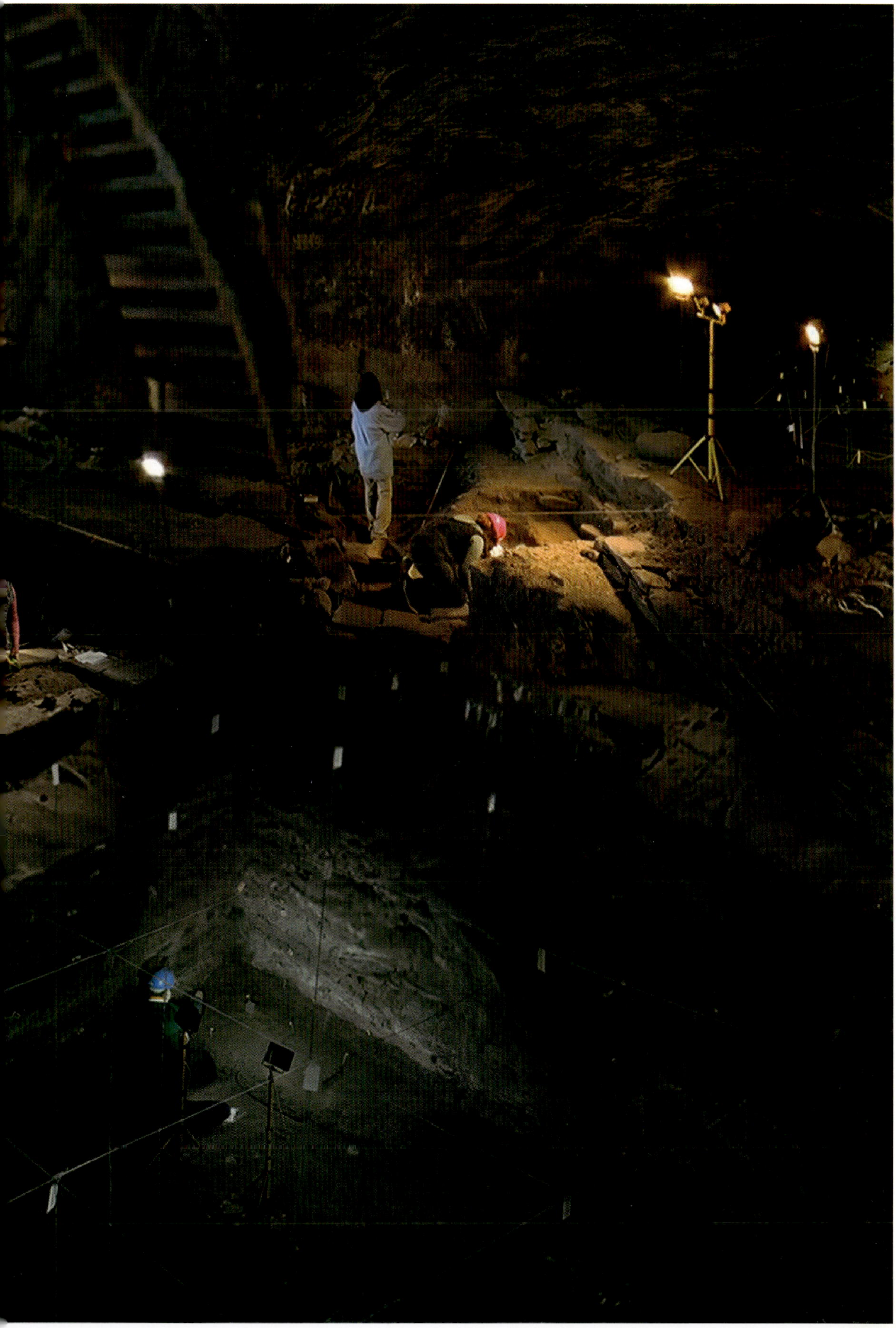

Eden, 2019
Huile sur toile / Oil on canvas, dimensions variables / dimensions variable

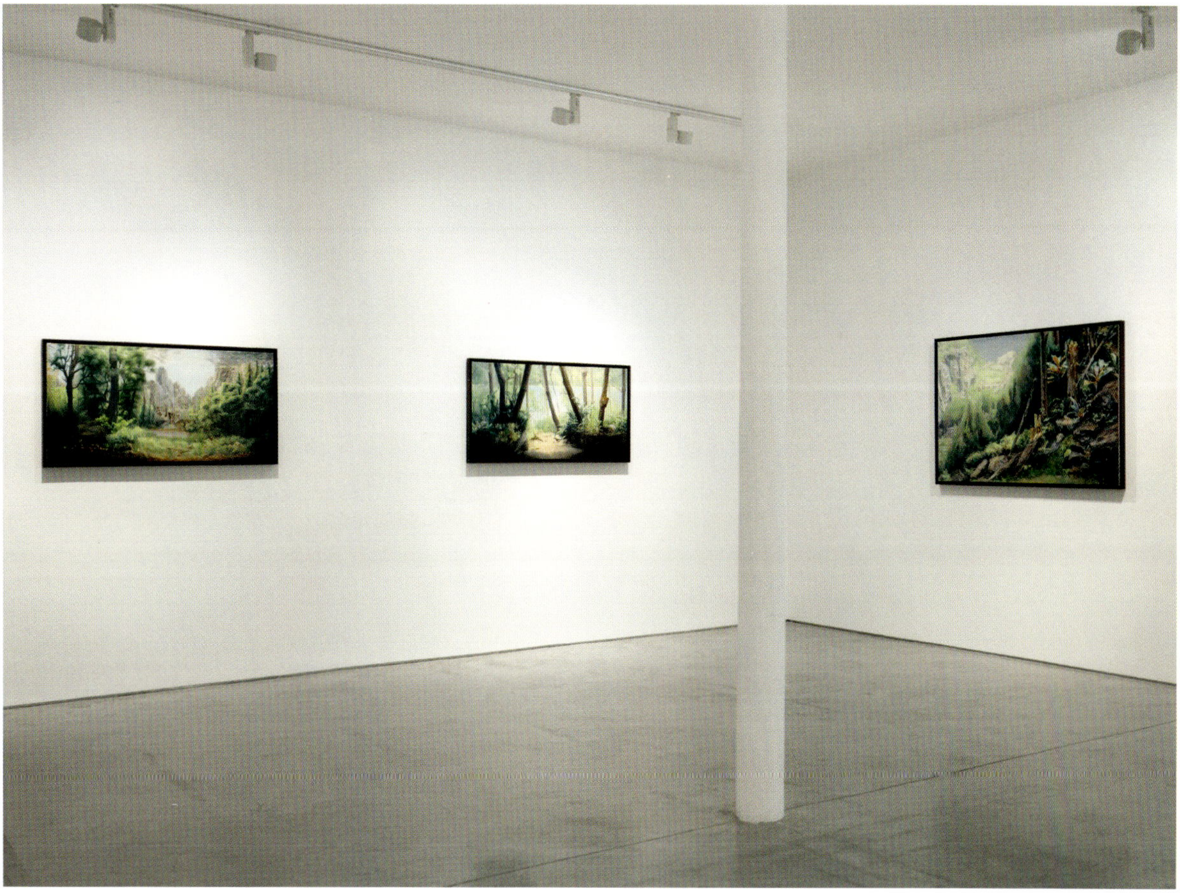

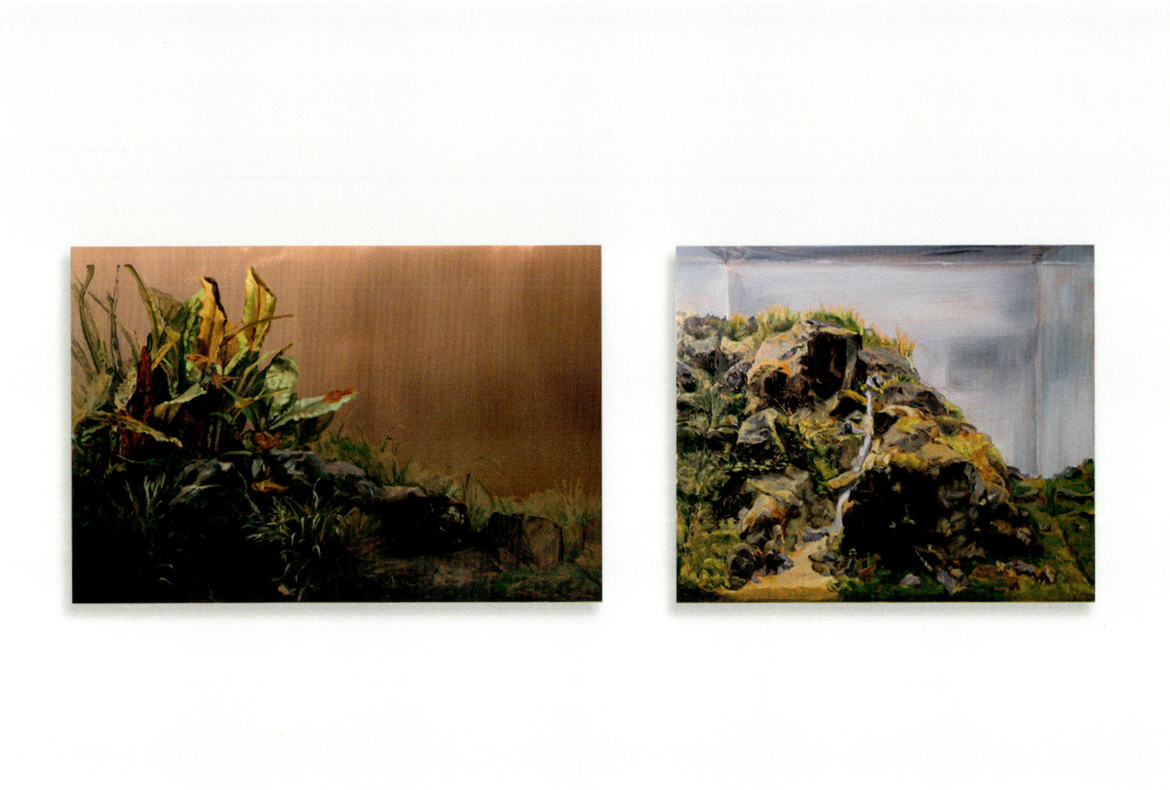

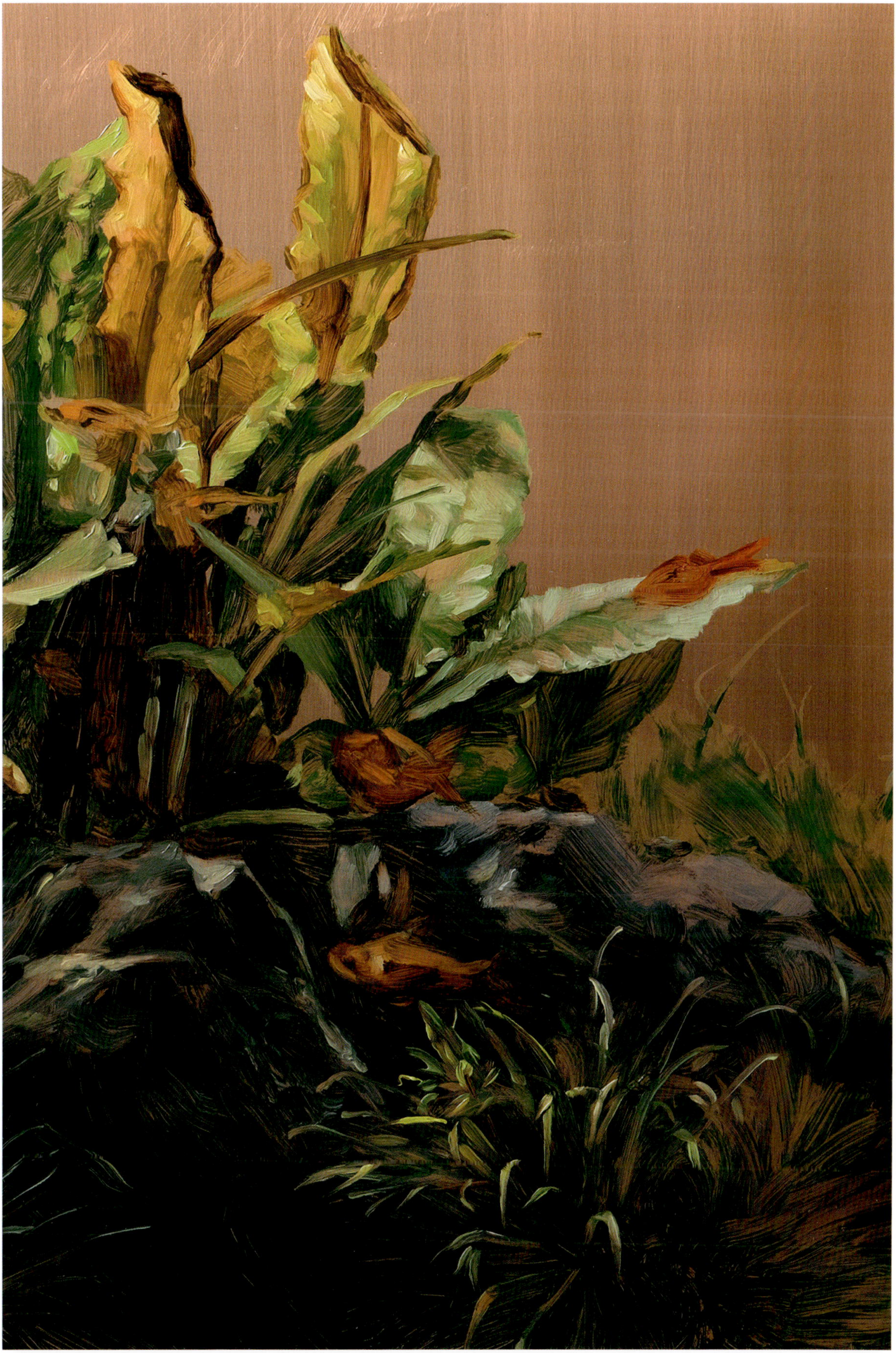

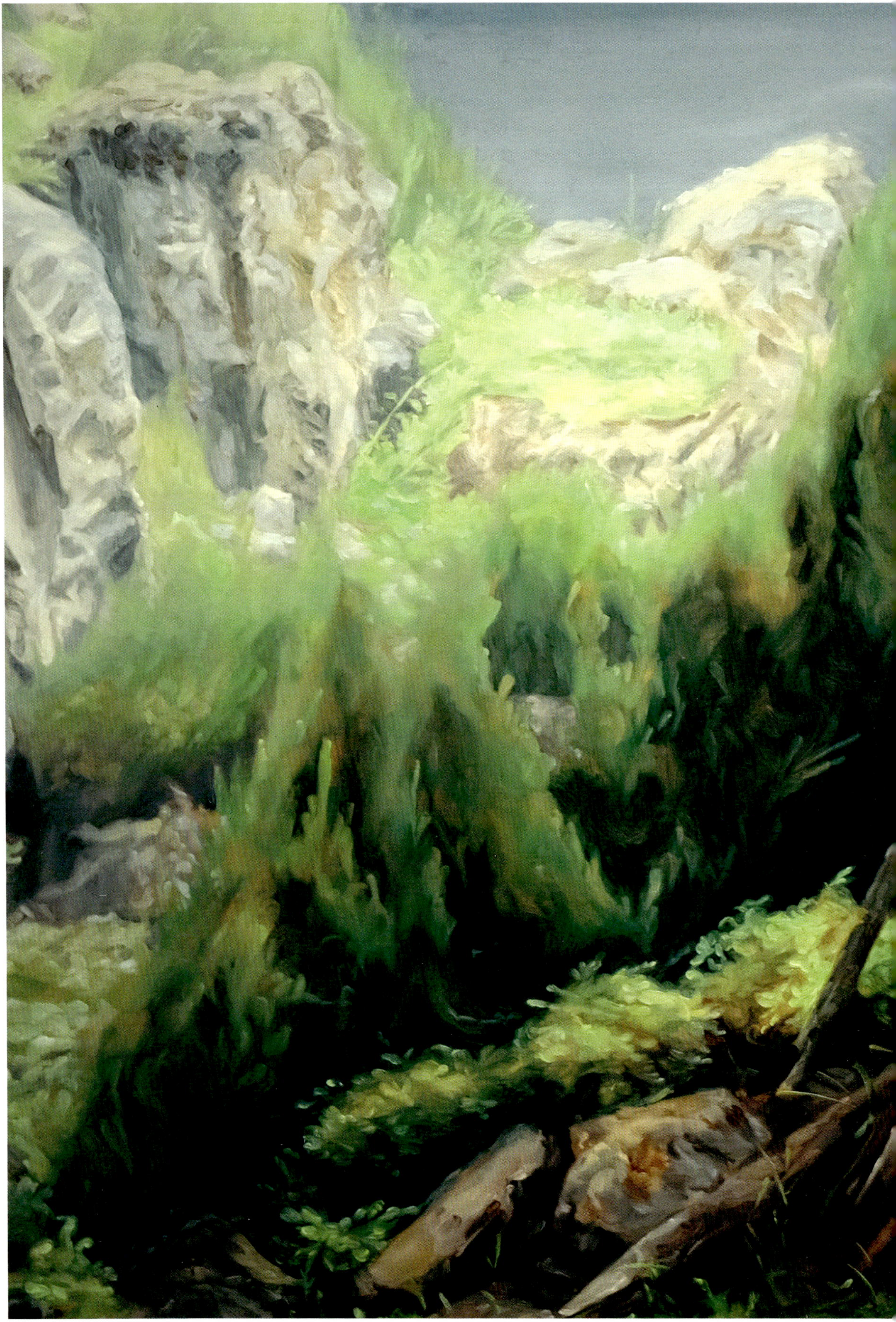

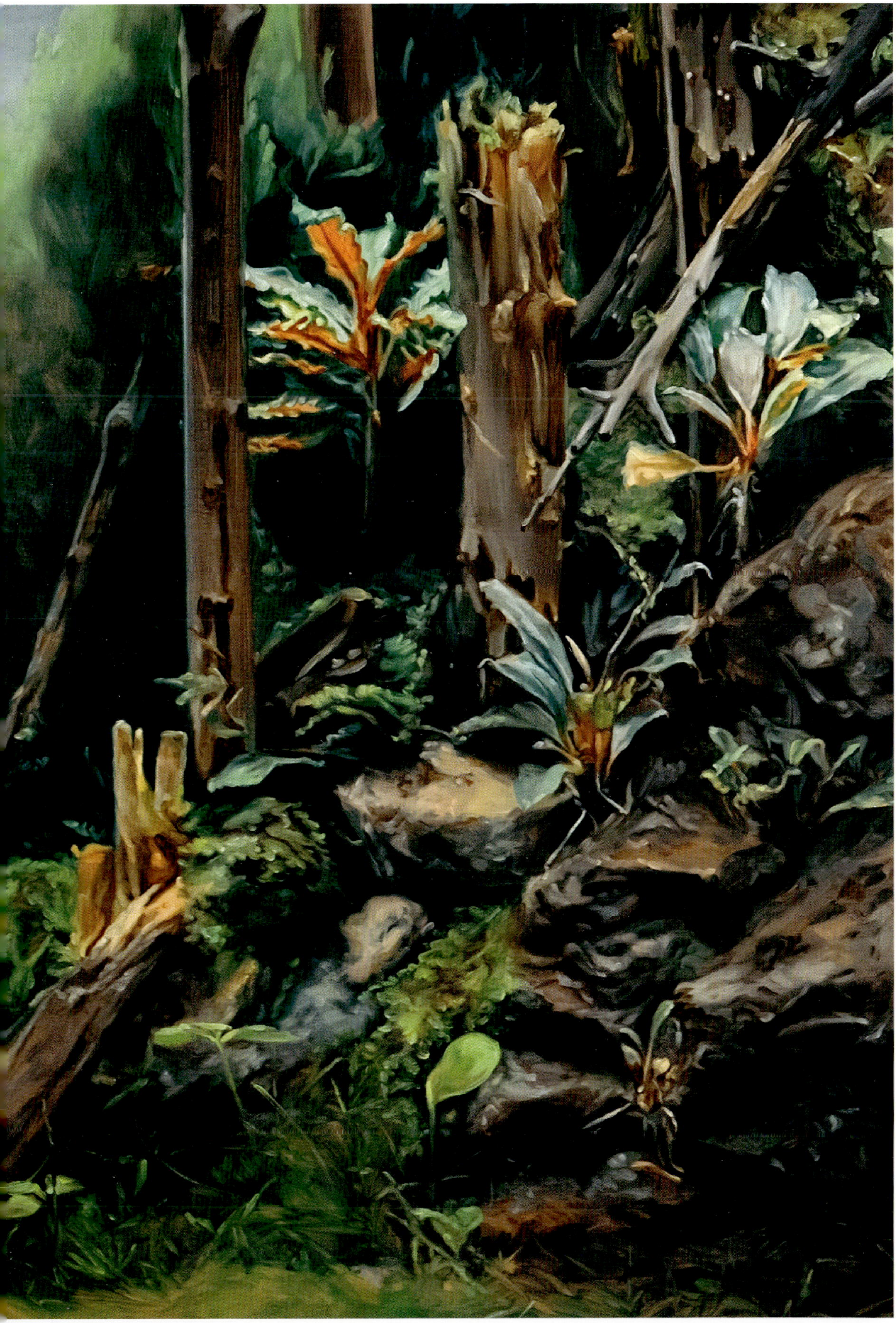

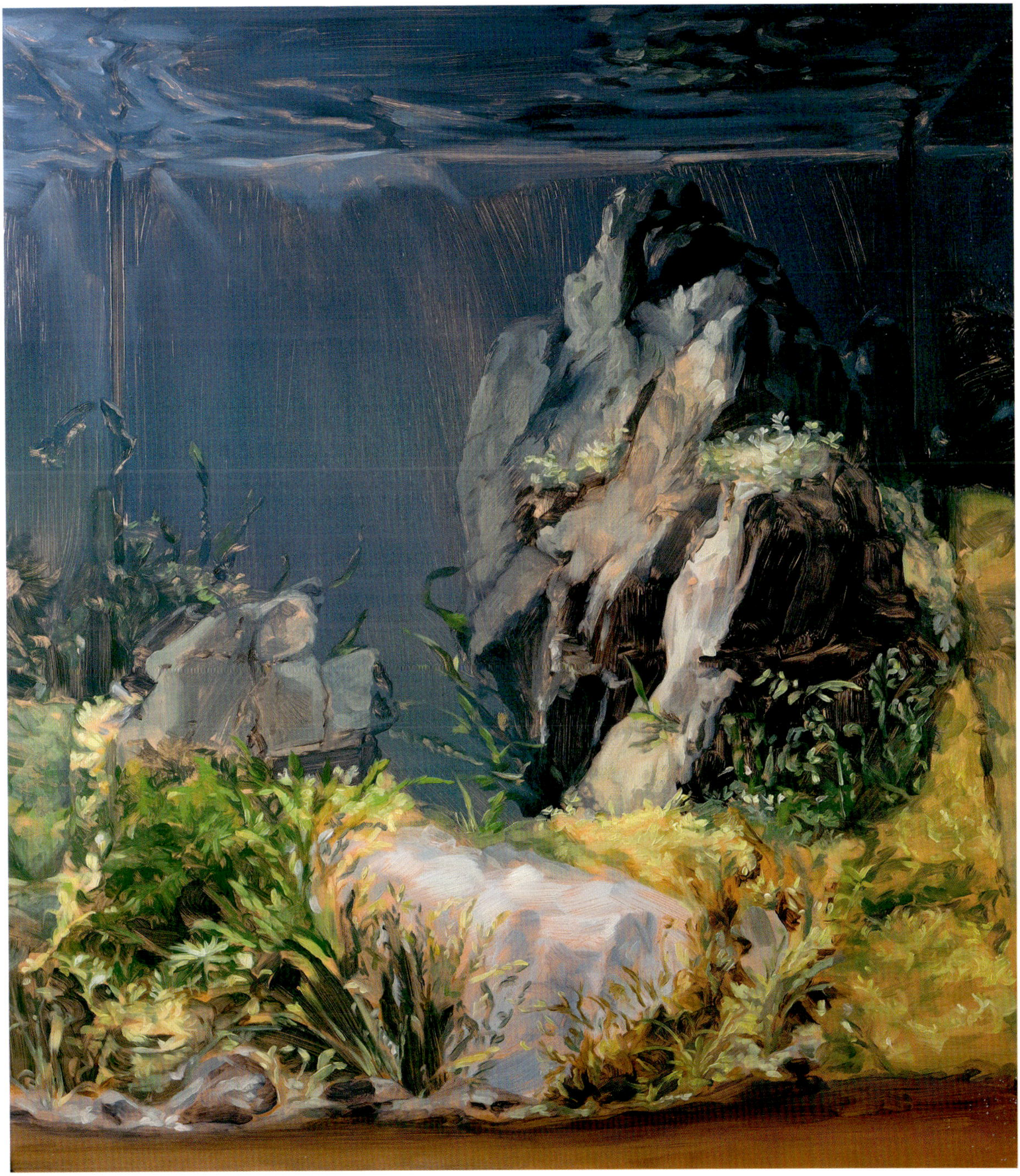

Livres, 2003
Tirage photographique par contact sur bromure d'argent / Contact print on silver bromide, 50 × 50 cm

CHRONOLOGIE / TIMELINE

2002–5

60 œuvres irréalisées
Tirage photographique par contact sur bromure d'argent / Contact print on silver bromide
29.7 × 21 cm
Photo: Julien Audebert

Les lignes horizontales, formatées comme sur une page de carnet A4, rassemblent deux années de notes et écrits (projets d'œuvres non réalisés). Cette première photographie de texte par contact sur papier bromure présente déjà les caractéristiques principales des photographies textuelles qui vont suivre (taille de la police de caractère, support, film négatif et tirage contact).

For more than two years, Audebert collected notes and writings (ideas for works never achieved), then formatted them according to the lines and size of a blank A4 notebook page. This first contact photograph of text on bromide paper, which laid the groundwork for subsequent textual photographs (font size, support, negative film, contact print).

2003

Parasites
Tirage photographique par contact sur bromure d'argent / Contact print on silver bromide
58.5 × 40 cm
Photo: Julien Audebert

Ce tirage unique rassemble des dessins d'acariens domestiques « dermatophagoïdes » représentés à l'échelle 1:1. Séparés par des intervalles réguliers, ils reproduisent le maillage d'un vêtement. Le motif animal devient la trame de dentelles et passementeries qui n'habillent aucun corps. « Au moment où mon intérêt se portait sur la "chose imprimée" et les techniques de photogravure alors en train de disparaître, ces dessins d'acariens mettaient à l'épreuve la limite physique du papier photo. Le lien entre texte et textile a été un laboratoire pour mes travaux sur le texte qui suivirent. »

This unique print consists of a set of drawings of "dermatophagoides" (domestic mites) at 1:1 scale. They re-create the intervals of the mesh of a suit. The animal motif acts as a raster, revealing the laces and trimmings of an empty piece of garment. "At a time where my interest lay in printed matter and photoengraving techniques that were about to disappear, these drawings of house mites challenged the physical limit of photographic paper. The link between text and textile became a sort of workshop for my subsequent works."

Livres
Tirage photographique par contact sur bromure d'argent / Contact print on silver bromide
50 × 50 cm
Collection Frac Occitanie Montpellier
Collections privées / Private collections
Photo: Fabrice Gousset

L'intégralité de l'Ancien Testament est condensée dans un carré de 50 cm de côté. Tous les différents noms de Dieu ont été effacés et remplacés par un vide équivalent à la longueur des mots. Cet effacement apparaît en trouées blanches irrégulières dans la surface du texte, le révélant comme image.

This is the entire Old Testament condensed into a 50 cm square. All of God's names have been erased and replaced by a blank equivalent the length of the word. This erasure appears as irregular white holes in the surface of the text, revealing it as an image.

L'œuvre d'art à l'époque de sa reproduction mécanisée (pour W. Benjamin)
Tirage photographique par contact sur bromure d'argent / Contact print on silver bromide
21 × 29.7 cm
Collection Frac Occitanie Montpellier
Collections privées / Private collections
Photo: Fabrice Gousset

Le texte célèbre de Walter Benjamin est condensé sur une seule page, réalisant le rêve du philosophe d'écrire un livre entier sur une feuille de papier. Sans la contrainte de la pagination, le texte est illisible à moins d'avoir recours à des instruments grossissants. Il apparaît dans sa forme organique, condensant un double mouvement de contraction extrême et de déploiement.

Walter Benjamin's famous text is here condensed onto a single page, fulfilling the philosopher's dream of writing an entire book on a single sheet of paper. Without the constraint of pagination, it is no longer legible without the use of magnifying tools. It appears in its organic form, condensed in a double movement of extreme contraction and extension.

BPM
Tirage photographique par contact sur bromure d'argent / Contact print on silver bromide
47 × 85 cm
Collection FRAC des Pays de la Loire, Carquefou
Collections privées / Private collections
Photo: Fabrice Gousset

BPM est un rythme – l'encéphalogramme textuel de la folie – et l'acronyme d'un pamphlet de Louis-Ferdinand Céline. Document d'histoire témoignant de l'avant-guerre et de la catastrophe qui s'y annonce.

BPM is a rhythm, a textual encephalogram of madness, and the acronym of one of Louis-Ferdinand Céline's pamphlets. A historical document testifying to the prewar period and the catastrophe to come.

2004

Reconstitution du meurtre d'Elsie Beckmann
Tirage Lambda / Lambda print
60 × 240 cm
Collection Frac Occitanie Montpellier
Photo: Nicolas Lafon

A partir des plans en extérieur du film de Fritz Lang *M Le Maudit* (1931), l'artiste a reconstitué le lieu de disparition d'Elsie Beckmann qui est au centre de l'investigation policière développée par le cinéaste. Le geste de démontage déploie l'espace du film tout en écrasant sa temporalité, dans un instant photographique où tous les protagonistes cohabitent simultanément, comme autant de témoins et suspects du drame.

Using the exterior shots of Fritz Lang's *M* (1931), the artist reconstructed the location of Elsie Beckmann's disappearance, around which the movie's police investigation is built. This dismantling unfolds the film location while crushing its temporality in a photographic moment that all the protagonists cohabit simultaneously, as both witnesses to and suspects in the crime.

2005

Landschaft
Tirage Lambda sur papier baryté / Lambda print on baryta paper
120 × 144 cm
Collection Sammlung

Goetz, Munich
Collections privées / Private collections
Photo: Fabrice Gousset

Landschaft expose une temporalité écrasée au sein du paysage montagneux reconstitué du *Nosferatu* de F. W. Murnau – chef d'œuvre du cinéma muet d'épouvante tourné en décor naturel. Cette géographie fictive, produite par la reconstruction des plans dans l'espace, déploie jusque dans le lointain le cheminement du jeune clerc de notaire Hutter dans une nature de plus en plus sauvage et étrangère. « C'est avec ce photomontage que j'ai découvert une aberration visuelle qui résultait de ce remontage des plans. Une inversion s'opère, la netteté se faisant dans le lointain. »

Landschaft shows a flattened temporality within the reconstructed mountainous landscape of F. W. Murnau's *Nosferatu*, a masterpiece of silent horror cinema shot in natural settings. The fictional geography, constructed by the spatial reconstruction of the shots, unfolds the journey of the young notary clerk Hutter into the distance, in an increasingly wild and strange nature. "Thanks to this photomontage I discovered a visual aberration resulting from this reassembling of the shots. An inversion takes place, such that the focus is set in the distance."

Royal Albert Hall
Tirage Lambda / Lambda print
57 × 200 cm
Collection FRAC Normandie Rouen
Collection Sammlung Goetz, Munich
Collections privées / Private collections
Photo: Fabrice Gousset

Cette photographie du Royal Albert Hall a été réalisée à partir des deux versions de *L'homme qui en savait trop* d'Alfred Hitchcock – celle de 1934 tournée en Angleterre (avec Peter Lorre notamment, qui joua *M le Maudit*) et son « remake » hollywoodien de 1956. L'artiste a conservé des deux versions la scène d'assassinat, raté, d'un ministre dans la salle de concert. La photographie condense le même moment précédant le coup de feu… un coup que feu qui, d'une certaine manière, dure 20 ans.

This photograph of Royal Albert Hall was took from the two versions of Alfred Hitchcock's *The Man Who Knew Too Much*—the 1934 version shot in England (starring Peter Lorre, who played *M*) and the 1956 Hollywood remake. Of the two versions, the artist kept the failed assassination scene of a minister in the concert hall. The photograph condenses the same moment right before the gunshot—a gunshot that, in a way, lasted for twenty years.

2006

Campagne Première
Tirage Lambda / Lambda print
77 × 121 cm
Collection Sammlung Goetz, Munich
Collection FRAC-Artothèque Nouvelle Aquitaine
Collection Fond municipal d'art contemporain, Paris
Collections privées / Private collections
Photo: Fabrice Gousset

Cette photographie est une reconstruction de la rue Campagne-Première à Paris, depuis la scène finale d'*A bout de souffle* de Jean-Luc Godard. Le point de netteté, au fond de la rue et au bout du travelling, correspond à l'endroit où s'effondre Poiccard, abattu d'une balle dans le dos par l'inspecteur Vital.

This photograph is a reconstruction of rue Campagne-Première in Paris, from the final scene of Jean-Luc Godard's *Breathless*. The focal point, at the end of the street and at the end of the tracking shot, corresponds to the place where Poiccard collapses, shot in the back by Inspector Vital.

Studio
Tirage Lambda / Lambda print
90 × 190 cm
Collection FRAC des Pays de la Loire, Carquefou
Collections privées / Private collections
Photo: Fabrice Gousset

Photographie réalisée à partir de *La Corde* d'Alfred Hitchcock, un « faux » plan séquence de 1h30 dans un appartement reconstitué. En réduisant le film à une seule image, la photographie oscille entre ce lieu fictif et le lieu réel du tournage, le studio qui lui préexiste. Tout en condensant par collages et mises à l'échelle la totalité des plans du film, l'image donne à voir cet espace selon un point de vue nouveau : la position du mort, caché dans une malle dans les premières séquences. Cette perspective inédite est à la fois celle du mort et celle de l'équipe technique sur le plateau.

Photograph made from Alfred Hitchcock's movie *The Rope*, a "fake" ninety-minute sequence shot in a reconstructed flat. By reducing the film to a single image, the photograph oscillates between fiction and the real location, the studio, which existed prior to the film. By condensing the totality of the film's shots via collage and scaling, the image gives us a view of the place from a new vantage point: the position of the dead man, hidden at the beginning of the film in a trunk. This new perspective is both his and that of the technical crew on set.

L'Éternité par les astres
Tirage photographique par contact sur bromure d'argent / Contact print on silver bromide on aluminum
23 × 29.7 cm
FMAC, Fonds d'arts contemporain – Paris Collection
Collections privées / Private collections
Photo: Fabrice Gousset

La théorie astronomique de Louis Auguste Blanqui est ici réécrite et justifiée en son centre. Ce texte, rédigé par le révolutionnaire en prison, est influencé par la lecture des théories mécanistes de Pierre-Simon de Laplace. Auguste Blanqui se soumet ici à la pensée dominante bourgeoise de son époque avec une telle radicalité qu'il lui renvoie, selon Walter Benjamin, « le réquisitoire le plus terrible qui puisse être prononcé à l'encontre d'une société qui projette dans le ciel cette image cosmique d'elle-même. » Une atomisation du monde en clones se démultipliant dans le Même à l'infini.

The astronomical theory of Louis Auguste Blanqui is here rewritten in a justified centered page layout. This text, written by the revolutionary while in prison, is influenced by Pierre-Simon de Laplace's mechanistic theories. Auguste Blanqui submits here to the dominant bourgeois thinking of his time with enough radicalism to throw back at it "the most terrible indictment that can be pronounced against a society that projects this cosmic image of itself into the sky," according to Walter Benjamin. An atomization of the world into clones that is infinitely multiplied within itself into oblivion.

2007

Dream never end
Tirage Lambda / Lambda print
78 × 103 cm
Photo: Fabrice Gousset

La photographie reconstitue en une seule image le premier concert de New Order dans Taras Shevchenko filmé à New York en novembre 1981. Il s'agit de la première apparition du groupe sans Ian Curtis, chanteur de Joy Division, décédé un an auparavant.

This is a single-shot reconstruction of New Order's concert filmed at Taras Shevchenko, New York, in November 1981. It was the band's first appearance without Ian Curtis, lead singer of Joy Division, who had died a year before.

Odyssée
Texte d'Homère kinéscopé sur film 35 mm / Homer's text transferred to 35 mm film
Longueur / Length: 307 m

Collection Sammlung Goetz, Munich
Photo: Fabrice Gousset

La circularité achevée du mythe rencontre ici la pellicule de cinéma. À la manière d'un long générique de film, l'artiste a transféré l'intégralité de l'*Odyssée* sur une pellicule 35 mm. L'objet est présenté au mur, la succession des chants lisible dans la partie déroulée.

The completed circularity of myth meets film here. In the manner of a long film credit, the artist transferred the entire *Odyssey* onto 35 mm film. The object is presented on the wall, the succession of books readable in the unrolled part.

2008

La Règle du jeu
Tirage Lambda / Lambda print
57 × 77 cm
Collection FRAC-Artothèque Nouvelle Aquitaine
Collections privées / Private collections
Photo: Fabrice Gousset

En 1939, avant la guerre, Jean Renoir tourne *La Règle du jeu*. Il filme une scène centrale où la haute société s'adonne à une partie de chasse. Tous les plans du film sont condensés en un instant unique où tous les animaux semblent tomber simultanément, un moment qui préfigure les événements à venir.

In 1939, before the war, Jean Renoir filmed *La Règle du jeu*. In one pivotal scene, high society goes hunting. These shots have been compressed into a single moment where all the animals seem to fall at the same time—a moment that foreshadows the events to come.

1925-1964
Tirage Lambda / Lambda print
123 × 143 cm
Collection Sammlung Goetz, Munich
Collections privées / Private collections
Photo: Fabrice Gousset

Deux moments insurrectionnels convergent dans un escalier, celui d'Odessa, filmé dans la célèbre scène du *Cuirassé Potemkine* (Sergueï Eisenstein, 1925), et celui de la manifestation étudiante réprimée de *Soy Cuba* (Mikhaïl Kalatozov, 1964). L'espace de l'escalier crée une continuité artificielle entre les deux événements historiques (respectivement Odessa en 1905 et Cuba en 1957). Dans un mouvement ascendant et descendant, les prémices du soulèvement de 1905 apparaissent au fond de l'image et les chevaux d'Odessa cohabitent avec les voitures de la Havane au premier plan. Cette collision produit une temporalité nouvelle et discontinue qui est celle du moment révolutionnaire.

Two moments of insurrection converge on an Odessa staircase: the famous scene from *Battleship Potemkin* (Sergei Eisenstein, 1925), and that of the oppressed student uprising in *I Am Cuba* (Mikhail Kalatozov, 1964). The space of the staircase weaves an artificial continuity between the two historical events (Odessa in 1905 and Cuba in 1957). In an ascending and descending movement, the beginnings of the 1905 uprising appear in the background while the hoses in Odessa cohabit with the cars in Havana in the foreground. This collision produces a new, discontinuous temporality—that of the revolutionary moment.

Inside the letter (The clue)
La Lettre volée d'Edgar Allan Poe tamponnée sur mur, ektachrome (*bladerunnerblowup*) sur socle avec table lumineuse / Edgar Allan Poe's *The Purloined Letter* stamped on wall, illuminated Ektachrome on plinth
Murs / Walls: 540 × 540 × 270 cm
Socle / Plinth: 101 × 51 × 39 cm
Collection FRAC Auvergne, Clermont-Ferrand
Collection Sammlung Goetz, Munich
Photo: Ludovic Combe

Déploiement de *La Lettre volée* d'Edgar Allan Poe en une ligne courant sur 54 mètres, le texte définit un espace labyrinthique dans lequel lecture et déambulation se confondent. En lisant l'intrigue, ou plutôt en la pratiquant, le spectateur est alors physiquement pris dans la recherche de l'indice disparu, qui pourtant était là posé aux yeux de tous, sur le bureau du ministre D. Au centre du labyrinthe, un socle qui paraît vide, l'indice : la photographie d'une chambre. C'est une histoire de recherche, de rapport à l'objet d'art et du regard aveuglé qui ne voit rien.

The text of Edgar Allan Poe's *The Purloined Letter* is spread out in a single line fifty-four meters long, defining a labyrinthine space in which reading and wandering merge. By reading through the plot, or rather by living through it, the spectator is physically caught up in the search for the missing clue, which was always there for all to see on Minister D's desk. In the center of the labyrinth, on a seemingly empty pedestal, lies the clue: the photograph of a room. It is a story of research, of the relationship to the art object and of the blinded eye that sees nothing.

The clue (bladerunnerblowup)
Plan-film ektachrome / Ektachrome sheet film
13 × 18 cm
Collections privées / Private collections
Photo: Ludovic Combe

Inside the Letter, au centre de la lettre, au cœur du labyrinthe où conduit le fil du récit, se trouve la photographie d'une investigation policière : reconstruction à l'échelle 1:1 d'une photo dans *Blade Runner* dans laquelle le détective Deckard réalise un grossissement impossible afin de trouver l'indice, la femme tatouée qu'il devra éliminer. L'artiste a reconstruit cet espace en utilisant les plans de Ridley Scott et des éléments assemblés en studio. Le transfert photographique sur film ektachrome autorise la présence réelle, dans le fond du miroir, de la femme endormie.

Inside the Letter, at the heart of the labyrinth where the storyline leads us is the photograph of a police investigation: a 1:1 reconstruction of a photo from *Blade Runner* in which Detective Deckard performs an impossible magnification to find the clue, the tattooed woman he must kill. The artist reconstructed this space by using Ridley Scott's shots with elements assembled in the studio. The photographic transfer on Ektachrome film allows the real presence of the sleeping woman in the mirror.

Julius Magneticus (H)
Poussière de fer, aimants et aluminium anodisé / Iron dust, magnets, and anodized aluminum
91 × 69 × 4 cm
Photo: Fabrice Gousset

C'est un « objet typographique » qui renvoie au langage : des aimants agencés constituent, par agrégation, des lettres, des mots, puis des phrases. Au recto d'une plaque non conductrice, Audebert a déposé de la poussière de fer, faisant apparaître le spectre du texte, champ magnétique des mots. Devenus aimants, ils s'attirent ou se repoussent et déterminent ainsi l'espace des mots. Privée de tout sens narratif, la lettre raconte sa propre histoire, son mode d'apparition. Il s'agit d'un « Lorem ipsum », généré aléatoirement par un traitement de texte – texte de substitution ou « texte muet » utilisé traditionnellement par les imprimeurs.

This is a "typographic object" that refers to language: magnets have been arranged to form letters, words, and sentences by aggregation. On the front of a non-conductive plate, Audebert placed iron dust, making the ghost of the text appear, a magnetic field of words. The words become magnets, attracting or repelling one another and thus determining the spacing between the words. Deprived of any narrative sense, the letter tells its own story, its own apparition. It is a "Lorem Ipsum"—the placeholder or "silent" text traditionally used by printers.

Written ornaments – Shelf
Encre sur mur, étagère en chêne peinte / Ink on wall, painted oak shelf
Dimensions variables / Dimensions variable
Photo: Galerie Joanna Kamm

L'essai *Ornement et crime* de l'architecte Adolf Loos est le matériau premier de cette installation murale. Ce texte polémique et radical de la modernité, écrit au début du XXe siècle, est ramené à une fonction ornementale. Mis en page à la mesure du mur, seuls les termes du titre (les ornements et « le » crime) sont inscrits avec un tampon, selon leur position et récurrence dans le texte. Ce passage littéral de la théorie à la pratique développe une dialectique du lisible et du visible. Application stricte et paradoxale du texte, elle agit comme l'évocation d'une modernité devenue désincarnée, passée de la subversion révolutionnaire à la nouvelle esthétique dominante. L'épure minimale n'est-elle pas aujourd'hui l'équivalent, en terme de bon goût, de la sécession viennoise tant décriée par Adolf Loos ? Une étagère en chêne, peinture en trompe l'œil selon une imitation de chêne, s'insère dans ce mur d'ornements.

The essay *Ornament and Crime* by the architect Adolf Loos is the primary material for this wall installation. This polemical and radical text of modernity, written at the beginning of the twentieth century, is reduced to an ornamental function. Layered to the size of the wall, only the terms of the title (the ornament and "the" crime) are stamped, according to their position and recurrence in the text. This literal passage from theory to practice develops a dialectic of the legible and of the visible. As a strict and paradoxical application of the text, it evokes a modernity that has become disembodied, passed from revolutionary subversion to the new dominant aesthetic. Isn't minimalist purity today's equivalent, in terms of good taste, of the Viennese Secession so decried by Loos? An oak shelf, painted in trompe l'oeil in imitation of oak, is inserted into this ornamental wall.

2009

nwsfrmnwhr
La Città del Sole, Tommaso Campanella
A New View of Society, Robert Owen
Nova Atlantis, Francis Bacon
News from Nowhere, William Morris
Utopia, Thomas More
Le Nouveau Monde Amoureux, Charles Fourier
Théorie des quatres mouvements et des destinées générales, Charles Fourier
Hygeia, Benjamin Ward Richardson
Les 500 millions de la Bégum, Jules Verne
Polyptyque de 9, tirages photographiques par contact sur bromure d'argent / Polyptych of 9, contact print on silver bromide
Chaque / Each: 23 × 31.5 cm encadrées / framed
Collections privées / Private collections
Photo: Fabrice Gousset

Neuf utopies, réécrites et micrographiées par procédé photographique (fabrication d'un négatif et tirage par contact) se déploient dans des cadres identiques, créant différentes marges de vide. Elles sont disposées selon une ligne au mur, horizon d'attente ou collection de mondes clos, « utopies prises aux limites de l'épreuve photographique » (Morad Montazami).

Nine micrographed utopias, rewritten by the photographic process (making a negative and printing by contact), are laid out in identical frames, thus creating different empty margins. They are arranged on the wall along a line as a horizon of expectation or a collection of enclosed worlds, "utopias taken from the limits of the photographic print" (Morad Montazami).

Julius Magneticus (Circa 2410)
Poussière de fer, aimants et aluminium anodisé / Iron dust, magnets, and anodized aluminum
31.5 × 50 cm
Collection FDAC, le Fond départemental d'art contemporain de Chamarande
Photo: Marc Domage

« Élevage de poussière » métallique agrégée pour signifier une simple date, celle de la disparition future du texte par démagnétisation.

An aggregated metallic "dust breeding" signifies a simple date: that of the future disappearance of the text once demagnetized.

Narcisse/Echo
Carte postale imprimée sur maille drapeau, projecteur de diapositives, diapositive / Postcard print on flag mesh, slide projector, slide
Production spécifique / Site-specific production
Domaine départemental de Chamarande
Dimensions variables / Dimensions variable
Photo: Marc Domage

L'artiste a agrandi une carte postale du début du XIXe siècle représentant l'escalier d'Odessa, vide de toute présence. Imprimé sur une toile lourde, le poids entraîne le motif de l'escalier vers le sol, dans une succession de plis. Au verso, la projection d'une diapositive ; un aphorisme de Karl Kraus : « Rien n'est un meilleur substitut à l'amour que la représentation. » Reflétée dans le grand miroir du château de Chamarande et lisible à sa surface, la phrase se reflète au verso du rideau, le projecteur occultant le « n' » donnant alors à lire dans l'espace physique « Rien est un meilleur substitut à l'amour que la représentation. »

The artist enlarged a postcard from the beginning of the nineteenth century representing a vacant Odessa staircase. Printed on a heavy canvas, its weight drags the staircase motif to the ground in a succession of folds. On the back, an aphorism by Karl Kraus is projected: "Nothing is a better substitute for love than representation." Reflected in the large mirror of the Château de Chamarande and readable on its surface, the sentence is reflected on the back of the curtain, the projector obscuring the "n," thus giving the physical space to read "nothing *as* a better substitute for love than representation," changing the meaning of the phrase in French to "Nothingness *itself* is a better substitute for love than representation."

Screenshot sequence
Toile occultante, tir au fusil / Blackout canvas, rifle shooting
200 × 280 cm
Photo: Sébastien Camboulive

Élément d'une exposition intitulée *Fort du Taureau* qui consistait en la réduction spatiale de la galerie In extenso à Clermont-Ferrand. Le spectateur se retrouvait, dans un sas exigu, face au texte réalisé d'après Auguste Blanqui *L'Éternité par les astres*. Un décrochement du mur permettait de se faufiler derrière. On pouvait y découvrir la photographie de la « Règle du jeu » où tombent les animaux morts, et tout au fond, dans un espace plus dégagé, un grand rideau noir. « Le rideau fut plié en 7 et en 4, puis j'ai tiré dedans au fusil de chasse. Le coup de feu unique essaimant les plombs se déploie alors comme une carte céleste, reproduisant le même coup sur la totalité de la toile. »

This was part of an exhibition entitled *Fort du Taureau* (The Bull's Fortress), which consisted of a spatial reduction of the In extenso gallery in Clermont-Ferrand. The spectators found themselves in a confined airlock, facing the text inspired by Auguste Blanqui's *L'Éternité par les astres*. A narrow opening in the wall allowed the viewer to slip behind it. There was a photograph of the *Règle du jeu* where the dead animals fall, and in the back, in a more open space, a large black curtain. "The curtain was folded in sevens and fours, then I fired a shotgun into it. When unfolded, the single shot spread out like a celestial map, reproducing the same shot across the whole canvas."

2009–10

Searchers
Impression digigraphie sur papier photo / Digigraphic print on photo paper
86 × 304 cm
Collection CNAP Centre national d'arts plastiques / Collection The Israel Museum, Jerusalem / Collections privées / Private collections
Photo: Fabrice Gousset

La prisonnière du désert (John Ford, 1956) et le documentaire relatant son tournage. En reconstituant le site de Monument Valley à partir de la fiction et son tournage, *Searchers* révèle en creux la fabrication du mythe de l'Ouest et de l'idéologie qu'il a durablement installées dans l'imaginaire collectif. La reprise du titre original *Searchers* renverse le sens initial de la recherche en convoquant le spectateur même comme chercheur dont le regard est mis en abyme.

A documentary filming of *The Searchers* (John Ford, 1956) relating to its location. By reconstructing the site of Monument Valley from the fictional film and its shooting, *Searchers* explores the making of the myth of the West and the ideology that that myth has permanently embedded in the collective imagination. The use of the original English title pivots the initial meaning of the research by summoning the spectators themselves as researchera, whose gaze becomes a mise en abyme.

2010

L'Élan pour l'Amérique
Film négatif (*Histoire de France* de Jules Michelet), néon / Negative film (*Histoire de France* by Jules Michelet), neon light
81.5 × 113.5 cm
Collections privées / Private collections
Photo: Fabrice Gousset

Le rêve américain préexiste à l'Amérique, c'est un espace utopique à investir. L'Amérique n'existe pas. Photographie de l'Histoire : celle, monumentale, de Jules Michelet, l'*Histoire de France*, qu'il rédigea pendant trente ans aux archives nationales. C'est une photographie avant son tirage, son négatif. Le chapitre "L'Élan pour l'Amérique" n'apparaît pas sur le film. Il laisse un espace vide, comme une biffure horizontale dans la masse du texte. Un néon éclaire cet espace manquant.

The American dream preexisted America as a utopian space to be conquered. America doesn't exist. A photograph of history: Jules Michelet's monumental *Histoire de France*, which he wrote for more than thirty years in the National Archives. It is a photograph used before its printing, its negative. The chapter "L'Élan pour l'Amérique" does not appear on the film paper. It leaves an empty space, like a horizontal strike-through in the mass of text. A neon light highlights this missing space.

2011

Chant 23
Film 15/70 mm (chant 23 de l'*Iliade* d'Homère), disque en marbre de Thassos, socle en bois / 70 mm film (Chant 23 of Homer's *Iliad*), marble slab, and wood pedestal
Socle / Plinth: 132 × 67 cm
Photo: Fabrice Gousset

« La notion de *kairos* m'intéressait particulièrement lorsque j'ai réalisé le *Chant 23*, qui consiste en un passage de *L'Iliade*, kinescopé sur le plus grand format de film existant (du 70 mm à défilement horizontal). » Le *kairos*, ou « moment opportun » est central dans ce passage où Antiloque, à l'occasion des Jeux funéraires organisés par Achille, remporte une course de char en doublant son rival au bon moment.

"The notion of *kairos* was of particular interest to me when I made *Chant 23*, which consists of a passage from the *Iliad* kinescoped onto the widest film format available (70 mm horizontal roll)." The *kairos*, or "opportune moment," is central to this passage where Antilochus, on the occasion of the Funeral Games organized by Achilles, wins a chariot race by overtaking his rival at the right time.

Red sunset over a lake
211 cartes postales, tir à la carabine / 211 postcards, carbine shooting
Photo: Aurélien Mole

« Il s'agit initialement d'une vidéo libre de droit d'un coucher de soleil, dont j'ai extrait 211 screenshots pour réaliser un ensemble de cartes postales. J'ai tiré un coup de revolver, de calibre 357 à 10 mètres, dans la pile de cartes, qui l'a traversée de part en part. Lors de l'exposition, les visiteurs pouvaient prendre une carte à l'entrée, rejouant ainsi sur la durée du vernissage une chronophotographie du tir traversant le soleil. »

"This was originally a royalty-free video of a sunset, from which I extracted 211 screenshots to make a set of postcards. I fired a 357-caliber revolver at a pile of cards from ten meters away, and it went right through it. During the exhibition, visitors could take a card at the entrance, thus replaying a chronophotography of the firing shot going through the sun."

Sandbagwal
Sacs militaires remplis de sable / Military sandbags filled with sand
160 × 325 × 35 cm
Photo: Fabrice Gousset

Le site de l'ancienne Babylone, rebaptisée Camp Alpha par les États-Unis, a été transformé durant la seconde guerre du Golfe en camp militaire ; enfoui sous le bitume pour construire des pistes d'atterrissage et diverses infrastructures militaires, la terre creusée et déplacée pour remplir des sacs. Cet événement a inspiré *Sandbagwal*, qui évoque cette transformation du site et ce grand retournement de terre. Le déplacement est au cœur de l'œuvre ; de la brique au sac, l'œuvre active, dans son immobilité de mur, un double mouvement. La figure mésopotamienne du lion en marche, reprise de la porte d'Ishtar, se voit alors investie d'un nouveau sens.

An ancient Babylon site, renamed Camp Alpha by the Americans, was turned into a military camp during the Second Gulf War. The site was buried under asphalt to build runways and other military facilities, the earth dug up and moved to fill bags. This event inspired *Sandbagwal*, which evokes this transformation of the site and its deadly tilth. Displacement is at the heart of the work; from the brick to the bag, the work activates, in its immobility as a wall, a double movement. The Mesopotamian figure of the lion in motion, taken from the Gate of Ishtar, is thus given new meaning.

2011–17

L'Histoire retournée
Feuille d'or 23 carats, photographie au verso, papier baryté / 23 carat gold leaf, photograph on reverse
18 × 15 cm
Photos: Julien Audebert

Verso de photographies prises pendant la Commune de Paris, où les barricadiers font face à l'objectif, posant devant leurs ouvrages de pierres et de pavés. Derrière l'image, la silhouette exacte de la barricade est reprise à la feuille d'or.

The reverse sides of photographs taken during the Paris Commune, where barricaders face the lens, posing in front of their stone and cobblestone structures. Behind the image, the exact silhouette of the barricade is reproduced in gold leaf.

2012

Est/Ouest
Tirage Lambda / Lambda print
111 × 396 cm
Collections privées / Private collections
Photo: Fabrice Gousset

« *Le Jour le plus long* (1962) et *Libération* (*Osvobozhdenie*) (1967-1971) : deux films qui décrivent la progression de l'occident et de l'URSS vers l'Europe, jusqu'à la prise de Berlin et le débarquement. J'ai retenu deux moments clé : la séquence du débarquement sur les plages normandes et la bataille de Koursk – deux épisodes qui, respectivement dans le roman national de chaque camp, figurent comme symboles de la victoire sur l'Allemagne. En procédant au "démontage" des deux films, j'ai assemblé les deux tournages dans une image unique, qui voit alors cohabiter ces deux épisodes. En faisant se rencontrer l'Atlantique et la steppe russe sur une Europe occultée (la seule plage normande fait la jonction entre la steppe et l'océan) se dessine une nouvelle géographie mentale : le paysage devient le lieu d'une conflagration entre l'Est et l'Ouest. Comme le bateau se meut sur l'eau et fait corps avec elle, c'est la mer qui progresse sur la terre, et comme le char, collé à la boue, se meut dans la steppe et fait corps avec elle, c'est toute la terre, le continent qui progresse vers la mer... dans cette grande ligne horizontale continue, qui est la figure centrale de l'œuvre. »

"*The Longest Day* (1962) and *Liberation (Osvobozhdenie)* (1967–71): two films that describe the progression of the West and the USSR toward Europe, until Berlin was seized and the Allied forces could land. I kept two key moments: the landing sequence on the Normandy beaches and the battle of Kursk—two events that respectively appear in the national story of each side as symbols of victory over Germany. By "dismantling" the two films, I have assembled them into a single image in order for these two events to cohabit. By arranging the Atlantic and the Russian steppe together on a hidden Europe (the only beach in Normandy is the junction between the steppe and the ocean), a new mental geography is shaped: the landscape becomes the site of a conflagration between East and West. Just as the boat moves on the water and becomes one with it, the sea progresses on the land, and just as the chariot, stuck to the mud, moves in the steppe and becomes one with it, it is the whole land, the continent, that progresses toward the sea, within this great continuous horizontal line, which is the central figure of the work."

Livres
Tirage photographique par contact sur papier, texte hébreu / Contact print on photographic paper, Hebrew text
50 × 50 cm
Collections privées / Private collections
Photo: Fabrice Gousset

Il s'agit d'une reprise de *Livres* de 2003, réécrit ici en hébreu.

This is a rework of *Livres* from 2003, rewritten here in Hebrew.

2013

L'Atelier fermé
Lames de bordé et membrures de barque
Tirage par contact sur papier photographique / Strip planking and ribs of boat, contact print on photographic paper
Dimensions variables / Dimensions variable
Collection FRAC Normandie Rouen
Photo: Jérémie Buchholtz

Cet ensemble, commande publique à l'occasion du cinquantième anniversaire de la mort de Georges Braque, prend sa source dans l'atelier abandonné de Braque à Varengeville-sur-Mer, lieu inaccessible au regard et au public. L'impossibilité de s'y rendre et de le photographier fut le motif premier du travail ; dans chacun des objets se joue cette dimension d'une visibilité altérée, transformée ou mise à distance. Cette figure est le fil qui relie l'ensemble, du paysage scellé – ou pénétré comme par effraction – au texte micrographié. « J'ai pensé cet agencement comme une constellation faite d'un paysage nocturne, d'une falaise, d'une page de texte et d'une photo de famille. Semblable au mur de l'atelier sur lequel des images ou des objets en attente constituent des configurations d'œuvres potentielles – œuvres dans lesquelles ces objets seront assimilés et transformés. À la différence de l'atelier du peintre, les images ici sont des objets achevés, qui condensent du temps et de l'espace ; chacune constitue une unité irréductible, close sur elle-même. Entre ces images l'œuvre dessine un espace mental, comme un lieu en suspens. »

This ensemble, a public commission on the occasion of the fiftieth anniversary of Georges Braque's death, originates from Braque's abandoned studio in Varengeville-sur-Mer, a place inaccessible to the public. The impossibility of going there and photographing it was the primary motive for the work; in each of the objects, this altered, transformed, or distanced visibility is played out. This figure is the thread that links the whole, from the sealed landscape—almost penetrated as if by a break-in—to the micrographic text. "I thought of this arrangement as a constellation made up of a night landscape, a cliff, a page of text, and a family photo, similar to the wall in the studio where awaiting images or objects presage potential works—works in which these objects will be assimilated and transformed. Unlike the painter's studio, the images here are finished objects, condensing time and space; each one constitutes an irreducible unit, closed in on itself. The work draws a mental space between these images, like a pending place."

2014

Tutto sta in un pugno
Impression digigraphie sur papier baryté / Digigraphic print on baryta paper
62 × 115 cm
Collections privées / Private collections
Photo: Dorine Potel

En 1963, Pier Paolo Pasolini réalise un repérage préalable au tournage de *l'Évangile selon saint Matthieu*. Au terme de ce documentaire tourné en Palestine, s'impose un constat d'échec : celui de l'impossibilité de tourner son film sur les lieux de la Passion, paysages et visages sont devenus trop modernes avec la création d'Israël. Il décidera finalement de tourner son *Évangile* dans le sud de l'Italie.
La photographie est une reconstruction du désert à partir du matériau pasolinien. Elle prend pour source ces images qui n'avaient pas trouvé leur but initial. Plus que la réalisation d'un « évangile photographique », l'image condense tout le voyage de Pasolini et du prêtre qui l'accompagne, depuis les rivages du lac Tibériade jusqu'à Jérusalem et Bethléem, l'endroit où leur périple s'achève mais « où l'histoire commence. » Le paysage est essaimé par leur conversation (les sous-titres du documentaire ont été conservés), conversation qui porte sur les lieux et les moments clé de la vie du Christ, ou bien des considérations sur la transformation du paysage. Cohabitent alors récit théologique et géopolitique, à l'intérieur d'un paysage qui « tient dans la paume d'une main. »

In 1963, Pier Paolo Pasolini scouted locations prior to the filming of *The Gospel According to St. Matthew*. At the end of this documentary, shot in Palestine, he came to the conclusion that it was impossible to shoot his film in the places where the Passion took place, as the landscape and faces had become too modern with the creation of Israel. He eventually decided to shoot his *Gospel* in southern Italy.
The photograph is a reconstruction of the desert from the Pasolinian material. It originates in those images that had not found their original purpose. More than the realization of a "photographic gospel," the image condenses the entire journey of Pasolini and the priest who accompanied him from the shores of Lake Tiberias to Jerusalem and Bethlehem, the place

where their journey ended but "where history begins." The landscape is swarmed by their conversation (the documentary's subtitles have been retained), a conversation that focuses on the key sites and moments in the life of Christ, or considerations on the landscape's transformation. Theological and geopolitical narratives coexist within a landscape that "fits in the palm of one hand."

2015

Danse américaine
Tirage Lambda /
Lambda print
35 × 216 cm
Photo: Claire Dorn

Trois chansons qui rythment *Un Américain à Paris* servent de trame à la reconstitution du Paris en technicolor filmé par Vincente Minelli en 1951. Un Paris artificiel où la butte Montmartre semble jouxter le quartier latin. En révélant l'image mentale qui se dérobe par l'effet du montage, *Danse américaine* dévoile le processus de domination culturelle enclenché à partir du plan Marshall et qui trouvera son allié parfait dans le cinéma. De part sa structure, (Gene Kelly disparaît dans la reconstitution, où ne restent que ses paroles) seuls subsistent ses partenaires de chant (la fleuriste, les enfants, la tenancière du bistrot), l'image évoque le genre pictural des danses macabres médiévales.

Three songs that give rhythm to *An American in Paris* serve as the framework for Paris as reconstructed in the Technicolor film by Vincente Minelli, made in 1951. It is an artificial Paris, where Montmartre's hill seems to adjoin the Latin Quarter. By revealing the mental image that is hidden by the editing effect, *Danse américaine* reveals the process of cultural domination set in motion by the Marshall Plan, which would find its perfect ally in cinema. Gene Kelly disappears in the reconstruction, and only his words and singing partners remain (the florist, the children, the bistro keeper), such that the image evokes the pictorial genre of the medieval *danse macabre*.

Nocturne (été)
Impression pigmentaire /
Pigment print
78 × 298 × 5 cm
Photo: Claire Dorn

Ces *Nocturnes* consistent en un long travail (sur deux périodes de l'année) sur les sites d'affrontements de la première guerre mondiale autour de Fleury-devant-Douaumont (proche de Verdun). L'artiste a repris une démarche initiée avec *L'Atelier fermé*, consistant en photographies du site en pose B, de nuit, à la lampe torche. La lumière y joue un double rôle : elle dévoile une géographie modelée par les bombes, (seuls les trous d'obus sont éclairés) tout en rejouant l'instant du bombardement. La nuit apparaît comme un film photographique non révélé, duquel vont émerger intentionnellement les formes par la prise de vue. "C'est la nuit, l'intérieur de la nature qui existe ici [...]. Surgit alors subitement une tête ensanglantée, là, une autre silhouette blanche, et elles disparaissent de même. C'est cette nuit qu'on découvre lorsqu'on regarde un homme dans les yeux, on plonge son regard dans la nuit qui devient effroyable, c'est la nuit du monde qui s'avance ici à la rencontre de chacun" (G. W. F. Hegel).

These *Nocturnes* consist of a long work (over two periods within a year) on World War I battle sites around Fleury-devant-Douaumont, near Verdun. The artist took an approach initiated with *L'Atelier fermé*, consisting of photographs of the site in B position, at night, with a torch. The light plays a double role: it reveals a geography shaped by the bombs (only the shell holes are lit) while replaying the moment of the bombing. The night appears to me as unrevealed photographic film, from which the forms will intentionally emerge through the shooting. "This [is] the night, the interior of nature, existing here—pure Self—[and] in phantasmagoric representations it is night everywhere: here a bloody head suddenly shoots up and there another white shape, only to disappear as suddenly. We see this night when we look a human being in the eye, looking into a night which turns terrifying. [For from his eyes] the night of the world hangs out toward us." (G. W. F. Hegel).

2015–16

Diagram of the sea
Huile sur toile /
Oil on canvas
Chaque / Each: 38 × 55 cm
Photo: Julien Audebert

Le vent qui souffle sur ces eaux incertaines est le même. C'est l'image de la mer comme un espace total, égal, c'est n'importe où et nulle part en même temps. Un obstacle au centre vient faire obstruction. À y voir de plus près il s'agit de navires, cadrés à l'identique et occupant à peu près la même surface peinte. Ces navires sont des copies rigoureusement exactes d'après des photos de presse. À la différence des ex-voto marins, où le portrait d'un bateau était installé dans l'église pour assurer sa protection, les navires représentés ici ont tous coulé, disparu, ou ont été victimes d'un incident civil ou militaire durant ces cent dernières années. Ils agissent alors comme des signes temporels précis, dessinant une certaine périodicité, un diagramme. Une telle histoire peinte par ces navires coulés, rassemble alors ces événements disparates dans un même continuum, où chacun devient l'occurrence d'un seul navire progressant à l'horizon. Cet ensemble m'a été inspiré par la figure de l'Ange de l'Histoire de Walter Benjamin : « Là où nous apparaît une chaîne d'évènements, il ne voit, lui, qu'une seule et unique catastrophe. »

The wind blowing on these uncertain waters is the same. It is the image of the sea as a total, equal space, anywhere and nowhere at the same time. An obstacle blocks the center. On closer inspection, it is made of ships, identically framed and occupying more or less the same painted surface. These ships are exact copies of press photos. Unlike marine ex-votos, where the portrait of a ship was installed in the church to ensure its protection, the ships represented here have all been sunk, lost in some civil or military incident over the past hundred years. They then act as precise temporal signs, drawing a certain periodicity, a diagram. Such a history painted by its sunken ships then gathers these disparate events into a single continuum, where each becomes the occurrence of a single ship progressing over the horizon. This ensemble was inspired by Walter Benjamin's figure of the Angel of History: "Where we see a chain of events, he sees a single catastrophe."

2016

Nocturne (printemps)
Impression pigmentaire /
Pigment print
151 × 136 × 5 cm
Collections privées /
Private collections
Photo: Claire Dorn

En suivant le même processus que pour *Nocturne (été)*, la *Nocturne (printemps)* fait apparaître les écosystèmes (faune et flore) qui se sont spontanément développés après la guerre dans ces cavités. La découverte de ces écosystèmes, avec des variétés de tritons, grenouilles mais aussi de fleurs « déplacées » par la guerre inspirera la série peinte des *Obsisdionales*.

Using the same process as *Nocturne (été)*, *Nocturne (printemps)* reveals the flora and fauna that spontaneously developed in these cavities after the war. The discovery of these ecosystems, with varieties of newts, frogs, but also flowers "displaced" by the conflict, would later inspire the *Obsisdionales* painting series.

Mars et Vénus, phases d'opposition
Film numérique 35 mm, couleur, son / 35 mm digital film, color, sound, 10:30 min.

Film réalisé avec la participation du Centre national des arts plastiques Production ARTER-VIVANTO en partenariat avec l'IMCCE-Observatoire de Paris / Film produced with Centre national des arts plastiques Production ARTER-VIVANTO 2016, in partnership with IMCCE-Observatoire de Paris
Interprétation: Alice Renavand, danseuse étoile de l'Opéra national de Paris / Performance: Alice Renavand, prima ballerina of the Opéra national de Paris
Collection CNAP Centre national d'arts plastiques

En reconstruisant la mécanique céleste avec la machinerie du cinéma, le film donne à voir le phénomène de la danse et la traque de Vénus par l'oeil de Mars. « J'ai filmé la danse nuptiale des deux astres qui, par intermittence, se rencontrent durant les 'oppositions', cet instant fugace où ils sont alignés et où Vénus semble effectuer une boucle, un mouvement rétrograde. Durant ce suspens, c'est l'antique question du réel et des apparences que l'on peut observer.
Ce troisième mouvement est celui perçu par l'illusoire point fixe d'un 'regardeur astronome'. »

By reconstructing celestial mechanics with the machinery of cinema, this film shows the phenomenon of the dance and the tracking of Venus under Mars's watchful eye. I filmed the nuptial dance of the two planets, which regularly meet during the 'opposition'—that fleeting moment when they are aligned and Venus seems to make a loop, a retrograde movement. During this lapse of time, the ancient question of reality and appearances can be pondered. This third movement is the one perceived by the illusory fixed point of an 'astronomical viewer'."

Summit
Tirage Lambda /
Lambda print
46.3 × 80.4 × 4 cm
Photo: Claire Dorn

« J'ai enregistré le streaming vidéo (sur 12 heures) du sommet de l'OTAN à Newport en 2014, afin d'en extraire essentiellement les contre-champs. J'ai produit l'image "négative" de la photo de famille où les chefs d'État posent devant le manoir pour la presse. Le nouveau point de vue se situe derrière leur tête, nous voyons alors les journalistes de face, puis dans le lointain le terrain de jeu des démonstrations militaires, sur le golf du Celtic Manor Resort. »

"I recorded the twelve-hour video stream of the 2014 NATO summit in Newport mainly in order to extract the reverse shots. I produced the 'negative' image of the group photo where the heads of state pose in front of the mansion for the press. The new viewpoint is behind their heads, so we see the journalists from the front, then in the distance the playground of the military demonstrations on the Celtic Manor Resort golf course."

2018

Le Chariot de Mars
Tirage pigmentaire noir et blanc / Black and white pigment print
150 × 354 cm
Photo: Julien Audebert

La perspective est doublement convoquée dans cette grande photographie, construite à partir du documentaire de 1956 qu'Alain Resnais tourna dans la Bibliothèque Nationale, *Toute la mémoire du monde*. Le film, comme archive lui-même de cette immense archive qu'est la bibliothèque, constitue le matériau central de cette image qui condense trois moments de la connaissance : le livre, le film et l'archive numérique. La photographie se développe selon une perspective à deux points de fuite, qui correspond au temps linéaire de cette accumulation de savoirs (les infinis rayonnages de livres qui s'abîment vers la silhouette de l'homme disparaissant dans l'encadrement d'une porte). En son sein se joue un autre mouvement, celui d'un livre dont on suit la trajectoire : un hypothétique ouvrage de vulgarisation astronomique sur la planète Mars, qui semble y effectuer une boucle, passant des étagères au chariot sur lequel le livre est déplacé. Le livre dessine une ligne courbe dans l'espace, laquelle, au lieu de se refermer, retrouve la ligne fuyante du point de fuite central. L'image d'un temps astronomique, cyclique, converge alors avec l'image du temps linéaire de cette bibliothèque-monde.

Perspective is invoked twice in this large photograph based on the 1956 documentary film that Alain Resnais shot in the Bibliothèque Nationale, *All the Memory in the World*. The film, as an archive of the immense archive that is the library itself, constitutes the central material of this photograph, which gathers three moments of knowledge: the book, the film, and the digital archive. The photograph develops in a perspective with two vanishing points, which corresponds to the linear time of this knowledge accumulation (the infinite shelves of books that collapse toward the silhouette of the man disappearing in the doorway). Within it, another movement plays out—that of a book whose trajectory we can follow: a hypothetical popular astronomy book on Mars, which seems to make a loop in it, passing from the shelves to the trolley on which it is moved. The book draws a curved line in space, which, instead of closing, returns to the central vanishing point line. The image of an astronomical, cyclical time then converges with the image of this library-world's linear time.

2019

Eden (Danien)
Huile sur toile /
Oil on canvas
64.5 × 124 cm
Photo: Romain Darnaud

Eden (Carbonifère)
Huile sur toile /
Oil on canvas
64.5 × 124 cm
Photo: Romain Darnaud

2019–

Obsidionales
Huile sur cuivre /
Oil on copper
18 × 15 cm
Collections privées /
Private collections
Photo: Romain Darnaud

L'artiste a amorcé cette série de peintures après avoir découvert ces variétés de plantes exogènes sur les champ de bataille de l'Est de la France. Déplacées par les semelles des soldats, les fourrages pour animaux ou par le chemin de fer, les obsidionales sont les traces botaniques de l'Histoire qui laboura le sol européen ces deux derniers siècles. J'ai peint ces fleurs dans un format domestique, de manière à pouvoir les tenir en main en les exécutant. Le cuivre, métal dont sont faits les obus, fut aussi un support privilégié pour la peinture de genre notamment en Flandre et en France.
Le contraste entre la dureté tranchante du cuivre et son usage domestique, préexiste dans l'artisanat des tranchées où les soldats recyclaient des douilles pour réaliser des objets décoratifs en attendant le prochain feu.

The artist began this series of paintings after discovering these exogenous plant varieties on the battlefields of eastern France. Displaced by the soles of soldiers, animals, or railways, obsidian plants are the botanical remnants of the history that has plagued European soil over the past two centuries.
I painted these flowers in a domestic format so that I could hold them in my hand while making them. Copper, the metal from which shells are made, was also a favored medium for genre painting, particularly in Flanders and France. The contrast between the sharpness of copper and its domestic use mirrors the situation in the trenches where soldiers recycled shells into decorative objects while waiting for the next assault.

2020–

Inclusion -1798
Tirage photographique par contact sur papier baryté / Contact printing on baryta paper
17 × 12 cm
Photo: Romain Darnaud

Inclusion -1798 est un montage entre l'*Essai sur le principe de population* de T. R. Malthus paru en 1798, et le Alien and Sedition act de 1798, texte de loi américain visant à protéger les États-Unis des « citoyens étrangers de puissances ennemies. »

Inclusion -1798 is a montage of T. R. Malthus's *Essay on the Principle of Population*, published in 1798, and the Alien and Sedition Act of 1798, a US law designed to protect the United States from "alien citizens of enemy powers."

La main invisible
Tirage photographique par contact sur papier baryté / Contact printing on baryta paper
33 × 41 cm
Photo: Romain Darnaud

La main invisible est un montage entre deux textes : l'essentiel est composé par la *Fable des abeilles* de Bernard Mandeville, précédé par la Genèse. Le collage des deux textes crée une continuité qui fait succéder à la Chute (expulsion d'Adam et Eve du jardin d'Eden) le premier texte d'économie libérale, où apparaît pour la première fois une naturalisation du Capital et des échanges.

La main invisible is a montage of two texts: the main one is composed by Bernard Mandeville's *The Fable of the Bees*, preceded by the Book of Genesis. The collage of the two texts creates a continuity that makes the Fall (Adam and Eve's expulsion from the Garden of Eden) succeed the first text of liberal economy, where a naturalization of capital and exchanges appears for the first time.

Eden (Deer forest)
Huile sur toile / Oil on canvas
93 × 134.5 cm
Collection privée / Private collection
Photo: Romain Darnaud

Eden (Montagne)
Huile sur cuivre / Oil on copper
45 × 54 cm
Collection privée / Private collection
Photo: Julien Audebert

Eden (Dévonien)
Huile sur cuivre / Oil on copper
55 × 49 cm
Collection privée / Private collection
Photo: Julien Audebert

2021

Eden (Jardin)
Huile sur cuivre / Oil on copper
30 × 45 cm
Photo: Julien Audebert

Eden (Plage)
Huile sur cuivre / Oil on copper
34 × 55 cm
Photo: Julien Audebert

Eden (Trompettes d'eau)
Huile sur cuivre / Oil on copper
35.5 × 55 cm
Collection FRAC-Artothèque Nouvelle Aquitaine
Photo: Julien Audebert

Ces tableaux, dans lesquels on retrouve des constantes de la peinture de genre paysagiste héritées du romantisme, procèdent par redoublement de l'objet qu'ils dépeignent : des aquarium domestiques, une nature sous verre ordonnancée et composée pour l'oeil. « Je vois dans l'aquarium une image spéculaire de la crise et le refuge naturaliste aux reconfigurations brutales de la sphère publique. C'est la toile de fond d'une ère, qui trouve son origine dans une nature dont elle crée d'un même geste les contours. »

These paintings, in which one finds the permanent features of the landscape genre inherited from Romanticism, proceed by redoubling the object they depict: domestic aquariums, nature under glass composed to be watched. "I see the aquarium as a specular image of the crisis, the naturalistic shelter away from the brutal reconfigurations of the public sphere. It is the backdrop of an era that originates in nature, whose contours it creates in the same gesture."

Le Tribut
Dyptique / Diptych
Huile sur cuivre / Oil on copper
Chacun / Each: 35 × 35 cm
Photo: Julien Audebert

Comme les fleurs obsidionales, ces *crepidula fornicata* ont été déplacées, collées aux coques des navires américains durant le débarquement. Elles ont colonisé le littoral et modifié l'écosystème en proliférant. Suétone raconte quelque part comment Caligula déclara la guerre à la mer. En guise de trésor de guerre il fit ramasser à ses troupes arrivées au bord de l'Angleterre les coquillages qui s'y trouvaient. « Enfin, comme pour terminer la guerre, il dirigea son front de bataille vers le rivage de l'Océan. Il disposa les machines, et les balistes, sans que personne connût ou pût deviner son dessein. Tout à coup il ordonna qu'on ramassât des coquillages, et qu'on en remplît les casques et les vêtements. C'étaient, disait-il, les dépouilles de l'Océan dont il fallait orner le Capitole et le palais des Césars. »

Like the obsidian flowers, these *Crepidula fornicata* were displaced, stuck to the hulls of US ships during World War II landing operations. They colonized the coastline and modified the ecosystem by proliferating. Suetonius tells somewhere how Caligula declared war on the sea. As a war treasure he had his troops collect shells from the coast of England. "At last, as if resolved to make war in earnest, he drew up his army upon the shore of the ocean, with his ballistae and other engines of war, and while no one could imagine what he intended to do, he suddenly commanded them to gather up the sea shells, and fill their helmets, and the folds of their dress with them, calling them 'the spoils of the ocean due to the Capitol and the Palatium.'"

Premier feu
Photographie numérique transférée sur plan-film ektachrome / Digital photograph transferred to Ektachrome sheet film
10 × 12 cm
Photo: Julien Audebert

L'artiste a accumulé plusieurs documentaires sur la recherche archéologique des premières traces d'activité humaine dans les grottes de Bruniquel, Castillo et Wonderwerk. La reconstruction par photomontage d'un site unique, fait cohabiter différents moments et lieux de la recherche. L'image est le transfert sur un plan-film argentique d'un espace immense qui contient en son sein, dans un détail infinitésimal, l'indice stratigraphique du premier feu. Mais le *sujet*, plus que la recherche des origines, n'est-il pas d'abord la mise en abyme du regard du spectateur, la recherche elle-même ?

The artist collected several documentaries on the archaeological search for the first traces of human activity in the caves of Bruniquel, Castillo, and Wonderwerk. The photomontage reconstruction of a unique site brings together different moments and places of the search. This image is the transfer onto a silver film plate of an immense space that contains within it, in infinitesimal detail, the stratigraphic index of the first fire. More than the search for the origins, isn't the *subject* the very mise en abyme of the spectator's gaze, the search itself?

Julien Audebert

Auteurs / Authors
Philippe-Alain Michaud
Corinne Rondeau

Résponsables d'édition /
Publishing Editors
Vittoria Mieli—Mousse
Irene Varano

Traductions / Translations
Emilie Lecatre

Relectures / Copy editing
and proofreading
Vittoria Mieli—Mousse
Lindsey Westbrook

Conception graphique /
Graphic design
Massimiliano Pace—Mousse

Publié par / Published by
Mousse Publishing
Contrappunto s.r.l.
via Decembrio, 28
20137, Milan–Italie / Italy

Distribution /
Available through
Mousse Publishing, Milan
moussemagazine.it
DAP | Distributed Art
Publishers, New York
artbook.com
Idea Books, Amsterdam
ideabooks.nl
Les presses du réel, Dijon
lespressesdureel.com
Antenne Books, Londres /
London
antennebooks.com

Avec le soutien du /
With the support of

FRAC–ARTOTHÈQUE NOUVELLE–AQUITAINE

Avec le soutien aux galeries / publication du Centre national des arts plastiques /
With the support of Centre national des arts plastiques (National Centre for Visual Arts), France

Première edition /
First edition
2022

Imprimé en Italie par /
Printed in Italy by
Artigiana Grafica, Vicenza

ISBN 978-88-6749-518-4

€ 27 / $ 30

Avec le soutien du /
With the support of the

adagp
Pour le droit des artistes

L'artiste tient à remercier / The artist would like to thank:
Ken Alpert, Olivier Antoine, Léonie Audebert, Loris Audebert, Artothèque de Villeurbanne, Erich Bachmann et Christina Sageros, Lola Calif Baude, Luc Bellier, Pascale Brun, Patricia Carette et Jean-Marc Urrea, Stéphane Chambaud, Nadège Champagne, Elie Colistro, Hubert Duprat, Sandrine Dusollier, Fabrice Gousset, Jean-Paul Guarino, Johanna Hagege, Grégoire Jeanblanc, Laboratoire LPH, Laurent Laclos, Emilie Lecatre, William Lowenstein, Primo Mazzoni, Philippe-Alain Michaud, Pierre Morio, Jonathan Nguyen, Jean-Philippe et Lydia Pasquier, Myriam et Jacques Salomon, Garret Siegel, Ida Simon-Raynaud, Corinne Rondeau, Alexandra Tarlinton, Irene Varano.